NEW STUDIES IN BONHOEFFER'S ETHICS

NEW STUDIES IN BONHOEFFER'S

ETHICS

Edited By
William J. Peck

Contributing Authors:
Clifford J. Green
Robin W. Lovin
Larry L. Rasmussen
William J. Peck
Gerard Th. Rothuizen
John D. Godsey
Charles C. West

Toronto Studies in Theology
Volume 30
Bonhoeffer Series
Number 3

The Edwin Mellen Press
Lewiston/Queenston

Library of Congress Cataloging-in-Publication Data

New studies in Bonhoeffer's Ethics.

(Toronto studies in theology ; v. 30)
Includes bibliographical references and index.
1. Bonhoeffer, Dietrich, 1906-1945. Ethik.
2. Christian ethics--History--20th century. I. Peck, William J. (William Jay) II. Series.
BJ1253.B6153N49 1987   241'.092'4   87-7944
ISBN 0-88946-775-7 (alk. paper)

This is volume 30 in the continuing series
Toronto Studies in Theology
Volume 30 ISBN 0-88946-775-7
TST Series ISBN 0-88946-975-X

Copyright © 1987 William J. Peck

All rights reserved. For information contact

The Edwin Mellen Press
P.O. Box 450
Lewiston, New York
USA 14092

The Edwin Mellen Press
P.O. Box 67
Queenston, Ontario
CANADA L0S 1L0

Printed in the United States of America

CONTENTS

Abbreviations vii
Editor's Preface ix

PART ONE: TEXT, CONTEXT AND METHOD

I. The Text of Bonhoeffer's <u>Ethics</u> 3
                        Clifford J. Green

II. Biographical Context 67
                        Robin W. Lovin

III. A Question of Method 103
                        Larry L. Rasmussen

PART TWO: STUDIES IN THE <u>ETHICS</u>

IV. The Euthanasia Text-Segment 141
                        William J. Peck

V. Who Am I? Bonhoeffer and Suicide 167
                        Gerard Th. Rothuizen

PART THREE: BONHOEFFER'S ETHICAL THEOLOGY

VI. The Doctrine of Love 189
                        John D. Godsey

VII. Ground Under Our Feet 235
                        Charles C. West

Works Cited 275
Index 279

ABBREVIATIONS

BOOKS BY DIETRICH BONHOEFFER

AB Act and Being. Trans. Bernard Noble. New York: Harper and Row, 1962. Reprint (same pagination); New York: Octagon Books, 1983.

CC Christ the Center. Revised translation by Edwin H. Robertson. New York: Harper & Row, 1978.

CD The Cost of Discipleship. Trans. R. H. Fuller, revised by Irmgard Booth. New York: Macmillan, 1963. Hardcover reissue, same pagination; Gloucester, MA: Peter Smith, 1983.

CF/T Creation and Fall. Temptation. Trans. John C. Fletcher and Kathleen Downham, respectively. New York: Macmillan, 1966. Hardcover reissue, same pagination; Gloucester, MA: Peter Smith, 1983.

CS The Communion of Saints. Trans. Ronald Gregor Smith et al. New York: Harper & Row, 1963.

E Ethics. Trans. Neville Horton Smith. Re-arranged edition. New York: Macmillan, 1965. [Note: this abbreviation refers to the 1969 and later printings which contain the "Editor's Preface to the Newly Arranged Sixth German Edition (1963)" that was omitted in earlier printings of the re-arranged edition. Although pagination for the body of the text is the same from 1965 onwards, both prefaces are necessary for Green's chapter, "The Text of Bonhoeffer's Ethics."] Hardcover reissue, same pagination; Gloucester, MA: Peter Smith, 1983.

Eg Ethik. Sixth edition. Herausgegeben von Eberhard Bethge. Munich: Chr. Kaiser Verlag, 1963.

FP Fiction from Prison. Ed. Renate & Eberhard Bethge, with Clifford Green (in the English edition); trans. Ursula Hoffmann. Philadelphia: Fortress Press, 1981.

GS Gesammelte Schriften, I-VI. Munich: Chr. Kaiser Verlag, 1958-1974.

LPP Letters and Papers from Prison. The Enlarged Edition. Edited by Eberhard Bethge. Trans. R. H. Fuller, John Bowden et al. New York: Macmillan, 1972.

LT Life Together. Trans. John W. Doberstein. New York: Harper & Row, 1954; paperback edition, same pagination, 1976.

NRS No Rusty Swords. Letters, Lectures and Notes, 1928-1936. Ed. Edwin H. Robertson. Revised edition. Translation revised by John Bowden and Eberhard Bethge. London: Collins, 1970; Cleveland: Collins-World, 1977.

TP True Patriotism. Letters, Lectures and Notes, 1939-1945. Ed. Edwin H. Robertson. Trans. Edwin H. Robertson and John Bowden. New York: Harper & Row, 1973. Paperback edition, same pagination: Cleveland: Collins-World, 1977.

WF The Way to Freedom. Letters, Lectures and Notes, 1935-1939. Ed. Edwin H. Robertson. Trans. Edwin H. Robertson and John Bowden. New York: Harper & Row, 1966. Paperback edition, same pagination: London: Collins, 1972; Cleveland: Collins-World, 1977.

SECONDARY LITERATURE

DB Eberhard Bethge, Dietrich Bonhoeffer. Man of Vision, Man of Courage. Edited by Edwin Robertson, trans. Eric Mosbacher et al. New York: Harper & Row, 1970; paperback edition, same pagination, 1977.

DBg Eberhard Bethge. Dietrich Bonhoeffer. Theologe, Christ, Zeitgenosse. Fifth edition. Munich: Chr. Kaiser Verlag, 1983. (Contains new Vorwort and Anhang but pagination in the body of the text is unaltered).

SCH Clifford J. Green, The Sociality of Christ and Humanity. Dietrich Bonhoeffer's Early Theology, 1927-1933. Missoula, MT: Scholars Press, 1975.

ER John D. Godsey and Geffrey B. Kelly, eds., Ethical Responsibility: Bonhoeffer's Legacy to the Churches, Toronto Studies in Theology, Volume 6, Bonhoeffer Series, Number 1 (New York and Toronto: The Edwin Mellen Press, 1981.

EDITOR'S PREFACE

"Bonhoeffer's Ethics, the writing of which he himself looked upon as the great task of his life, still seems to be his most neglected book."[1] Eberhard Bethge, its editor and Bonhoeffer's foremost interpreter, arrived at this assessment more than a decade ago. Its continuing validity led a group of scholars, members of the International Bonhoeffer Society, to plan and produce this volume. We suspected that the root problem was not simple neglect but, instead, certain features of the text which injected an element of uncertainty into the task of interpretation.

As Clifford Green's chapter demonstrates, even the revised published text of the Ethics (in both German and English editions), contains problems which must be resolved before interpreters can be confident about the development of Bonhoeffer's ideas from 1940 to 1943, and consequently about the full meaning of his argument. This notably contrasts with the status of scholarly opinion about works from earlier periods of his life. For example, careful observation and debate has evolved into a consensus that the early theology pivoted on the sociality of Christ and the structure of the Christian

---

1. Eberhard Bethge, Bonhoeffer: Exile and Martyr, ed. with an essay by John de Gruchy (New York: Seabury Press, 1975), 20.

community.2 We concluded that no such consensus existed about the Ethics and that a volume of fundamental and specialized studies, as well as more general essays, would be both timely and useful. That is the significance of our title.

Of course, the forthcoming German critical edition of Bonhoeffer's works (Dietrich Bonhoeffer Werke), the first volumes of which have recently been published will soon permit an enhanced level of accuracy and comprehensiveness in all Bonhoeffer scholarship. Meanwhile, this volume attempts to move study of the Ethics in that direction; indeed some of the work published here is simultaneously directly contributing to the new critical edition of the Ethik. But, rather than wait several years for the completion of that undertaking, the authors of this volume decided the importance of the issues, both technical and ethical, warranted an earlier publication date.

This volume is the third in a series of studies sponsored by the English Language Section of the International Bonhoeffer Society.3 One of the fundamental reasons for the existence of the Society, which was founded in 1971, is to foster research; indeed, its name originally included the terms "archive and research." Accordingly, it was no accident that our group coalesced around a project requiring extensive research. We soon began calling ourselves the "Bonhoeffer Ethics Working Group," and collaborated at several annual meetings

---

2. A number of strong articles and monographs had converged from various angles of approach to provide a genuine answer to the confusions into which Bonhoeffer scholarship had fallen during earlier phases--suffice it to mention DB; SCH; Ernst Feil, The Theology of Dietrich Bonhoeffer, trans. Martin Rumscheidt (Philadelphia: Fortress Press, 1985); and Jürgen Moltmann and Jürgen Weissbach, Two Studies in the Theology of Bonhoeffer, trans. Reginald H. Fuller and Ilse Fuller (New York: Charles Scribners Sons, 1967).

3. The previous volumes are John D. Godsey and Geffrey B. Kelly, eds., Ethical Responsibility: Bonhoeffer's Legacy to the Churches, Toronto Studies in Theology, Volume 6, Bonhoeffer Series, Number 1 (New York and Toronto: The Edwin Mellen Press, 1981), abbreviated ER; and Thomas I. Day, Dietrich Bonhoeffer on Christian Community and Common Sense, Toronto Studies in Theology, Volume 1, Bonhoeffer Series, Number 2, (New York and Toronto: The Edwin Mellen Press, 1982).

Editor's Preface

of the American Academy of Religion and at a productive three-day session in the Center for Continuing Education at Princeton Seminary.

Gradually the book took shape. The arrangement is in three sections. Part One, because we were seeking to place the study of Bonhoeffer's Ethics (and consequently of his ethical thought) on a new foundation, begins by concentrating on the text. In addition there are discussions of the interplay between text and biography (with special attention to Bonhoeffer's experiences in the resistance movement), and about Bonhoeffer's methods of approaching Christian Ethics.

In the first chapter, Clifford Green, who had worked with the Bonhoeffer papers in Germany before, presents the results of his work on the problems of the text. The reason text criticism is the point of departure for the whole book is that scholars need to know the order in which the chapters were written and how Bonhoeffer conceived the structure of his work and its argument before any other interpretation and evaluation is possible. Painstaking work with the original German manuscripts has yielded a new theory of the book's structure; this is presented in dialogue with previous arrangements made by Eberhard Bethge. Particularly striking is Green's argument for the relocation of the chapter on "Church and World"; its section on 'Christ and Good People' assumes much greater importance, and reveals the roots in the resistance movement of the 'religionless Christianity' project of the Letters and Papers from Prison.

Robin Lovin, who came to Bonhoeffer studies first through an essay on faith development, has authored the second chapter, which explores the linkages between biography, text and ideas. He introduces the reader to the background of Bonhoeffer's ethical ideas from World War I onwards, pointing out the role of Barth's early theology, certain parallels with Brunner, and the impact of his involvement in the Confessing Church. Then he offers a narrative account of the writing of the Ethics, noting the biographical and political events and influences which came to expression in the manuscripts for the various chapters. Of particular interest is Lovin's discussion of Bonhoeffer's nuanced conception of responsibility which he developed in support of his fellow conspirators. Finally, the treatment of the commandment of God serves as a bridge between the more technical discussions of the same topic in Green and Rasmussen.

The third chapter, by Larry Rasmussen, was originally written many years ago when he was engaged in his doctoral research on the relation of Bonhoeffer's ethical theology to his involvement in the resistance movement against Hitler. Rasmussen had argued that Chapter Seven of Bonhoeffer's Ethics appeared heavily influenced by volume II/2 of Karl Barth's Church Dogmatics, the section on ethics headed "The Command of God." What makes Rasmussen's essay especially timely is the recent discovery of previously unavailable letters between Bonhoeffer and Barth, decisively confirming Rasmussen's circumstantial evidence. Further, his discussion of different methods in Bonhoeffer's Ethics still raises issues relevant to contemporary ethical thought.

Part Two contains specialized studies of texts and issues within the Ethics. William Peck, while exploring Bonhoeffer's treatment of issues which today belong in the province of medical ethics, stumbled upon an anomaly in the text fragment on euthanasia. The term euthanasia, of course, arose for Bonhoeffer not out of our current interest in life-prolonging technologies, but out of the Nazi master-race theories. But the investigation moved away from the theory of euthanasia as such and focussed on the text itself and the problem of a "close reading" of a short text segment. Its conclusion illustrates, and in part is based upon, Green's discovery in Chapter One that the theme of Christ and good people is considerably more central than previously thought. The nub of the argument is that this brief text on a subject apparently unrelated to the "good people" theme discloses the force and importance of that theme for Bonhoeffer and connects it decisively with his fellow workers in the resistance movement.

A parallel piece was found in the discussion of Bonhoeffer and suicide by Gerard Rothuizen, one of the leading Dutch interpreters of Bonhoeffer. It is a special pleasure to publish a translation of the

Editor's Preface

Dutch original of this essay because up to now none of Rothuizen's scholarly writings have been available in English. I wish to thank Edwin Robertson for graciously making available his draft for the translation. The final version is a much revised result of transatlantic correspondence between the author and the editor.

The subject of suicide, like that of euthanasia, engenders a different set of issues when considered in the context of Nazi Germany. Rothuizen shows that Bonhoeffer's wrestling with the possibility of suicide after he was imprisoned is a much richer theme than we might have expected. After locating the theme within a network of traditional positions on suicide and interpreting Barth's views on the subject, he offers a sensitive exploration of Bonhoeffer's position in relation to the question of "being for others."

Part Three of this volume comprises two essays on Bonhoeffer's ethical thought as it unfolded in his authorship as a whole. John Godsey, a veteran in Bonhoeffer studies, fills a gap in the literature with his fresh and wide-ranging treatment of Bonhoeffer's doctrine of love. Any reader of this volume who is unfamiliar with the more technical aspects of Bonhoeffer studies ought to begin with this chapter, because Godsey opens with an introductory survey of the theme in modern ethical discussion and then explores, in chronological order, the things Bonhoeffer said about love. So central to Bonhoeffer is this theme that Godsey's treatment can almost serve as an introduction to his entire theology.

Charles West, too, provides a discussion of Bonhoeffer's ethical thought as a whole through the theme "Ground under Our Feet." The metaphor of being true to the earth and of keeping a firm footing on the ground appears frequently in Bonhoeffer's writings and West explores its wide and deep implications. Appropriately our concluding chapter is the most poetic and comprehensive, a reminder of the grand range of historical roots and aesthetic, political, ecclesiastical and familial ramifications for which Bonhoeffer took ethical responsibility. West not only connects and summarizes many levels of Bonhoeffer's own ethical theology, he also briefly goes outside it to the question of indebtedness to Luther and even to Calvin. In this way West's chapter constitutes a reminder of the questions about the place of the Ethics in its wider historical and philosophical contexts which this volume leaves unattended.

One matter which has concerned us at many points is the issue of inclusive language. Bonhoeffer belonged to a time before the consciousness of Western culture had been raised about sexist language. We have not changed quotations where Bonhoeffer's language is sexist, our thought being that by such intervention we would be creating an anachronism untrue to the particularity of our subject matter. However, when the English translation is more sexist than the German original, we have freely made improvements.

An editor soon learns to depend on the assistance of other people and organizations. I want to thank the American Philosophical Society for a travel grant which enabled me to check details in the Bonhoeffer archives and especially to thank Eberhard and Renate Bethge for access to those archives. I am deeply grateful for their generous gifts of time and patience in providing important facets of "living history."

The financial support of the University of North Carolina, through a grant from its University Research Council, through computer assistance from Todd Lewis, and the Microcomputer Support Center, and through the Department of Religious Studies' provision of time from the following research assistants has been crucial: Margot French Schultz, Tim Van der Wert, Lydia Hoyle, John Santucci, Meg Harper Pettis, and Roper Marks.

My colleagues in the "Bonhoeffer Ethics Working Group," including those whose names do not appear in the table of contents, have been helpful and long-suffering at every turn. Their institutional affiliations are as follows: Clifford Green, Hartford Seminary, and President of the International Bonhoeffer Society, English Language Section; Robin Lovin, University of Chicago; Larry Rasmussen, Union Theological Seminary, New York City; Gerard Rothuizen, Theological College of the Reformed Churches in the Netherlands at

Editor's Preface

Kampen; John Godsey, Wesley Theological Seminary, Washington, D.C.; Charles West, Princeton Theological Seminary. One of the Working Group members, Geffrey Kelly, is the secretary of the International Bonhoeffer Society, English Language Section. Anyone interested in information about the society and its services may reach him at La Salle University, Philadelphia, PA 19141.

William Jay Peck
Chapel Hill, NC
December 1986

PART ONE: TEXT, CONTEXT, AND METHOD

I

THE TEXT OF BONHOEFFER'S ETHICS

Clifford J. Green

All interpretations of Bonhoeffer's Ethics to date rest on an unstable foundation. It is an anomaly of Bonhoeffer studies that the problems of ordering the text have never been systematically addressed--though the book has been published and much discussed for over thirty-five years. Only in 1980 did several scholars begin to confront this issue.

From the first publication of the German edition in 1949, Eberhard Bethge, the editor, clearly pointed to these problems. The "book" consists of drafts of seven "chapters," rather than a complete, continuous, and integrated argument. Most chapters are incomplete, and there are uncertainties about the order in which some of them were written. The dating of some chapters is problematic. Further, there is a debate about which chapters Bonhoeffer regarded as "blocks," that is, chapters which he intended to belong together because they contain a continuity of argument and an integrity of theological perspective. The most obvious sign of these problems is the total re-arrangement of the volume that Bethge made in the sixth German edition published in 1963.

This essay is the first systematic analysis of the problems of ordering the text. My aim is to propose an arrangement of the Ethics which is based on careful study of the manuscripts as physical evidence, as well as of their content. My proposed arrangement differs significantly from Bethge's, but also results in the work appearing more coherent and less fragmentary than has been customary. It also clearly illuminates Bonhoeffer's theological development from the beginning of the ethics work to the <u>Letters and Papers from Prison</u>.

My interest in this problem began in 1969, but I first began serious research on it in 1980. Since then some preparatory work has been done for the critical German edition of Bonhoeffer's <u>Ethik</u> as part of the publication of the Dietrich Bonhoeffer Werke. In addition to research on Bonhoeffer's original manuscript I am also drawing upon his writing notes and outlines (Zettel) which have just been systematically revised. Further, we now have for the first time transcriptions of the deletions from Bonhoeffer's original handwritten manuscript. A catalogue of the paper types in the <u>Ethik</u> manuscript and Zettel, correlating them to dated use of the same paper types (as in letters), has also been prepared. And Dr. Ilse Tödt has recently circulated a fourteen page listing of variations in the printed text from the original manuscript.[1] We also have the benefit of some re-discovered correspondence between Bonhoeffer and Karl Barth which bears directly upon the <u>Ethics</u>.

This mass of evidence requires a good deal of digestion, especially the material that has just become available. I will be involved in this task as a member of the editorial team working on the critical edition. The following essay, therefore, is presented as a report in the mid-stream of ongoing research. We begin by reviewing how our present German and English texts came about, and what guided the arrangements Bethge made. (For the convenience of readers the Table of Contents of <u>Ethik</u> is appended to this essay.)[2]

---

1. Dr. Ilse Tödt, along with Eberhard Bethge and Dr. Herbert Anzinger, deserves special mention for her work with these preparatory studies.

2. See Appendix A, 61-64 below.

I. THE EMERGENCE AND ARRANGEMENTS OF THE ETHICS

"I've reproached myself for not having finished my Ethics," wrote Bonhoeffer to Bethge in his November 18, 1943 letter from Tegel.[3] Acknowledging that his "ideas were still incomplete," he apparently still wanted to finish the work, and expressed the hope that even if the manuscript had been confiscated, the essential ideas he had conveyed to Bethge would somehow emerge indirectly. But self-reproach did not drive him to the unfinished task. Instead he wrote the now lost essay on "The Feeling of Time"[4] and the essay "What is Meant by 'Telling the Truth'?"[5] Above all, he turned to the autobiographical literary efforts to gather up the past, now published as Fiction from Prison.[6]

More poignantly he wrote a month later: "I sometimes feel as if my life were more or less over, and as if all I had to do were to finish my Ethics."[7] But in January, Dilthey--a catalyst for what was to come--appears for the first time in the prison letters, and reappears regularly.[8] While ideas from the Ethics emerge occasionally (especially the discussion of the "mandates"[9]), as they did also in the fiction, the task of completing the Ethics is never mentioned again. Instead, April sees the articulation of the "non-religious Christianity" project which engaged his excited concentration for the rest of his imprisonment and led to work on a new book.

Ordering the material for publication thus fell to the editor. The

---

3. LPP, 129.

4. See the notes for this essay in LPP, 33-35.

5. E, 363-371.

6. FP.

7. 15 December 1943; LPP, 163.

8. LPP, 187.

9. LPP, 192-194.

Ethik was the first work of Bonhoeffer to appear posthumously. Eberhard Bethge's first Preface, which concludes by quoting the two comments from the prison letters, was dated "9th April 1948," and the book appeared early in 1949. Clearly the editor felt that, by making this an anniversary volume, he was presenting what at one point his friend believed to be the culmination of his theological work.[10]

Bethge made clear from the outset that the Ethics was not a finished work. The Preface began: "This book is not the Ethics which Dietrich Bonhoeffer intended to have published."[11] The chapters are "scattered drafts," he wrote elsewhere, and the book has an "incomplete and fragmentary character."[12] In spite of a later remark that he deciphered the drafts and "attempted... to arrange it so far as possible in the order of its origin,"[13] the first edition was not really governed by a consistent, chronological ordering of the chapters--that is, according to the order in which they were written. Rather, a systematic order was attempted for the first few chapters, based on an outline Bonhoeffer made in Autumn, 1940.[14] So, Bethge writes, "the first sections [i.e., chapters] have been arranged according to the outline... [and] the remaining sections... have been placed in the order in which they appear to have been written."[15] Apparently this means that the first three chapters of that edition (the present chapters III, V and IV) were placed according to the outline order, while the other four (the present I, II, VI and VII) followed in the presumed order of writing. This volume continued through five editions (actually reprintings); an English translation was published in 1955, with its

---

10. Cf. DB, 621.

11. E, 7.

12. "The Editing and Publishing of the Bonhoeffer Papers," Andover Newton Bulletin LII.2 (December, 1959), 2-3.

13. Ibid.

14. Cf. E, 8-9, and also below, 26-28; see also Appendix B, 65-66 below.

15. E, 9.

The Text of Bonhoeffer's *Ethics*

own idiosyncratic arrangement into two "parts" noted below.

In 1963 the sixth newly arranged German edition was published. The stimulus for this new edition was discussion of Bonhoeffer's theological development as this came to fruition in the prison letters.[16] (Hanfried Müller's controversial reading of the later Bonhoeffer was prominent at that time.[17]) The English translation also adopted this ordering in the Collins Fontana edition of 1964, the Macmillan paperback of 1965 and--with different pagination--the S.C.M. hardcover edition of 1971. Inexplicably, some printings omitted Bethge's new Preface explaining the re-arrangement; Macmillan's paperback edition, the one most widely used in the United States, first included it in 1969.

In this new edition Bethge attempted a strictly chronological ordering of the chapters. Further, as explained below, he proposed a fourfold scheme of organization, regarding the seven chapters as grouped into four Ansätze.[18] By this term he meant to convey the preliminary and unfinished character of the writings (as in "beginnings") and also an experimental character (as in "approaches" and "attempts"). But he also meant more, namely, that each Ansatz was a fairly coherent unit focused on a particular theological theme.

---

16. E, 11.

17. Müller, <u>Von der Kirche zur Welt</u>. Leipzig: Koehler & Amelang, 1961; 2nd edn. (Leipzig & Hamburg, 1966). In discussion of an earlier draft of this paper at the Third International Bonhoeffer Conference (Oxford, 1980), Bethge repeated the significance of Müller's impetus for the re-arrangement. See also Bethge's quotation from and comments upon a 1957 article by Müller in the East Berlin newspaper <u>Neue Zeit</u>: in Bethge, "The Editing and Publishing of the Bonhoeffer Papers," (note 13), 5-7. Müller did not debate the problems of ordering the text, but his controversial interpretation of the later Bonhoeffer prompted Bethge to attempt a *chronological* ordering to provide a textual basis for argument about Müller's thesis.

18. Eg, 14-15. In his Alden-Tuthill lectures at Chicago, Bethge called these Ansätze "four new and different attempts to approach ethics from 1940 to 1943"; cf. "The Challenge of Dietrich Bonhoeffer's Life and Theology," <u>Chicago Theological Seminary Register</u> LI.2 (February, 1961), 29. The biography also speaks of "four new beginnings" (viermaligen neuen Beginnen), of a third "Versuch" and a fourth "Neuansatz"; cf. DBg, 806-808; DB, 622-624.

Bethge's scheme is described in at least three places: his Alden-Tuthill lectures (1961), the Preface to the re-arranged edition (1963), and the biography (1967).[19] The scheme can be summarized, using the present chapter numbering, as follows.

(A) Chapters I and II. By comparing the theological ethos of this material to Nachfolge (published 1937), Bethge especially had in mind the emphasis on Christ's *lordship*, though with the new notes of the *breadth* of this dominion and the *unity* of God and the world in Christ. The Preface dates these chapters 1939-40 and says they were "probably broken off before August 1940"[20]; the biography attributes the beginning of the work on ethics to "1939 or 1940." In light of the discussion below, it is interesting to note that while Bethge does not explicitly mention Chapter II in his discussions of this first approach, he clearly intends to include it since he refers repeatedly to the theme of the exclusiveness and universality of Christ found in Chapter II.

(B) Chapter III. This writing is located at the von Kleist estate at Klein-Krössin in September-October, 1940. The Preface speaks of "conformation" (Gleichgestaltung) as the keyword: in the dialectic of transformation, Christ takes on the forms of worldly life in order to shape them to his own form. In the biography Bethge says this about the theological orientation of this chapter: "Bonhoeffer now took his theological stand on the incarnation."[21] This means that Bethge has given us two--perhaps related--theological themes for this second Ansatz, conformation and incarnation.

The Chicago lectures mention the strong "christological basis" which is spelled out to be Christ as "Lord and Redeemer of the world [who is] the center, reason and aim of all human reality and claims, therefore, all fields of human existence." At most the lectures may allude obliquely to the incarnation theme in the reference to "Christ's

---

19. "The Challenge"; Eg, 14-17; E, 11-14; DBg, 806-811; DB, 622-626.

20. E, 11; cf. E, 58.

21. DBg, 807; DB, 622.

conforming to this world."22

Bethge is certainly right that incarnation is an explicit, prominent category in this chapter; indeed, it is the basic one. But that means it is questionable to use the incarnation theme to identify later "new approaches." Also, it makes one question Bethge's assumption about *one* theological theme characterizing each Neuansatz.

Further, the problem of whether each Ansatz has a characteristic theological theme, and, if so, what it is for Chapter III, is compounded when the Preface describes the theological focus of the chapter as "conformation"23 while the biography first speaks of incarnation but then in the summary refers to conformation.24 The problem is highlighted when we juxtapose the Preface statement that the "theologischen Ausgangspunkt" of Chapter III is "Gleichgestaltung" with the biography statement that the "theologischen Standort" is "Inkarnation."25 If one attempts to resolve the problem as the Chicago lectures perhaps suggest (by hinting that incarnation is the christological basis for the theo-anthropological concept of conformation), then it is problematic to use incarnation as a distinctive theological category characteristic of the *fourth* "new approach" (see below).

(C) Chapter IV. This chapter, with its distinction of ultimate and penultimate leading to a discussion of natural life, is Bethge's third Neuansatz. He dates it late November, 1940 to mid-February, 1941 at the Benedictine monastery of Ettal near Munich. Both the Preface and the biography identify "justification" as its theological point of departure; the Chicago lectures and Oxford comments are consistent with this.

---

22. Bethge, "The Challenge," 29.

23. Eg, 15. Bethge repeated this in discussion at the Oxford conference.

24. Cp. DBg, 807 and 810.

25. Eg, 15; DBg, 807.

(D) Chapters V, VI and VII. Bethge notes uncertainty about the date of Chapter V, either the summer of 1940 or that of 1941 being possible. He prefers the latter and links it to Chapter VI because of continuous page numbering in the manuscripts. The theological "point of departure" is given as "incarnation." All Bethge's writings (and his Oxford comments as well) agree on this. The three chapters are dated from the summer of 1941 until the arrest in April, 1943, with Chapter V, and the beginning of work on Chapter VI, attributed to Klein-Krössin in the summer of 1941; Chapter VI exists in two versions and presumably the work on these is believed to have extended into 1942. Chapter VII, Bethge reports, is included in this fourth Ansatz because it was on Bonhoeffer's desk at the time of his arrest, and its writing notes were all marked by Bethge.

One further point about Bethge's arrangement should be noted. Elaborating on a point briefly mentioned in the biography,[26] Bethge stated at Oxford that in trying to re-arrange the manuscripts in historical order, he put the emphasis not so much on paper types and similar evidence, but rather on a double schema of *theological theme* and *place*. The result is that the four Ansätze are interpreted like this:

(A) Discipleship--Sigurdshof: the ethos is that of Finkenwalde where Bonhoeffer, as director of that theological seminary, looks back to <u>Nachfolge</u>.

(B) Conformation--Klein-Krössin: Bonhoeffer is here focusing on German church history, and seeing how the world represented by Klein-Krössin is going to pieces.

(C) Justification--Ettal: in the Catholic setting of the monastery Bonhoeffer thinks not only of "the natural" but also of the central Reformation doctrine.

(D) Incarnation--"Sigtuna": Sigtuna was Bonhoeffer's code name for his conspiracy and resistance work, and his involvement in that is to be seen under the theological-ethical rubric of incarnation.

---

26. DBg, 810; DB, 625.

The Text of Bonhoeffer's Ethics

This approach reminds us of others Bethge has used, from his early Alden-Tuthill lectures to the biography, and in other writings, to organize his exposition and interpretation by thematic summaries and periodizations. This can often be helpful, but here it is very risky. In historical-textual work attention must first focus on the detailed internal and external evidence of the manuscripts themselves. Otherwise textual evidence can be overridden by general schemas, distinctions can be made which don't correspond to the text, and crucial questions can be begged.

II. ISSUES OF TEXTUAL ORGANIZATION

Bethge's work is indispensable; yet we have already seen that his arrangement and interpretation raise several issues. So do analyses by Larry Rasmussen, Ernst Feil, Peter Möser and also my own research with the texts and manuscripts.[27] The chief textual issues are these: 1) What was the chronological order in which the chapters were written? Can we know if the present chapters were completed one by one, or did Bonhoeffer sometimes work on more than one simultaneously? In particular, when are Chapters II and V to be dated? 2) What were the time periods in which the various chapters were written? 3) Are any of the chapters to be regarded as "blocks"? By using "block" rather than Bethge's term "Ansatz," I choose a more neutral word which does not imply that a particular block is necessarily a "new approach" or that it is governed by a particular theological theme which is different from other blocks; but

---

27. See Rasmussen's chapter in this volume, originally written in 1968 with the title, "Bonhoeffer's Ethics: One Method or Two?" Ernst Feil, "Strukturen wirklichkeitsgemässen Handelns des Christen. Ein Beitrag zur Ethik Dietrich Bonhoeffers," lecture at Halle, November 3, 1981. Peter Möser, "Arbeitsschritte, Entscheidungsprobleme und klärende Vorüberlegungen zur Neuarbeitung von Bonhoeffers Ethik im Rahmen der geplanten Bonhoeffer-Werkausgabe," April, 1982. My own earlier working papers were "Bonhoeffer's Ethics: A Research Brief," written in March, 1980, and two supplements to it written in November, 1980 and December, 1981. (The papers of Feil and Möser, and my previous drafts, have not been published.)

nor does it exclude that possibility. Rather, "block" here means a chapter or group of chapters which Bonhoeffer intended to belong together in developing a set of ethical ideas. 4) Did Bonhoeffer regard the headings within the manuscripts as sections of chapters, or were some of these regarded as chapters themselves, comprised within a larger unit? These issues by no means exhaust the questions to be posed to the text as a whole; but the substantive questions presuppose answers to the textual issues of this paper.

Since the following argument is detailed and complex, readers may find it helpful to preview the summary of the results in the final section of the chapter.[28] Here I would simply offer the generalization that Bonhoeffer's Ethics must be considered a less fragmentary and much more coherent text than previously assumed. To be sure, the manuscripts do not constitute a finished and polished book; they retain an experimental character. But there is a purposeful development, both within the manuscripts themselves and from his writings in the later 1930's to the Letters and Papers from Prison.

III. DESCRIPTION OF THE MANUSCRIPTS

Analysis of the manuscripts requires an account of them, which will also yield some information helpful for studying the argument of the texts.

To start with, it can be stated confidently that we possess all the material that Bonhoeffer wrote for his Ethics. One could imagine from the editor's first Preface[29] that only "parts of the work" survived and that some were confiscated by the Gestapo. The Gestapo did indeed confiscate some of the manuscript (Chapter VII) from Bonhoeffer's family home prior to his arrest in 1943; but Bethge has informed me that this was returned, and that no other parts were lost or destroyed in the war. The complete set of manuscripts is therefore

---

28. See 58-59 below.

29. E, 7.

extant.

The originals, following Bonhoeffer's usual custom, consist of handwritten manuscripts. They reveal all the familiar signs of first drafts--material deleted, additions interleaved, parts relocated, and so forth.[30] Only one chapter was reworked, namely Chapter VI.[31] But even the second version is incomplete, and neither of them include all the sections projected in an outline for this chapter.

In addition to the manuscripts a large collection of note pages (Zettel)[32] is extant. The Nachlass contains 113 pages[33] with outlines, biblical references, occasional quotations, and so on. They are Bonhoeffer's working papers, and are written on about forty different sorts of paper including letter paper, typing paper, old calendar leaves, a bank letter and even a medical schedule. Prior to research for this essay, the Zettel collection had never been systematically checked, ordered or analyzed, though a draft transcription was made before 1948.[34] One cannot be certain, of course, that all the note pages from

---

30. The considerable volume of deleted material was first transcribed in 1985, in connection with research for this essay and in preparation for the new Ethik volume in the critical German edition of Bonhoeffer's works. A copy of this material, and of the new Zettel transcriptions (see note 34 below), has been deposited in the Bonhoeffer Archive at the Burke Library, Union Theological Seminary, New York.

31. For the first version, see GS III, 455-477.

32. The word "Zettel" has the same form for singular and plural.

33. While the Zettel collection is numbered 1-123, Bethge never possessed 123 Zettel. Even though the numbering spreads over that range, ten numbers (90-99) were reserved during the initial ordering for future use but never assigned to specific notes. It is also important to realize that a number of the Zettel in this collection do *not* belong to the work on the Ethik. (See also footnote 34.)

34. Those using the microfilm copies of the Bonhoeffer papers made at Harvard Divinity School in 1958, and even the more recent microfiche set produced by the Bundesarchiv in Koblenz, should be warned that the original typed transcriptions of the Zettel on these films have never been systematically revised since they were made in the mid 1940's. There are omissions and inaccuracies. The chapter identifications on most of them were supplied by the transcriber, Frau Lindner, not Eberhard Bethge; some of these are uncertain or erroneous. Late in 1984 Dr. Herbert Anzinger (Dielheim-Heidelberg) began to make a new, systematic

Bonhoeffer's hand have survived since it is quite possible that he might have lost or discarded some; Bethge reports that he himself gave special care to these papers, including marking those on the desk in connection with the work on Chapter VII which was in process at the time of the arrest. Given the considerable number of Zettel and their spread across all the chapters (and even some "appendices"), it seems probable that most of them survived the hazards of war.

Both the German and English publications of the Ethics contain five other essays on ethical and theological subjects. Some of these are quite closely related to themes in the chapters of the Ethics proper, and come from the same period of work, 1940 to 1943. Others have only a general relationship, one of them certainly (and another possibly) dating from Tegel. These pieces are appropriately printed in the German editions as an appendix, and incorrectly in the English editions as "Part Two." But there is no evidence that Bonhoeffer regarded these pieces as draft chapters for his Ethik.

The manuscripts are all handwritten on twenty four different types of paper, some types being used a great deal, others only a little. As now found in the Nachlass they appear to fall into eight groups (counting the two versions of Chapter VI) which have been printed as chapters; there are cases, discussed below, where what appears to be a separate chapter (e.g., Chapter II) in fact is not so. Each chapter is identified by a title on its first page (Chapter V has an alternative title as well), and by a numbering sequence on its pages. The chapters as such are not numbered, so we have no clue to their chronological or conceptual order from markings like that. There is only one case in which numbers appear to run from one chapter to another: Chapter V, "Christ, Reality and Good," ends with a page numbered 14a. and Chapter VI, "History and Good," begins with a page numbered 15; this is true for *both* versions of Chapter VI (hereafter VI/1 and VI/2).[35]

---

transcription of the Ethik Zettel collection; this work was continued by Anzinger, Bethge and Ilse Tödt in 1985, and may be finished late in 1986.

35. VI/1 refers to the first-written version (GS III, 455-477), VI/2 to the second version which is included in Ethics.

Chapter VI is the only one in which material obviously exists in two drafts. The first version is shorter but covers more of the outline Bonhoeffer made for this chapter; the second is longer and more detailed and doesn't cover as much of the outline. The chapter titles, as noted, are Bonhoeffer's. So are the main chapter divisions in Chapters III, VI and VII. In Chapter IV the section heading "Das Natürliche," introducing the following seven sub-sections, derives from the editor, not Bonhoeffer; but each of the printed sub-section headings is found in the manuscript. In Chapter VI/2, the last page has a new heading "Liebe und Verantwortung," but no text appears under it.[36] All the other sub-section headings, printed in small type in both German and English editions, were supplied by the editor who derived them from the sense of the texts.

Before proceeding further we need to consider the significance of similarity of paper types as evidence for questions of dating and writing sequence. For example, Bethge connects Chapter II to Chapter I largely because the same paper was used for the beginning of the former as for the end of the latter. Möser questions the deduction somewhat, saying that such paper evidence only proves "that Chapter II was written after Chapter I, not that these two chapters belong together."[37] But can such evidence, by itself, really prove sequence or succession? The answer must be a definite negative. Consider two parallel cases to that example. Both versions of "History and Good" begin with the same paper that Chapter VII ends with; so do Appendices 1 and 5. But that does not mean that they were all necessarily written later. In fact we know that VI/1 and VI/2 were definitely written *earlier* than Chapter VII, and so was Appendix 1. Appendix 5, on the other hand, was written later; however, we know that not from evidence of paper type but rather

---

36. See the outline for the continuation of this chapter, E, 262. Also note the omission in the translation of 2. (c) of the words "Sichzurechnen, Einzelner sein" after "Schuldübernahme"; cf. Eg, 278.

37. Möser, 12.

from a remark in a letter from prison. Another parallel case concerns Chapter I and Appendix 2; the former begins with the same paper as the latter ends with. But this doesn't prove temporal sequence either. While other evidence from content does connect these two pieces, neither paper nor content is sufficient in this case to establish temporal sequence.

This is not to deny that use of similar papers *may* indeed reflect the fact that material was written in a particular period of time. So paper *may* be evidence of temporal proximity, though other evidence is needed to prove it. But what needs much clearer recognition is that paper types are as often *place*-specific as *time*-specific. If one examines a catalogue of the manuscript papers[38] and concentrates on chapters whose date and provenance are secure, it is striking to see that the papers are all *place*-specific. Thus Chapters I, III and IV are written on papers which are all different from one another; we also know that the work on these chapters was done in three different places, Berlin, Klein-Krössin, and Ettal. So we can safely call the three papers of Chapter I "Berlin papers," the six papers of Chapter III "Klein-Krössin papers" and the two papers of Chapter IV "Ettal papers." The evidence is not only from the chapters written during Bonhoeffer's first work periods in these places after beginning on his ethics. It is also found from other periods of work when Bonhoeffer returns to those same places. Accordingly, Chapter V is written on Klein-Krössin paper, as Bethge pointed out in the second Preface. And the Eichberger paper (one of the "Berlin" types used in Chapter I) is also used in several other chapters, two appendices and also in writings produced during the imprisonment at Tegel.

A natural comment is that paper is easily portable and is not necessarily fixed in one place. True enough; we even have a letter in which Ruth von Kleist-Retzow offers to send 700 sheets of paper

---

38. I have made such a detailed catalogue and copies will be available from the Bonhoeffer Archive at the Burke Library of Union Theological Seminary, New York, and through the Bonhoeffer Society.

The Text of Bonhoeffer's Ethics

from Klein-Krössin to Berlin.³⁹ Still, a correlation of types of paper with places of work demonstrates that Bonhoeffer did not use Berlin papers at Klein-Krössin in the autumn of 1940, nor did he use Berlin or Klein-Krössin papers at Ettal in the winter of 1940-41. However, I am not arguing an absolute point, that paper is *only* place-specific; rather, I am arguing that the evidence proves it is sufficiently place-specific that one cannot simply assume that same paper means same time. It can just as easily mean same place, different time.⁴⁰

I will now take up the questions of the order and arrangement of the text, beginning with Chapter I of the present arrangement. This order of analysis does not, however, presuppose anything about the writing chronology or possible "blocks." It is simply a convenient way to proceed.

IV. CHAPTER I

Since questions have been raised about the status of Chapter II, I will not make an assumption about its relation to Chapter I, though Bethge has consistently linked them together as his first Ansatz. Bethge initially gave 1940 as the beginning of the ethics work, then in the second Preface mentioned "1939/40"; the biography identified both "1939 or 1940" and the spring of 1940: "It was then [late March, early April] that Bonhoeffer began to write his Ethics." ⁴¹

The later date seems much more likely. During the 1939-1940 winter and up to mid-March, Bonhoeffer was working with the Sammelvikariat in Pomerania. In his literary activity he wrote intensely on Psalm 119 at Sigurdshof, continuing work begun earlier and completing a substantial manuscript; in addition he was involved

---

39. Letter of 12 December 1941; cf. DBg, 792; DB, 609.

40. The picture could be somewhat different for the Zettel papers since Bonhoeffer may have taken notes and outlines prepared in one place to continue working with them in another location.

41. E, 7, 11; DBg, 806, 760, 765, DB, 522, 580, 603.

in the Beckmann-Eichholz project of Predigt-Meditationen volumes, and he also had to write Das Gebetbuch der Bibel, which was published in 1940.[42] Feil, who independently pointed to some of these facts, also pointed out that, as he returned from America in 1939, Bonhoeffer was invited to give the Croall Lectures in Edinburgh the following winter; on August 24 he gave John Baillie the theme, not ethics, but "Death in the Christian Message," and read several works on this subject in the latter part of the year.[43] Further, on September 19, 1941, Bonhoeffer wrote to his sister in England that he had been working on a book on ethics "for about a year."[44] Bethge also indicates that the Zettel for Chapter I are on types of paper Bonhoeffer used for letters "in the spring and summer of 1940."[45]

All of the above evidence points to Bethge's later date, rather than 1939, as the time when Bonhoeffer began writing his ethics. After Köslin and Sigurdshof were closed by the Gestapo on March 17, 1940, Bonhoeffer spent the rest of the spring in Berlin. He was also there in the summer, and made two trips to East Prussia in June and July. Hence mid-March, 1940, is the most likely terminus a quo for beginning work on the ethics.

What evidence is there that the present Chapter I derives from spring-summer, 1940, and that it was actually the first that Bonhoeffer wrote? Negatively, it does not explicitly refer back to any previously written chapters, and does not mention any outline in which other material precedes it; nor does it forecast discussion in other chapters which will follow it. By itself, however, this is not decisive evidence.

Secondly, its beginning certainly qualifies as an opening statement for an initial chapter in Christian ethics. "The first task of Christian ethics is to negate and overcome [aufheben]" the virtually

---

42. Cf. GS IV, 480-569; DB, 571-572.

43. Feil, Halle lecture, 7; cf. DBg, 743.

44. GS VI, 542.

45. E, 11.

unquestioned idea in all other approaches that "the knowledge of good and evil seems to be the aim of all ethical reflection.... Christian ethics claims to discuss the origin of the whole problematic of ethics, and thus professes to be a critique of all ethics as such."[46] If this certainly sounds like an opening statement, it nevertheless does not give us a date.

Positively, Bethge reports that the Zettel for this chapter contain "types of paper which Bonhoeffer used for letters in the spring and summer of 1940."[47] And there is a further piece of evidence which points to summer, 1940, namely the critique of Dilschneider, "'Personal' und 'Sach' Ethos." This is written on the same paper as the first half of Chapter I (also found in some of Chapter II). But the stronger connection between the two pieces is the very clear allusion to Dilschneider's categories and approach. In Bonhoeffer's discussion of love we find this passage:

> Nor is love the direct personal relation, participation in the personal and the individual, in contrast to the law of the institutional [Sachlichen], the impersonal order. Quite apart from the fact that here the 'personal' and the 'institutional' ['Persönliches,' 'Sachliches'] are in a quite unbiblical and abstract manner torn apart from each other, love becomes here a human attitude, and only a partial one at that.[48]

Here Bonhoeffer is using Dilschneider's very own language, and giving the same critique as found in the review. Dilschneider's Die Evangelische Tat was almost certainly published in May, 1940.[49]

---

46. Eg, 19, translation mine; cf. E, 17.

47. Eg, 14; E, 11.

48. Eg, 54, translation mine; cf. E, 49.

49. The Preface is dated March 28, 1940 and the Deutsche Bücherei (as reported in their letter to me of October 15, 1985) inventoried its copy June 13, 1940; this indicates, they conclude, a publication date before June 1, 1940.

Bethge reports that Bonhoeffer's critique was written "soon after it was published,"[50] that is, June-July, 1940. Of course, we can't be sure whether the critique or the chapter material was written first. But the connection of the two pieces does seem to locate Chapter I about the middle of 1940, rather than in 1939, or at a much later date after he had time to work on the material we know for certain was written in autumn, 1940.

Is the theological focus of Chapter I a clue to its date? Bethge's characterization of a *discipleship* ethos in this chapter (also, or indeed, especially in Chapter II as he reads it) is a broad one by which he links it to an earlier stage. So far as Chapter I is concerned, there are certainly several explicit references to "Nachfolge Jesu" and "Christusnachfolge."[51] Even more, the style of *exegetical commentary* on verses from the gospels and epistles is strongly reminiscent of The Cost of Discipleship. Nevertheless, this should not disguise the fact that the exegesis takes place within a controlling systematic-theological perspective. The problem of ethics is the problem of disunity and conflict, as the title makes plain: "God's Love and the Disintegration of the World." This is rooted in alienation from the origin which is manifested socially in shame and individually in conscience. Christ, the "crucified and risen God," is the revelation of the *love* of the living God; he is the "new humanity" [neuen Menschen], and conformation [Gleichgestaltung] with his form overcomes the disunity with God so that Christian ethics can then be simple doing of the one will of God.[52]

This impresses me as even more an anticipation of later chapters than a reminiscence of Nachfolge. Indeed, it is obvious that the repetition of themes from Creation and Fall and also the

---

50. Eg, 17.

51. Eg, 40-41, 53; E, 37, 48.

52. Eg, 37, 41-42; E, 34, 37-38.

The Text of Bonhoeffer's Ethics

problematic of the 1932-related "soteriological passages"[53] is also at least as strong as reminiscences of Nachfolge. And that means a notably different focus here from Nachfolge. In the latter the problematic is grace without obedience, faith without ethics, justification without sanctification; the theological themes are discipleship which involves renunciation and obedience to the command of Christ. Here the problematic is disunity, judging and inaction in a conflicted ethic of good and evil which aims to secure one's goodness through knowledge of good and evil; the theological themes are God's love, reconciliation, and conformation to Christ which enables simple, unified, free action. In short, the themes of this chapter sound much more related to Bonhoeffer's situation at the beginning of the war than to 1932 when the problematic of Nachfolge was first crystallized.[54]

Invoking The Cost of Discipleship, then, must be heavily relativized. But we can still say that the exegetical methodology of this chapter does echo that book, just as the christology equally contains themes which are more fully developed in later chapters of the Ethics. Taking both together, the theology of this chapter is consistent with a position prior to other chapters like III-VI. More definite dating evidence than this is not provided by the theological content of this chapter.

In summary, then, the evidence from the Zettel papers and the Dilschneider critique points most clearly to a date in spring-summer, 1940, and the other pieces of evidence are not inconsistent with this. I therefore agree with Bethge to the extent of regarding Chapter I as the "first block." This raises the question of Chapter II.

---

53. Cf. Green, SCH, esp. 145-160.

54. Cf. Green, SCH, Chapter IV, especially reference to the November, 1932 address "Christus und der Friede."

V. CHAPTER II

The distinctive theme of this chapter is rooted in the humanist opposition to Nazism and in the Kirchenkampf. Humanists who support values like reason, culture, humanity, freedom, law, tolerance, autonomy, and human rights find themselves allied with Christians in resisting barbarity, violence, arbitrariness, and irrationality. Christ is the origin of these human values and the protector of secularized humanists who, like the Confessing Church, suffer for the cause of justice, goodness, and humanity. The Christ whose church is to make an exclusive and uncompromised confession of faith gives the protection of his name, by affirming their cause, to those who work for humanity even though they themselves may not work in Christ's name. Hence the relationship of the church to the world must be presented in terms of Christ as the origin of human values, the crucified Christ who justifies humane behavior; and the church's relation to the world will be shaped by the theme that "to know and find Christ one must first become righteous like those who strive and suffer for the sake of justice, truth, and humanity."[55] In short, the topic of 'church and world' is pursued under the rubric 'Christ and good people'.

Bethge points out that the notes (Zettel) for this chapter are on calendar leaves for 1939. There are twelve of these leaves, one from April 25 and the rest from the first half of May. If Bonhoeffer used them after the whole calendar was finished, this would be 1940 at the earliest. So far as paper is concerned, the first four pages are on a Doppelbogen of a paper type which Bonhoeffer used for the last ten pages of Chapter I. Another ten pages are on paper only used elsewhere in Chapter I and in "'Personal' und 'Sach' Ethos," and there is a two page insert on letter paper perhaps used in 1941 and for an

---

55. E, 61.

The Text of Bonhoeffer's Ethics 23

essay fragment which may date from 1940.[56] This evidence might be construed, as Bethge does, to establish a somewhat tenuous link to Chapter I and the year 1940.

Ernst Feil regards Chapter V as a "doublet" of Chapter II and attributes I, II and V to the period May through summer, 1940; this view will be taken up below. For present purposes it suffices to say that Feil presents no independent evidence for dating Chapter II or placing it after Chapter I; he appears simply to accept Bethge's judgment, with the additional comment that Chapter V represents a "christological deepening" of Chapter II.[57]

Peter Möser, however, has strongly questioned Bethge's linking of Chapter II to Chapter I. Möser's skepticism is not primarily based on the fact that the heading "Church and World" comes in *fourth* place in the Autumn, 1940 outline (i.e., *after* the material now in Chapter III). Rather, he argues, "thematically and in content Chapters I and II have nothing to do with each other, whereas there are many commonalities and connections between Chapters II and III."[58] Möser also points out that Bonhoeffer calls this piece of writing a "section" (Abschnitt), not a chapter, and wonders if it should perhaps be regarded as the last main section of Chapter III, as the 1940 outline might suggest. (He notes that if it were so placed this would conform Chapter III to the "normal" condition of all other chapters except Chapter V, namely, that they are all broken off incomplete; but he admits that this is hardly a decisive argument.)[59] Regarding the manuscript papers, he concludes that the use of the same paper for the

---

56. GS III, 416-417.

57. Feil, 7-8.

58. Möser, letter to Green, June 27, 1982. Day also calls Chapter II "a chapter appended and not integral to his beginning essay"; cf. Thomas Day, Dietrich Bonhoeffer on Christian Community and Common Sense (New York: Edwin Mellen Press, 1983), 149. Day also notes that the Christian community is central in Chapters III and II but not in Chapter I.

59. Möser, "Vorüberlegungen," 11-12.

beginning of Chapter II as for the end of Chapter I shows "only that Chapter II was written after Chapter I, not that these two chapters belong together."[60] And the use of the 1939 calendar leaves for notes, given the paper shortage of wartime, does not convince Möser of an early dating, since they could have been used much later.[61]

Möser's point about the difference in content of Chapters I and II is well taken, if somewhat overstated. Further, Chapter II is not a necessary or obvious continuation of the argument in Chapter I, though it does not contradict it either; the subject is simply different. The concept of the "origin" (Ursprung) is found in both chapters. Christologically Chapter II stresses Christ as the center of humanity, reason, justice, and culture as well as of the Bible, church, and theology, particularly emphasizing the crucified Christ as the protector of these threatened human values.

It is very questionable, therefore, whether Chapter II, together with Chapter I, comprises the first Ansatz as Bethge has proposed. Certainly Chapter II is not an obvious continuation of Chapter I. So there are three possibilities: (a) that Chapter II was a section written about the same time as Chapter I, but at most only loosely related to it; (b) that Chapter II belongs to another "block," perhaps following the three sections of the present Chapter III as Möser has suggested; (c) that Chapter II is an independent and free-floating Abschnitt, that is, an idea that Bonhoeffer developed on the basis of important experience, but did not integrate into other material. More discussion below will demonstrate that option (b) is correct.

VI. CHAPTER III

Bethge confidently dates the beginning of this chapter as September, 1940 and locates it at Klein-Krössin, where Bonhoeffer

---

60. Ibid. Even though both judgments are correct, they are not substantiated by the paper types; see my discussion above, 15-17.

61. Cf. Möser, "Vorüberlegungen," 11-12.

The Text of Bonhoeffer's Ethics

stayed in September-October of that year.[62] Feil concurs, as does Möser.[63] While Bethge does not detail his evidence, we can safely surmise that paper is part of it. For Chapter III is written on paper (six types, four of them used a good deal) completely different from Chapter I with which he began in Berlin, and different also from Chapter II. This period was Bonhoeffer's first extensive and intensive time to work on his ethics away from Berlin.

Further evidence is a letter, probably from October 9, 1940, where Bonhoeffer mentions that he had written an outline of the whole work, which pleased him because he always found that task difficult.[64] This outline (on two Zettel, 38 and 1) is on the same paper as the first pages of the chapter. And on another Zettel of the same paper types as this chapter we find notes and outlines on several sections of the chapter--"Ethik als Gestaltung," "Erbe und Verfall," and "Schuld, Rechtfertigung, Wiedergeburt." Bethge has good reason to be confident in his judgment.[65]

Möser also sees in the content of Chapter III references to contemporary events, concluding that it was written shortly after the German victory over France, and that it alludes to Hitler as one of the "successful people" Bonhoeffer criticizes and to imperialistic conquest politics.[66]

In this chapter we find the sketch of different ethical postures (reason, fanaticism, conscience, duty free responsibility and private

---

62. Eg, 14; E, 12.

63. Feil, 8; Möser, 7, 9, 13.

64. GS II, 375-376; Eg, 14, 12; E, 12, 8.

65. The biography states that when Bonhoeffer went to Klein-Krössin "he worked hard for four weeks on the *first chapters* [ersten Kapiteln] of Ethics" (DBg, 785, DB, 603, my italics). Bethge cannot mean that the ethics work *began* at this time. Rather, this phrase seems to refer to the fact that much of "Ethik als Gestaltung" which was written then at Klein-Krössin was originally the first chapter of the Ethics, i.e., before the revised edition re-numbered it Chapter III.

66. Möser, 9, citing Eg, 79-83, 125 and 72 on Don Quixote.

virtue) that Bonhoeffer includes almost word for word in his essay "After Ten Years" which he gave as a Christmas present in 1942 to Oster, Dohnanyi, and Bethge.[67] This repetition suggests that these concerns and criticisms remained important for Bonhoeffer as his reflections on ethics continued.

We surely have a new approach to ethics in this chapter. First, it does not refer back to previous writing nor obviously continue discussion of issues and theological themes considered before. And the outline obviously projects the several "sections" now printed as Chapter III as themselves chapters in a multi-chapter book.

The outline is important, even though it doesn't represent Bonhoeffer's final thoughts on the structure of the book; indeed, as he wrote his way into the outline (actually, into the first half), new sections, such as that on natural life, come into the discussion. The form of the outline Bethge has printed in the first Preface is a composite of two Zettel. Furthermore, the printed version in the Ethics[68] is not exactly what Bonhoeffer originally projected, but is adapted to what he actually wrote. Bethge's outline is as follows.

I. GRUNDLAGEN
Ethik als Gestaltung
Erbe und Verfall
Schuld und Rechtfertigung
Kirche und Welt, Christus und die Gebote
Die vorletzten und die letzten Dinge
Der neue Mensch

II. AUFBAU
Der Aufbau des persönlichen Lebens

---

67. Cp. Eg, 69-72, E, 65-67, and LPP, 3-17.

68. Eg, 12; E, 8. See Appendix B, on page 65 below, for a copy of the original handwritten Zettel outlining the sections of "Grundlagen"; the appendix also contains the original typed transcription of this Zettel from which Bethge worked.

The Text of Bonhoeffer's Ethics

Der Aufbau der Stände und Aemter
Der Aufbau der Gemeinschaften
Der Aufbau der Kirche
Aufbau des christlichen Lebens in der Welt

It is important to compare this to Bonhoeffer's actual outline. A copy of an original page appears as Appendix B to this chapter; the main headings are given here.

Grundlagen und Aufbau der mit Gott versöhnten
(einer künftigen) Welt
Versuch einer christlichen Ethik

Grundlagen:
Ethik als Gestaltung
Erbe und Verfall[69]
Schuld und Rechtfertigung
Kirche und Welt[70]
Die Gesetze und die Gnade, Christus und die Gebote
[Die ewigen Grundlagen des Handelns: deleted]
Die vorletzten und die letzten Dinge
Der neue Mensch

Aufbau:
1.) Der Aufbau des persönlichen Lebens

---

69. Immediately above is written, then deleted, "Das Erbe und der Verfall." To judge from the spacing of the page, that was probably the original formulation.

70. "Die Gesetze und die Gnade" was added in *below* "Kirche und Welt (Gestaltung)" and above the now deleted "Die ewigen Grundlagen des Handelns." In the left margin is written "Christus u. d. Gebote" with a line connecting it to "Die Gesetze und die Gnade"; it appears that the latter is an alternative formulation to the former. Also in the left margin, and now deleted, stand the two following phrases "Erneuerung u. Heiligung" (to the left of "Kirche und Welt") and below it "Erneuerung d. Handelns" (to the left of "Die ewigen Grundlagen des Handelns").

2.) Der Aufbau der[71] Aemter? Berufe?
3.) Der Aufbau der Gemeinschaften
4.) Der Aufbau der Kirche
5.) Aufbau des christlichen Lebens in der Welt

Additional notes are found on each page of the outline, elaborating some main headings.

In contrast to Bonhoeffer's headings in the first part, Bethge gives the fourth as "Kirche und Welt, Christus und die Gebote"; this has led some such as Feil, to speculate whether Chapter V, with its subtitle "Christus, Kirche und Welt,"[72] might be intended or related. But on the handwritten Zettel; the other headings definitely come below "Kirche und Welt," not beside it. While the next two lines, due to deletions and additions, are not quite so clear, there is no uncertainty about "Kirche und Welt" on the handwritten original.[73] It stands alone, in fourth place, and "Die Gesetze und die Gnade, Christus und die Gebote" come under it.

Study of the original version of the outline yields two conclusions. First, Chapter III is clearly linked to Chapter IV as a sequence in one block; this is demonstrated by the explicit mention of "Die vorletzten und die letzten Dinge" (Chapter IV) in sequence after the other sections of Chapter III. Second, the original reference to

---

71. Here the deleted word "Stände" follows. There is some uncertainty about the punctuation of the two following words: it seems that each word is followed by a question mark, as here; and this is the reading adopted in the 1985 Zettel transcription.

72. In fact it was this chapter, now numbered V, which Bethge printed as the second chapter (following "Ethics as Formation") in the old edition. His conflation of the outline headings, and the subtitle of this chapter, surely combined in this result. Was it the subheading of this chapter that prompted the conflation?

73. The error of connecting "Kirche und Welt" with "Christus und die Gebote" appears already in Bethge's handwritten Vorwort prior to publication (see the Harvard microfilm). It surely derives from working with the typed transcription rather than from the original Zettel; the former is confusing while the latter is clear.

"Kirche und Welt" (no longer confused by joining it to "Christus und die Gebote") gives us, along with other evidence, a convincing solution to the proper location of the so-called Chapter II on that subject: I am confident that it is the fourth section (Abschnitt) projected in the outline.

If the original Outline gives a clear location for "Kirche und Welt," the content of Chapter III already contains in the section on "Inheritance and Decay" an anticipation of the argument of "Church and World." Bonhoeffer had argued that the form and unity of the West derived from Christ, but that this unity had been broken at the Reformation. While the French Revolution created a new, secular unity, the crisis in which he wrote was one of Western godlessness[74] which, on the one hand, glorified the Germanic past and dreamed of the coming millenium while exhibiting personal and political decay at the brink of the void; on the other hand, however, there was also a promising godlessness which is anti-church but has not completely broken with the possibility of a genuine faith in God. Presumably these are those of whom he says:

> Justice, truth, science, art, culture, humanity, freedom, patriotism, after long straying from the path, are finding their way back to their origin [Ursprung]. The more focused the message of the church, the more effectual it will be; and the church's suffering is infinitely more dangerous to the spirit of destruction than whatever political power she may retain.... The church does not reject those who come to her, seeking sanctuary.[75]

Of course, this is precisely the central theme of Chapter II. The same "goods" are specified; Christ is identified as the "Ursprung"; the reference to the uncompromising theology of the Confessing Church

---

74. Eg, 109; E, 102.

75. Eg, 116, translation mine; cf. E, 109. Cf. Eg, 60, E, 56 for the notion of sanctuary, refuge and similar metaphors.

is unmistakable; and the theme of the suffering church giving protection to humanity is also present.

If "ethics as formation" is concerned with how the form of Christ takes shape in a particular historical situation and rests upon the presence of Christ in the church, then the church-world relation is not only crucial but must address the question of "Christ and good people," the origin of human "goods" and goodness in Christ. In short, the logic of the argument does point to an Abschnitt like Chapter II appearing in this "block," this sequence of reflections.

And the paper, of the Berlin type like Chapter I, most probably means this: that Bonhoeffer wrote the first three sections listed in the outline in Klein-Krössin on the paper characteristic of that place, and then spent some time in Berlin in the first half of November. That Bonhoeffer was indeed back in Berlin for some days in the first half of November we know certainly from letters.[76] There he resumed using the paper types he had used before, now writing on the theme that appears as the fourth section of the Zettel outline. This would make sense of his calling it an "Abschnitt." And since it is quite short and uncomplicated, it wouldn't have taken long to write. The theme is also one that has a natural Sitz im Leben among his resistance colleagues in Berlin.

If "Church and World" belongs in the fourth place, then the section on "Guilt, Justification and Renewal" would quite naturally have come before it in the third place. Theologically, these themes follow Bonhoeffer's logic that the church is the community where Christ's form is taking shape among people, and confession is the beginning of the process by which one is conformed to Christ.[77] And right in the midst of Bonhoeffer's graphic confession we find yet another reference to Christ as the origin of truth, science and justice. The church, he writes,

---

76. Cf. November 13, 1940, GS VI, 486; November 4 and 13, 1940, GS II, 377-378.

77. Eg, 118; E, 111.

has not witnessed to the truth of God such that all pursuit of truth, all science [Wissenschaft], acknowledges its origin in this truth; it has not proclaimed God's righteousness such that all true justice must see in it the source of its own essential nature.[78]

In short, it would be an appropriate development of the argument for the Abschnitt on "Church and World" (Chapter II) to come after "Guilt, Justification and Renewal" and before Chapter IV, "The Ultimate and the Penultimate." And that, of course, is exactly how the outline has the sequence.

A conclusive proof demonstrating "Chapter" II as the fourth section (Abschnitt) of Chapter III would be if we found Zettel with notes for it on the same Klein-Krössin paper used for Chapter III and its notes. For that would confirm that Bonhoeffer did not write it in Berlin at the same time as Chapter I, but that he worked on the ideas for it at Klein-Krössin. Further study of the Zettel is needed to check this possibility; but the absence of such Zettel is not a disproof.

What of Feil's suggestion that Chapter V is a "doublet" of Chapter II in a writing sequence I, II, V in the period May-summer, 1940? This suggestion is not at all convincing. First, Feil did not discuss the evidence Möser addressed which appears to link Chapter II much more closely to Chapter III than to Chapter I. Second, the subtitle of Chapter V, namely "Christus, Kirche und Welt," while similar to Bethge's version of the outline, does not correspond to the actual outline in the Zettel--that compels one to draw a quite different conclusion.[79] Third, Chapter V does not deal at all with the theme of "Christ and Good People" which is the focus and raison d'être of Chapter II; this surely would be necessary for it to qualify as a

---

78. Eg, 122, translation mine; cf. E, 115.

79. One wonders if Bethge's rendering of the fourth subheading of the outline as "Kirche und Welt, Christus und die Gebote" was influenced by his decision to print Chapter V (entitled "Christus, die Wirklichkeit und das Gute," and carrying the alternate title "Christus, Kirche und Welt") in that position in the first edition.

doublet. Fourth, the evidence for another location of Chapter V (see below) is persuasive, in comparison to which Feil's suggestion is quite hypothetical. Finally, Feil's point about a "christological deepening" in Chapter V is too broad a generalization to decide a textual question--and in any case, Chapter II has an ecclesiological title but is strongly christological in content.

To conclude this section, then, I believe that the evidence convincingly places "Chapter" II in the second "block" rather than the first, locates it after the three sections of Chapter III, and dates it most likely in the first half of November in Berlin. If this is correct, then the actual texts corresponding to the first half of the outline would be:

>Ethik als Gestaltung (III.a)
>Erbe und Verfall (III.b)
>Schuld, Rechtfertigung, Erneuerung (III.c)
>Kirche und Welt (II)
>Die letzten und die vorletzten Dinge (IV,
> at least the first part)

We have no sections or chapters that certainly correspond to the second part of the outline (unless the second half of Chapter IV on "the natural life" qualified for that on "personal life"), but we can be confident that Bonhoeffer's thinking about "mandates" would have appeared in this part.

VII. CHAPTER IV

How much more elegant the translation would have been had it simply read "The Ultimate and the Penultimate"! This chapter can be dated with certainty. It was written in the Benedictine monastery at Ettal where Bonhoeffer stayed from November 17, 1940 to February 23, 1941. Two types of paper were used, both of them different from the papers used in Berlin and at Klein-Krössin. In the Ethics these papers were only used for this chapter, and for letters to his parents and to Bethge from Ettal. The letters (on other types of paper as well) refer repeatedly to work in progress.[80] Shortly after he arrives at Ettal there is a reference to "vorletzte"; on December 10 he reports that he is beginning the part on "natural life," and on February 22, 1941 he refers to his ideas about suicide.

If the dating of this work is certain, what needs further analysis is its relation to previous and later writings. This matter is highlighted by Bethge's opinion that this chapter constitutes a third approach (dritten Neuansatz).[81] I do not consider that the evidence supports this view; rather it seems to me that this chapter is clearly a continuation of the second block which begins with Chapter III.

First, I have already noted that the outline contains the heading "Die Vorletzten und die letzten Dinge" in the order that this chapter follows. Further, we know that Bonhoeffer was sketching ideas on this theme during his earlier work at Klein-Krössin. Bethge refers to this, and the Zettel show not only the heading in the outline but also a sketch devoted to this subject.[82] Thus to say that it was *written* in Ettal is not to say that it was all *conceived* there, for that honor belongs to Klein-Krössin, certainly for the first section on "The Ultimate and the Penultimate." And while the outline written at Klein-Krössin contains no headings on, or references to, "the natural life" nor to the particular topics in that section, there is a Zettel on Klein-Krössin paper headed "Das natürliche Leben" and containing other keywords such as "suum cuique"; this suggests that this material too was initially conceived at Klein-Krössin. (Of course, it is also possible that some blank paper was taken from Klein-Krössin to Ettal.)

---

80. Cf. GS VI, 488 (Vorletzte); GS II, 389 (Natürliche); GS IV, 509 (Unschuld); GS II, 394 (Euthanasie); GS VI, 518, 521 (Ehe); GS VI, 524 (Selbstmord); and GS VI, 492 ("Wegbereitung und Einzug" as a possible title for the book). I am here largely following Feil's helpful grouping of these references; cf. Feil, 5.

81. Eg, 15.

82. Eg, 15; E, 12. Cf. Zettel 61, "Die Vorletzten Dinge," on Klein-Krössin paper.

Given this evidence on Chapter IV as a continuation of Chapter III, why would Bethge regard this chapter as a new beginning? His answer is given in the Preface and in the biography, and he also confirmed it in conversations with me in August, 1969 and April, 1980. It is the contention that Bonhoeffer focuses on a new theological theme here, namely justification; here we see the impact of Bethge's double scheme of theological theme and place, mentioned above.

To this it must be replied, first, that this is a quite different type of evidence from the literary-critical data used elsewhere in the Preface to establish dates, sequences and organization of the material, and that the latter evidence militates strongly against seeing this as a new approach. Second, the statement in the biography that "he now began with justification, and from that he achieved his new and fruitful distinction between the ultimate and penultimate..."[83] contradicts the fact that this distinction was clearly in Bonhoeffer's mind earlier when working on "Chapter" III and the outline. Further, if Bonhoeffer begins Chapter III with the theme of formation and conformation, its third section is on precisely--justification! And this is just what the outline predicted.

Indeed, the treatment of justification in the end of Chapter III has intrinsic connection to the discussion of the ultimate-penultimate relation in Chapter IV, and warrants closer inspection. The intrinsic connection of conformation to Christ and justification is seen in the section on "Guilt, Justification and Renewal" which Bonhoeffer begins by recalling that "our concern is with the taking form among us of the form of Christ."[84] This leads straight into the discussion of guilt, justification and forgiveness of Christians and the church as they encounter the Gestalt Christi.

What is especially interesting for the connection of justification to the ultimate-penultimate relation is Bonhoeffer's treatment of

---

83. DBg, 807; DB, 623.

84. Eg, 117; E, 110.

history, politics and nations (i.e., "the Western world") at the end of this section. The argument goes as follows. The church is justified directly through confession to and forgiveness by Christ, while the "Western world" is justified only indirectly.

> The western world, as a historical and political form, can be 'justified and renewed' only indirectly, through the faith of the Church. The Church experiences in faith the forgiveness of all her sins and a new beginning through grace. For the nations there is only a healing of the wound, a cicatrization of guilt, in the return to order, to justice, to peace, and to the granting of free passage to the Church's proclamation of Jesus Christ (für die Volker gibt es nur ein Vernarben des Schuld in der Ruckkehr zur Ordnung, zum Recht, zum Frieden...).[85]

Now precisely this discussion of "order, justice, [and] peace" is a discussion of the penultimate. Granted, Bonhoeffer does not in these pages explicitly use the term "penultimate" when speaking of Vernarbung as "a faint shadow of forgiveness," that is, of justification. But we know from the outline that the idea was in his mind. And when we read in Chapter IV about the ultimate-penultimate relation, his treatment is clearly continuous with what we have just seen. Justification is the ultimate, the last word, while the penultimate is comprised of "being human and being good" [Menschsein, Gutsein].[86] And what does that involve? Not surprisingly, justice and rights (Recht), order and discipline (Ordnung), freedom, food, house, community, and so on.[87] In short, the penultimate things which prepare the way for the ultimate word of justification are precisely the

---

85. Eg, 125-126; E, 117.

86. Eg, 142, translation mine; cf. E, 133-134. Cf. also Eg, 147, 151; E, 139, 143.

87. Eg, 142-149; E, 133-140.

same as those involved in "healing the wounds."[88] That is to say, the thinking on the role of justification in the dimensions of ultimate and penultimate is the same in both chapters.

Nor would locating "Church and World" (the so-called Chapter II) between III.c and IV.a weaken this connection and continuity. To begin with, this is proposed by the Zettel outline--and paper types do not constitute counter evidence. But above all, "Church and World" contains discussions of justification very appropriate to this context. Certainly, the content of "Church and World" differs from conventional treatments of justification. But Bonhoeffer has already explained that in times when lawlessness and evil triumph, the gospel appeals especially to those who are just, truthful and humane; the church must preach not that people should become evil like the tax-collector and prostitute in order to know Christ, but that they should become righteous like those who struggle and suffer for truth, justice and humanity. To be sure, the evil and the good alike are sinners before God and have alike fallen away from the origin. Yet Christ belongs to both. At this point Bonhoeffer explicitly draws in the theme of justification. Christ "calls them [i.e., both evil and good people] back to the origin that they be no longer evil and good but *justified* and *sanctified* sinners."[89] Nor is this the only reference to justification, for a statement immediately follows which seems a broad hint predicting that a significant discussion of justification will soon follow.

> But before we express this *ultimate* [Letzte] in which evil people and good are one before Christ and in which the distinction between all times is transcended [aufgehoben] before Christ, we must not avoid the

---

88. The concept of "geschichtlichen Vernarbung" was taken over from the historical writer Reinhold Schneider; cf. DBg, 803.

89. Eg, 65; E, 61, emphasis mine. Note that the Zettel outline refers to both Rechtfertigung and Heiligung in the vicinity of "Kirche und Welt."

question posed by our own experience and time, namely, what is the meaning of the fact that good people find Christ, in other words, *what is the relationship of Jesus Christ to good people and human goods.*[90]

Since there is no discussion of the ultimate in the remaining pages of this chapter, and since that is exactly how Chapter IV begins, it is quite proper to regard the discussion of the Letzte foreshadowed here as that which follows in Chapter IV.

Further, the other central themes of "Church and World" are repeated in Chapter IV, as one might expect when one "chapter" follows another. Like the former, the latter warns against preaching as if there were a method leading to justification, as if everyone should first become like Mary Magdalene or the thief on the cross, "these biblically 'peripheral figures'."[91] This is consistent with the argument in "Church and World" that in these times preaching should rather claim good people for Christ. Indeed, Bonhoeffer reiterates the main argument of Chapter II. Loss of distinction between "'good' and 'evil'" is an obstacle to the reception of Christ--in addition to the general sinfulness of the world.[92] In Western Christendom, where ultimate and penultimate have existed in a dialectical relationship, each strengthening the other, there has been during the past two hundred years a mutual weakening of each. Nevertheless

---

90. Eg, 65, translation mine; cf. E, 61; Bonhoeffer's italics at the end of the quotation. Note, too, that the Ursprung theme also reappears right at the beginning of Chapter IV. (Perhaps we can also see allusions to previous discussions in Chapter III when this section refers to the Middle Ages and to falling away from the origin; cp. Eg, 63, 65; E, 59, 61, with Eg, 94-116; E, 88-109.)

91. Eg, 132; E, 123. (Text correction: 'biblischen,' not 'blassen.'

92. E, 139.

> there are to be found in Western Christendom today large numbers of those who do indeed hold fast to the penultimate [Menschsein, Gutsein],... but who do not clearly perceive, or at any rate do not resolutely accept, the connection of the penultimate with the ultimate, even though their attitude to this ultimate is not in any way hostile.... Whatever humanity and goodness is found in this fallen world must be on the side of Jesus Christ. It is nothing less than a curtailment of the gospel if the nearness of Jesus Christ is proclaimed only to what is broken and evil.... Humanity and goodness... should and shall be claimed for Jesus Christ, especially in cases where they persist as an unconscious residue of a former attachment to the ultimate.... It will be more Christian to claim precisely that man as a Christian who would no longer dare to call himself a Christian, and then with much patience to help him to the profession of faith in Christ. It is from this perspective that both the following chapters are to be understood.[93]

This obviously builds on the ideas first expressed in Chapter III and in "Kirche und Welt."

These considerations convince me not to regard Chapter IV as a new beginning, or its discussion of justification as a new theological theme; on the contrary, it clearly looks like the continuation of a logically outlined writing sequence or block. Pressed on this evidence of continuity in discussions at Oxford, Bethge contended that while justification was indeed in both the end of Chapter III and the beginning of Chapter IV, in the latter it had a different "tone." Such a judgment, however, is very subjective compared to objective literary-critical evidence. That evidence, and the content, convinces me that there is no new theological beginning in Chapter IV but that its

---

93. Eg, 151-152; E, 142-143, translation altered.

The Text of Bonhoeffer's Ethics   39

discussion of "The Ultimate and the Penultimate" and justification continues and develops the discussion in Chapter III and "Chapter" II. The theological focus, the central terms and the argumentation are the same. And, as the outline shows, this is just what Bonhoeffer intended. So Chapter IV should be regarded as a continuation of the second block, not as a third new beginning. Very strong evidence of the literary-critical type, strong enough to overcome the supporting evidence we have, would be necessary to dispute this judgment.

Turning now in the other direction, the connection of this chapter to writing which follows it, we find in Chapter IV the first explicit comments in the manuscripts where Bonhoeffer links one piece of writing to other chapters. They are all securely located in the chapter manuscripts themselves.

One of these refers to a future chapter which in all likelihood was never written. In a discussion under "The Natural Life" of types of slavery and exploiting "the bodily forces of the workman," Bonhoeffer says that "this subject is treated more fully in the chapter entitled Labour."[94] Bethge indicates that there is no extant chapter on this subject. Bonhoeffer's reference, while not unambiguous, suggests more an anticipated chapter than one already written. Of course, the pattern of the mandates was in Bonhoeffer's mind throughout his writing of the Ethics chapters, and labor was regularly mentioned as one of the four mandates. The more extensive treatments are found in Chapter V and Chapter VII. But the former only has one paragraph devoted to labor. And the latter not only breaks off in the middle of discussing the church mandate before getting to the others; it also changes the category from labor to culture--and in addition is found in a new approach (block) and that the last to be started. Accordingly, neither of these are candidates for the chapter Bonhoeffer projects. I think we can confidently conclude that it was never written as part of this block.

A second explicit comment is straightforward. At the end of

---

94. Eg, 196-197; E, 185.

the discussion on "The Ultimate and the Penultimate" (IV.a) we find a paragraph on claiming humanity and goodness for Christ. Then Bonhoeffer states: "It is from this perspective that both the following chapters are to be understood."[95] In the manuscript the second side of that page is left blank and, in typical Bonhoeffer fashion, a new heading appears at the top of a fresh sheet, "Das Natürliche Leben." The pagination continues right on. So there is no question that this is the first of the two chapters Bonhoeffer had in mind.

It is very important to observe that here we come upon a novelty in the writing plan. Bonhoeffer has worked his way through the first half of his outline, modifying the later sections somewhat as he went; but we do not have any material under headings projected for the second half of the book. Rather, we have new material on "the natural life," and mention of a chapter on "labor." It is clear that Bonhoeffer is branching off in directions not anticipated when the outline was made several months earlier. In other words, after writing the material projected in the outline on "the penultimate and the ultimate," Bonhoeffer enters a transition into new areas of thought not initially anticipated; this is important for understanding Chapter V.

The third explicit comment informs us about the second of the two chapters just as forecast. A few pages after the first mention of the two chapters, the manuscript contains a pencilled note that the issue of resolving conflicts between natural rights "needs developing later! At the end of the chapter on natural rights or in the next chapter about the good."[96] I do not doubt that Bonhoeffer is speaking of the same two chapters here as he did a few pages earlier. And if there is no question that the chapter on the natural is the first of the two, this comment makes it plain that he intends to follow it by a chapter on the good. Though the chapter on natural rights is unfinished, Bonhoeffer did not write according to a rigid plan, so it is necessary to ask if any of the chapters we now have qualify as the projected chapter on good.

---

95. Eg, 152, translation mine; cf. E, 143.

96. Eg, 162, translation mine; E, 153.

The Text of Bonhoeffer's Ethics 41

From their titles, the two obvious candidates are Chapter V and Chapter VI.

VIII. CHAPTER V

Several questions surround this chapter. (1) What is its writing date? Bethge says that either the summer of 1940, or that of 1941, is possible, and inclines to the latter.[97] (2) What is its relation to the forecast in Chapter IV of "the next chapter about the good"? (3) What is its relation to the following chapter "History and Good," both manuscripts of which appear to continue the pagination of Chapter V? (4) Is it the beginning of a new Ansatz, as Bethge has suggested, or is it part of a continuing block?

So far as date is concerned, Bethge is surely right in preferring the summer of 1941. One clue is the paper. It is written exclusively on Klein-Krössin paper. There are three types used in this chapter, and each of them had been used for "Ethik als Gestaltung" when Bonhoeffer was in Klein-Krössin during September and October, 1940. Why not, then, consider that this might have been written then also? First, Chapter III was a considerable writing project for that period. And, as we have seen above, Bonhoeffer was back in Berlin when he wrote the fourth section of the outline, "Kirche und Welt"; therefore, the autumn, 1940, work at Klein-Krössin comprised the three sections of Chapter III. Second, this chapter is nowhere found in the outline from that time. But, third, it is projected in Chapter IV, when Bonhoeffer was writing in Ettal--unless we assume it has no relation to the prediction of "the next chapter about the good," a very implausible assumption indeed. So it has to come after the Ettal work. The next time Bonhoeffer was in Klein-Krössin was in the period May to August 27, 1941.[98] Möser also locates Chapter V in this

---

97. Eg, 15, E, 12.

98. The biography (DBg, 770) records that Bonhoeffer was in Klein-Krössin, Berlin and occasionally Munich during this time; the paper very strongly suggests

period.[99]

In seeking to identify the predicted chapter on "the good," there is no chapter with just that title nor, given Bonhoeffer's theological approach, would we really expect one. Rather, we have "Christ, Reality and Good" and "History and Good." Regarding Chapter V, it is notable that there are many statements about "the good" and "the question of the good" in the opening pages. Consider the following. "The problem of ethics is not 'How can I be good?' and 'How can I do good'?" "All concern with ethics will have as its starting-point that God shows himself to be good...." "Any enquiry about one's own goodness, or the goodness of the world, is now impossible unless enquiry has first been made about the goodness of God." "The question of good can find its answer only in Christ." "The question of good becomes the question of participating in the divine reality which is revealed in Christ." "Good is the real itself..., the real which possesses reality only in God." "The question of good must not be reduced to an examination of the motives or consequences of actions...." "Good is reality itself, reality seen and recognized in God." "The question of good... embraces reality as a whole, as it is held in being by God.... This indivisible whole... is what the question of good has in view." "*Participation in the indivisible whole of the divine reality--this is the sense and purpose of the Christian question about the good.*" "Participation in this reality [Christ] is the true sense and purpose of the question about the good."[100]

Indeed, the whole first section of this chapter is an argument linking "the good" and "reality" together as christological concepts, just as the title indicates; on this basis the argument develops into the polemic against "Thinking in Terms of Two Spheres," followed by the constructive alternative, an exposition of "The Four Mandates."

Certainly, when we inspect both versions of Chapter VI, we

---

that the writing was done in Klein-Krössin.

99. Möser, 12.

100. Eg, 200-208, Bonhoeffer's italics, translation mine; cf. E, 188-195.

The Text of Bonhoeffer's *Ethics*

also find there a number of references to issues related to "good" and (in VI/2, though not in VI/1) some explicit references to "the question about the good"; the focus of these chapters, as both title and text indicate, is the issue of the good in history. So we can tentatively conclude that Bonhoeffer had Chapter V or Chapters V and VI in view when he forecast "the next chapter on the good." Discussion of this matter will be concluded in the analysis of Chapter VI.

Bethge regards Chapter V as beginning a new Ansatz, the fourth. Evidence for this judgment is not spelled out, though he appears to detect "incarnation" as a new theological theme.[101]

The language can also be read as sounding like a new beginning.

> An unparalleled demand must be confronted by anyone who intends to face the problem of a Christian ethic, namely the demand that he abandon as improper the two very questions which have led him to engage the ethical problem at all....

"Where there is faith in God as the ultimate reality, the origin [Ursprung] of all ethical endeavor is the fact that God is revealed to be good...."

> The origin [Ursprung] of Christian ethics is not the reality of one's own self, or the reality of the world, nor the reality of norms and values, but the reality of God revealed in Jesus Christ. That is the extraordinary demand which in all honesty must be made of anyone who wants to be concerned with the problem of a Christian ethic.... *The problem of Christian ethics is the realization among God's creatures of the revelational reality of God in Christ.*[102]

---

101. Eg, 15; E, 13.

102. Eg, 200-202, Bonhoeffer's italics, translation mine; cf. E, 188-190.

Of course, if Bonhoeffer were settling in to a new writing period and getting his mind re-oriented to the subject, it may be that such opening phrases would be written without signalling a new beginning. Further, there is strong reason to doubt that this is a new beginning. It is the simple fact that in the previous chapter Bonhoeffer had already predicted a sequel, namely "the next chapter on the good."

Because of the links of subject and pagination between Chapters V and VI/1-VI/2, we will carry forward the unresolved issues of their relation to the analysis of Chapter VI.

IX. CHAPTER VI (VI/1, VI/2)

This chapter exists in two versions, both with the same title; the first is printed in the Gesammelte Schriften,[103] and the case can easily be made that in the critical edition it should be printed with the rest of the text as an appendix. The Zettel contain an outline for this chapter,[104] though none of its headings actually appears in the manuscript for VI/1 and only three of them appear in VI/2;[105] of course, many of the subjects in the outline are discussed in both versions--in VI/2 seven subheadings are covered plus two not found in the outline. The first version is much shorter and covers more of the outline; the second is longer and more detailed, covering less of the outline. Because of this it seems evident that the version printed in Ethik really is the second version.

On the relation of Chapter VI to Chapter V, I mentioned above that VI/2 (though not VI/1) sometimes uses the explicit phrase, "the question about the good." However, this, and related formulations,

---

103. GS III, 455-477. It has not been translated.

104. Cf. Eg, 278; E, 262. The English text omits from 2. (c) the words "Sichzurechnen, Einzelner sein."

105. Though not printed in the book (cf. Bethge's note, Eg, 278), the heading "Liebe und Verantwortung" was the last line to be written in the manuscript of VI/2.

The Text of Bonhoeffer's *Ethics* 45

are not so frequent in either version of Chapter VI as they are in Chapter V. This suggests that the issue of "the good" has already been introduced in Chapter V and is here being continued. Indeed, we have a singular piece of evidence proving that this is so, namely the pagination which links Chapter V with Chapter VI. The manuscript of Chapter V ends with a page numbered 14a, while VI/1 begins with a page numbered 15 and VI/2 also begins with a page numbered 15. It is impossible for this to be an accident. Nor is there any other chapter manuscript ending with a page 14 which could conceivably be the antecedent. Furthermore, there is no other "chapter" which begins with a page number other than 1. In fact, so singular is this evidence that we must seriously consider whether Bonhoeffer regarded the presently numbered V and VI as two chapters, or whether he envisaged these as two parts of *one* chapter. After all, in every other case consecutive numbering is only found *within* single chapters.

Continuity may also be indicated by the fact that, unlike most, "Chapter" V is finished. It is concluded with two paragraphs which are clearly a concluding summary. Furthermore, study of the actual manuscripts reveals that this summary was originally located earlier in the chapter and then was adapted and moved to its final place to make room for an insert. Thus "Chapter" V is finished and related to Chapter VI like the opening sections of Chapter III which are also connected together by pagination as well as the outline. This may be an additional indication that V-VI/2 should be regarded as one chapter.

I am inclined, then, to regard V and VI as one chapter, not two. But however one decides, pagination proves indisputably that V-VI is a sequence. From *this* perspective it does not matter whether we regard the forecast of "the next chapter about the good" as referring only to "Christ, Reality and Good" or to both that and " History and Good" because they were considered to be one chapter.

The distinctive emphasis of this part (or chapter) is given by Bonhoeffer in both versions. In VI/2 he begins by saying that "the question about the good always finds us in a situation we cannot reverse: we are alive"; and this means that we are historical beings. He continues:

> The question about the good belongs intrinsically to our life, just as our life is inseparable from the question about the good. The question about the good is posed and decided in the midst of each definite yet incomplete, unique and fluid situation of our lives, in the midst of our living bonds to people, things, institutions and powers, that is, in the midst of our historical existence. So *the question about the good cannot be severed from* the question about life--that is to say, *the question about history.*[106]

The same linking of the good with historical life is found in the first version.[107] From there the discussion in both versions moves into various dimensions of "the responsible life."

The responsibility theme connects with the question of date, and one piece of evidence is found in the newly-discovered Bonhoeffer-Barth correspondence.[108] In her letter of September 22, 1941 to Pastor Paul Vogt, Charlotte von Kirschbaum refers to Bonhoeffer's proposal of a Christmas pamphlet in the <u>Bekennende Kirche</u> series. Bonhoeffer's suggestions were that Barth should write on "Christian Responsibility," Vischer on "History and Eschatology" and de Quervain on "Forgiveness of Sins." Most of "History and Good" was outlined under the heading "Verantwortung" and it is not surprising that Bonhoeffer should assign this subject to Karl Barth! The subjects assigned to Vischer and de Quervain also relate closely to topics in Bonhoeffer's outline and paragraphs. "History and

---

106. Eg, 227-228, italics and translation mine; cf. E, 214.

107. Cf. especially GS III, 455-456, 461-462, 463-464 and 470: "When, after these reflections, we go back to *the question about the good in human historical action*" (470, emphasis mine) we see that it is resolved into the claim of Jesus Christ, the Incarnate One, who himself is the ultimate reality of history.

108. See note 138 below.

Eschatology" is right on Bonhoeffer's theme and connects to topics he discussed such as politics, realism, freedom and meaning; likewise, "Forgiveness of Sins" is related to topics such as "acceptance of guilt," "deputyship," "the commandments" and "free responsibility." This request to the Swiss, then, strongly suggests that Bonhoeffer was working on one version or another of VI before the autumn of 1941. Bethge dates the beginning of work on "History and Good" in summer, 1941; Möser appears to agree, arguing that VI/1 was begun toward the end of work-period four (March 25 to August 27, 1941) and that it was completed, and then VI/2 written, in period five (September 17, 1941 to April 9, 1942).[109]

What can we learn from the paper types? In VI/1 there are four types, including the Eichberger which is consistently associated with Berlin; in VI/2 there are two types, again including the Eichberger. Bethge connects some VI/1 paper with Klein-Krössin. Further examination of papers may be fruitful; the consistent Eichberger connection with Berlin may indicate at least two locations for work on these chapters.

We must now return to the question of whether, seen from the perspective of Chapter VI, Chapter V should be regarded as a new Ansatz. If Chapter IV predicts "the next chapter about the good," and if this at the very least means V, or more probably V-VI, this seems to count strongly against Bethge's view. What other evidence can illuminate this issue?

One important statement which must be clarified is found early in VI/1. Bonhoeffer refers to a previous writing. He begins by saying that the abstraction of an isolated individual person making ethical decisions by reference to an absolute criterion and thus choosing between clearly perceived goods and evils "is something we have left behind us *on the basis of everything that has been said.*"[110] A couple of pages later comes the following quite specific reference in a

---

109. Bethge: Eg, 16; E, 13. Möser, 10.

110. GS III, 455; italics mine.

discussion of reality and responsibility: "for the most original reality is the reality of the incarnate God--*here we take up what was said back in the first chapter.*"[111] In an earlier draft I argued that the reference to the "first chapter" is to the first section of Chapter III, "Ethics as Formation." The argument went as follows.

Many quotations from the first section of Chapter III could be given to anchor this reference to the "first chapter." Just as in "History and Good" (VI/1) Bonhoeffer speaks of the incarnation as "the most original reality" so in Chapter III he says that God's bodily taking on humanity (Menschheit) in the flesh of Jesus Christ is the most profound assertion.[112] The theological argument of "Ethics as Formation" is, without neglecting cross and resurrection, that the incarnate God is the Reconciler.

> Ecce homo!--Behold the God who has become man, the unfathomable mystery of the love of God for the world. God loves man. God loves the world. Not an ideal man, but man as he is; not an ideal world but the real world.... God became man, real man [wirklicher Mensch].[113]

And again: "The reason why we can love as real men and can love the real man at our side is to be found solely in the incarnation of God, in the unfathomable love of God for man."[114] And finally a decisive passage in which Bonhoeffer summarizes "Ethics as Formation":

> Christ does not sublimate [aufheben] human reality [Wirklichkeit] for the sake of an idea which demands realization contrary to everything real, but Christ empowers that very reality. He affirms it, indeed *he*

---

111. GS III, 458; italics mine.

112. Eg, 76; E, 72.

113. Eg, 75-76; E, 71; translation altered.

114. Eg, 79; E, 74.

The Text of Bonhoeffer's Ethics 49

> *himself is precisely the real man and so the foundation of all human reality* [Wirklichkeit]. So conformation to the Gestalt Christi has this double aspect: that the Gestalt Christi remains one and the same... in its own uniqueness as the form of the *incarnate, crucified* and *risen God*; and that precisely for the sake of Christ's form is the form of the real man preserved such that the real man receives the form of Christ. [115]

Here is surely a strong contender for the explicit reference back to the "first chapter" which interprets "Wirklichkeit" on the basis of the "Menschwerdung Gottes."

We need to ask if another chapter might qualify as the one Bonhoeffer refers to. Bethge's identification of Chapter IV as being the third new Ansatz requires us to examine it first. But it can be quickly dismissed. As Bethge agrees, and as the analysis above confirms, its theme is justification, not incarnation. Nor is reality [Wirklichkeit] a central theme. Granted, there is a paragraph on the theme of the humanity of Christ, and one sentence alluding to the incarnation of God in created reality,[116] but this simply cannot compare with the prominence of the incarnation-reality theme in the first section of Chapter III.

What, then, of Chapter V which Bethge regards as another new Ansatz? Plainly the idea of Wirklichkeit is highlighted in its very title. And the opening paragraphs speak of God as ultimate reality [letzte Wirklichkeit] who is revealed to be good. "That God is revealed as good... leads to the origin [Ursprung] of ethical endeavor, namely believing in God as the ultimate reality."[117] And God-- Creator, Reconciler, Redeemer--is revealed in Jesus Christ, so only in him can the question about the good find its answer. In spite of this,

---

115. Eg, 91, translation and emphasis mine; cf. E, 85.

116. Eg, 139-140; E, 131.

117. Eg, 201, translation mine; cf. E, 188-189.

we do not find that incarnation is the dominant and controlling category for interpretation here. Certainly there are several references later in the chapter,[118] but the central and dominant category by which Bonhoeffer links the reality of God and the reality of the world is *revelation* in Christ.[119] Typical is his programmatic and italicized statement: *"The problem of a Christian ethic is the realization [Wirklichwerden] among the creatures of the revelational reality of God in Christ [Offenbarungswirklichkeit Gottes in Christus].*[120]

While I consider that the evidence I presented above makes a strong case on the relation of Chapter VI/1 to Chapter III, a couple of other considerations should be noted. The first is that VI/1 has clear echoes of justification as the ultimate word as it is found in the latter part of Chapter III and the beginning of Chapter IV.[121] Also, the theme of the love of God is discussed very similarly in "Ethics as Formation" and in the first version of "History and Good."[122]

Möser, however, regards the statement in VI/1 as referring back to Chapter V, not Chapter III. One objection he raises to regarding III-VI/1-2 as a sequence is that this would make the second block about 80% of the text and would give the first and third blocks (Chapters I and VII) the character of prologue and epilogue.[123] But the second assertion is a non sequitur, and the objection in the first begs the question. We have no a priori knowledge of how much material should be grouped in a given block; that can only be concluded from other evidence. There is no rule telling us in advance how much material we should find in each block.

---

118. Eg, 218-219, 224-225; E, 205-206, 211-212.

119. See numerous statements in Eg, 200-208; E, 188-195.

120. Eg, 202, translation mine; cf. E, 190.

121. Cf. GS III, 460-461, 463.

122. Cp. GS III, 466-469; E, 70-73.

123. Möser, 16.

Secondly, Möser points out that there are several references to the incarnation category in the latter part of Chapter V.[124] But only twice is the idea of Wirklichkeit related to incarnation in these statements. There is no sustained argument on this relation such as we find in Chapter III. Is that because the argument had already been made and these are then references to an established point? Further, in most cases the reference to incarnation occurs in a phrase which also includes cross and resurrection. So one could as easily argue that the theological theme of resurrection--or cross--was formative for this chapter. But in fact Bonhoeffer is using them, as he does elsewhere in this and other works, in a normal if not conventional way; no special function is played in Chapter V by the incarnation theme--rather, *revelation* is predominant here, while *incarnation* is central and fundamental in Chapter III.

Third, Möser holds that two elements in the sentence referring back to the "first chapter" are very typical of the thinking in Chapter V. One is the idea of the "ursprünglichste Wirklichkeit," which he considers a leitmotif throughout Chapter V. The other is Bonhoeffer's thesis that "in action which really accords with reality, acknowledgement of the factual and contradiction of the factual are indissolubly bound to each other."[125] The former Möser finds in Bonhoeffer's discussion of a "positivistic-empirical" ethic, the latter in his critique of idealistic ethics.[126] The synthesis for Möser occurs in the passage where Bonhoeffer says that "in Jesus Christ the reality of God entered into the reality of this world,"[127] because this is an incarnational passage.

Given this reading, Möser holds that the reference in the first

---

124. Möser, 10.

125. "...Anerkennung des Faktischen und Widerspruch gegen das Faktische sind in echt wirklichkeitsgemässen Handeln miteinander unlösbar verbunden." GS III, 458; cf. Möser, letter to Green, June 27, 1982.

126. Cf. Eg, 206; E, 193-194. Eg, 202-206; E, 190-193.

127. Eg, 207; E, 194.

sentence of VI/1 to "nach allem Gesagten" (and its modified form in VI/2)[128] is to Chapter V, for there Bonhoeffer disposed of "the abstraction of the isolated individual man" as well as an abstract understanding of good and evil.[129] This is supported, Möser feels, by the use of the phrase "nach allem Gesagten"; in German usage this phrase would normally refer back to the preceeding pages but hardly to a train of thought one hundred pages earlier. That may be so, but we cannot make a conclusive argument from this one phrase; here the content has to be much more decisive.

In making this case Möser nevertheless concedes that there is other evidence supporting the III-VI/1-2 sequence, especially the prediction of "the next chapter about the good" in Chapter IV. (Möser now accepts my argument that Chapter IV continues after Chapter III and is not, as Bethge proposed, a new Ansatz.) It should also be observed that Möser does not consider that V-VI might in fact be *one* chapter; on that presupposition one could not regard the VI/1 mention of the "first chapter" as a reference back to "Chapter" V.

What, then, of the content evidence Möser has adduced? Admittedly it has some plausibility. At the same time these ideas are to be found in Chapter III. The isolated individuals choosing between clear goods and evils by absolute norms could certainly be those types of moralists discussed at the opening of the chapter;[130] we know that these were concrete types of people Bonhoeffer was concerned about, and that these concerns stayed in his mind. See, too, the statement about a concrete rather than an abstract ethic; a concrete, Christian ethic seeks to overcome both formalistic and casuistic ethics (i.e. idealistic and empirical) which both presuppose a conflict between the good and the real.[131] Further, the critique against idealistic ethics

---

128. Eg, 228; E, 214-215.

129. Letter of June 27, 1983, citing especially Eg, 203-205 (E, 190-193).

130. Eg, 69-72; E, 65-68.

131. Eg, 91; E, 85-86.

abounds in Chapter III: Christ is not a principle for shaping the world; Jesus did not proclaim a timeless system; God did not become an idea, principle, program, etc. but a human being.[132] Further, the critique of a positivistic ethic is surely the basis--christologically developed--for the treatment of those who are despisers of the human, worshippers of success, or idolizers of death.[133] The theological alternative to the idealistic-factual dichotomy, which gives each its due by transforming them both, is the incarnational understanding of reality.

> Christ does not sublimate human reality for the sake of an idea which demands realization contrary to everything real, but Christ empowers that very reality. He affirms it, indeed, he himself is precisely the real man and so the foundation of all human reality [der Grund aller menschlichen Wirklichkeit]. So conformation to the Gestalt Christi has this double aspect: that the Gestalt Christi remains one and the same, not as a general idea but in its own uniqueness as the form of the incarnate, crucified and risen God; and that precisely for the sake of Christ's form is the form of the real man preserved such that the real man receives the form of Christ.[134]

Here, too, we have the "ursprünglichste Wirklichkeit," though not in that exact wording.

Summing up this discussion of the two versions of Chapter VI, and their relation to Chapter V, we have the following results. Assuming that VI/2 supersedes VI/1, Chapter V belongs together with Chapter VI/2 so that together they constitute "the next chapter on the good"--or, two chapters on that subject. Chapter V is not the

---

132. Eg, 89-91; E, 84-85.

133. Eg, 75-79; E, 71-74.

134. Eg, 91, translation mine; cf. E, 85.

beginning of a new Ansatz but a continuation of the argument in Chapter IV; along with Chapter VI, it constitutes "the next chapter on the good." Further, Chapter VI/1 refers back to Chapter III as "the first chapter"; this is a second link which ties Chapters V and VI in to the second block. Admittedly, this block now is somewhat different from what was first sketched in the outline, since the material on the natural and the good has appeared after five parts of the outline had been written. But the links forward and backward indicate that Bonhoeffer himself saw them in one framework.

Now we must turn to the last chapter, then gather the results of the analysis in a final conclusion.

X. CHAPTER VII

There is no doubt that this is the latest chapter on which Bonhoeffer worked; it was the one on his desk when he was arrested, the one confiscated and returned by the Gestapo. Further, the working notepapers (Zettel) for this chapter were collected from the desk by Bethge and marked in pencil "Schreibtisch" or "Schrbt."

Nor are there links to previous chapters such as continuity of page numbering, outlines, or projections in earlier chapters of subjects treated in this one. It also sounds like a fresh start. It begins:

> A Christian ethic will have to begin by asking whether and to what extent it is possible at all to treat the 'ethical' and the 'Christian' as a theme.... We cannot, in fact, even set foot in the field of Christian ethics until we have first of all recognized how extremely questionable a course we are pursuing....[135]

Some pages later we read: "This brings us to the only possible object of a 'Christian ethic', an object which lies beyond the 'ethical',

---

135. Eg, 279; E, 263.

namely the commandment of God.... God's commandment is the only warrant for ethical discourse."[136] To be sure, there are other instances where what sounds like a new start is not in fact that; but other evidence proves that this chapter is a new beginning.

Next, this chapter has a distinctive approach to the subject which, while not alien to Bonhoeffer's theology, is not typical of the earlier chapters. That is the focus on the *commandment of God* as "the only warrant for ethical discourse." It was the prominence of this theme that led Rasmussen in his 1968 paper[137] to ask if Bonhoeffer's ethics "book" contained "one method or two"?

Rasmussen went further and argued a strong case that Chapter VII seemed to be heavily dependent on Barth's ethics, especially in Church Dogmatics II/2. The theme of God's command is found in both Barth and Bonhoeffer's chapter. Further, Rasmussen shows, there are a number of striking instances in which Bonhoeffer's sentences are virtual quotations, or paraphrases, of Barth's statements. And in one case even the same biblical examples are appealed to by Bonhoeffer following Barth. To an obvious objection that Bonhoeffer read Barth's II/2 in prison and thus could not have been borrowing from it when working on Chapter VII, Rasmussen asks the obvious question: where is the evidence that Bonhoeffer had never seen this volume before? In fact, we now have evidence that the opposite is the case.

In the summer of 1981, previously unknown correspondence between Bonhoeffer and Barth was discovered in Basel. In a letter to Barth during his third trip to Switzerland, written on May 13, 1942, Bonhoeffer reports that he is reading the galleys of Church Dogmatics II/2:

> Armed with the galley-proofs of your new volume of

---

[136]. Eg, 393; E, 277.

[137]. It is now published for the first time in this volume.

the <u>Dogmatics</u>... I want to spend about eight days on the way to Geneva in complete peace and quiet in a boarding house on Lake Geneva.... There I want to work through at least the second half of your volume.... On the way back, then, I would very much like to visit with you.[138]

The second half, of course, is the ethics particular to Barth's doctrine of God. It is entitled "The Command of God."

Now we have proof that Rasmussen was right, and that the parallels were too great to be coincidental. And we know with certainty when Bonhoeffer first studied this section of Barth, namely in the middle of May, 1942. Before he knew of this correspondence, Bethge dated the work on this chapter "during the winter of 1942/43."[139] This recent discovery raises the possibility that Bonhoeffer began to work on it even earlier, perhaps in the summer of 1942. Indeed, the biography refers to work on the ethics in June and August of 1942.[140] At least some of this work was probably preparation for the synod commission on the Fifth Commandment which met in Magdeburg first on August 10, 1942 and then on March 15, 1943; Bonhoeffer was working on "The Doctrine of the Primus Usus Legis..." for this commission and Bethge thinks he "probably presented his work at the second session."[141] But given the fact that Bonhoeffer had read Barth in May (and surely discussed it with him on his visit), and that he was obviously strongly influenced at the time

---

138. Cf. Bonhoeffer, <u>Schweizer Korrespondenz 1941/42. Im Gespräch mit Karl Barth</u>, ed. Eberhard Bethge (München: Chr. Kaiser, 1982; <u>Theologische Existenz Heute</u>, N. 214). See John Godsey's translation in the Bonhoeffer Society <u>Newsletter</u>, Number 22, (June 1982).

139. Eg, 16; E, 13.

140. DB, 625, 677.

141. Eg, 16; E, 14. The biography is definite about the second session (DBg, 796; DB, 613).

by Barth's approach to Christian ethics, we at least have to consider that Barth's impact might have prompted him to begin this writing soon after May, 1942.

The Eichberger paper used throughout Chapter VII was also used for the first half of "Primus Usus Legis." It was also used in some of Chapters I, VI/1 and VI/2, in one Doppelbogen of the novel fragment and most of the truth-telling essay, both from Tegel; and it was used in Bonhoeffer's funeral address for Hans Friedrich von Kleist-Retzow on August 3, 1941, and for his own will written on September 20, 1942. Although this shows that Bonhoeffer was using this paper during 1942 after he read Barth, it does not allow us to say when he began working on Chapter VII; but it does provide negative evidence, in the sense that the paper does not contra-indicate a start in the summer of 1942, particularly since he also used it for some of the "Primus Usus Legis" essay which may also have been begun in the summer of 1942. If, indeed, he presented his paper to the commission in March, 1943, then it is most likely that he simultaneously worked on both pieces.[142]

The foregoing evidence leads me to conclude not only that Chapter VII was the last written but also that it constitutes by itself the final "block," rather than a continuation of a fourth Ansatz beginning at Chapter V, as Bethge suggested. The outer limits of the writing period must be May, 1942 and April, 1943.

To regard this as the latest block which is indeed a new approach does not, however, mean that Bonhoeffer rejected all that he had written before. He not only took up again his distinctive approach to the "mandates" which had been discussed in Chapters V and VI; he also employed again his characteristic ideas. For the mandates are forms of the commandment of God, its social actuality in the

---

142. Indeed, references to the Fifth Commandment, to the fact that the church does not proclaim two messages (natural law for unbelievers and the christian message for believers), to the twofold service of the church, to the various "offices" of proclamation (E, 316), to the appropriate "autonomy" of worldly orders (E, 317: Ordnungen, cf. mandates) are all found in both pieces.

historical world. And God's commandment is understood christologically, so here the central theological themes of the earlier chapters return.[143] For the eternal Son with the Father (Barth!) is the "incarnate God," so that "divine being cannot be found otherwise than in human form" and, consistently, in Christ one is set free to be really human before God--the Christian element not being an additive or an alienation but a humanization whereby living is not a being for self but simultaneously a being there for God and for others.[144] Likewise, the incarnate God is the crucified, so that the reality of the world is not simply its godlessness, but its godforsakenness is taken up in the cross of reconciliation, enabling "life in genuine worldliness," "life before God in the midst of the godless world." In this way the risen and ascended Lord is not a "foreign power" but the world's creator, reconciler and redeemer whose "commandment... sets creation free for the fulfillment of the law which is its own."[145]

In summary we can say that the distinction between the "ethical" and the "commandment of God" is new in this block. But while "commandment" as a central category is new here, its christological content is quite familiar, as is its social form in the mandates.

XI. CONCLUSIONS

I will now attempt to summarize the main results of the whole analysis.

1. Bonhoeffer's Ethics should be arranged into three blocks:
   A. Chapter I
   B. Chapters III, II, IV, V and VI/2
   C. Chapter VII

---

143. Eg, 313-316; E, 296-299.

144. Eg, 214.

145. Eg, 313-316; E, 298.

The Text of Bonhoeffer's Ethics 59

2. Chapter I is the first written, and was probably written between mid-March and summer, 1940. It obviously antedates the Autumn, 1940 outline and its more comprehensive conceptualization of the project. It can therefore be viewed as a preliminary attempt which is superseded by the second block--though this does not imply that all the ideas and issues in Chapter I were no longer important.

3. The bulk of the book is constituted by the second block. The first part of this is governed by the Autumn, 1940 outline. We have five of the seven parts Bonhoeffer projected for the first division of the book, but none from the second division. (Chapters III and IV should not be regarded as separate Ansätze.)

4. Chapter II is the fourth part (Abschnitt) of this block and belongs after the three parts in Chapter III and before the beginning of Chapter IV. It does not belong with and after Chapter I.

5. Chapter IV, in its opening discussion of "the ultimate and the penultimate," is a continuation of the argument being presented in Chapters III and II. However, there is clearly a new development of thought leading into the discussions of "the natural" and "the good." But while Bonhoeffer has now gone beyond his outline into new subjects, he also ties the new material into the previous argument.

6. Chapters V and VI should probably be regarded as one chapter. In any case they together constitute the discussion about "the good" forecast in Chapter IV.

7. Chapter VI/1, by its reference back to Chapter III as the "first chapter," shows that it is part of the same second block, though now expanded from its original conception. Chapter VI/2 is obviously a rewrite of VI/1 and is to be seen as supplanting it in the second block.

8. Chapter VII is a separate block, inspired by Karl Barth. It is not so much a radical departure from the ideas in the second block as an experiment in the foundations of Christian ethics based on the distinction and relation of the "ethical" and the "commandment of

God."

The aim of this study has been to place the analysis of Bonhoeffer's Ethics on a secure textual basis. While all issues may not yet be resolved, the construction and pattern of the book is now clearer than it has ever been. The new critical German edition--and hopefully an English counterpart--will build upon the research into textual issues. Meanwhile scholars can certainly look at the argument of the Ethics with new eyes.[146] It may be that, after forty years, the book will win new attention. That attention will not be as a source for some catchy phrases, nor as an antecedent of the Letters and Papers from Prison, nor as a fragmentary collection of stimulating but ad hoc reflections. Rather, the book needs to be studied as a substantive contribution to Christian ethics born in a creative and paradigmatic moment of our momentous times.

---

146. See, for example, my paper on "Bonhoeffer's 'Non-Religious Christianity' as Public Theology" which argues that "Kirche und Welt" discloses the social and intellectual roots of the prison theology in the resistance movement.

Appendix A: Ethik, Table of Contents

INHALT

Vorwort 11

I
Die Liebe Gottes und der Zerfall der Welt . 19
- Die Welt der Konflikte 19
- Die Scham 22
- Scham und Gewissen 26
- Die Welt der wiedergefundenen Einheit 29
- Der Pharisäer 29
- Das Prüfen 41
- Das Tun 47
- Die Liebe 53

II
Kirche und Welt 59
- Der Ganzheits- und Ausschließlichkeitsanspruch Christi 61
- Christus und die Guten 64

III
Ethik als Gestaltung 68
- Der theoretische Ethiker und die Wirklichkeit . . . 68
- Ecce homo 74
- Der Menschenverächter 75
- Der Erfolgreiche 79
- Die Todesvergötzung 83
- Gleichgestaltung 85
- Der konkrete Ort 91

Erbe und Verfall 94
Schuld, Rechtfertigung, Erneuerung 117
- Das Schuldbekenntnis 117
- Rechtfertigung und Vernarbung 124

IV

DIE LETZTEN UND DIE VORLETZTEN DINGE . . . 128
    Rechtfertigung als das letzte Wort 128
    Das Vorletzte 133
    Wegbereitung 142
Das Natürliche 152
    Das natürliche Leben 158
    Suum cuique 161
    Das Recht auf das leibliche Leben 165
    Der Selbstmord 176
    Fortpflanzung und werdendes Leben 184
    Freiheit des leiblichen Lebens 195
    Die natürlichen Rechte des geistigen Lebens . . . 198

V

CHRISTUS, DIE WIRKLICHKEIT UND DAS GUTE . . 200
(Christus, Kirche und Welt)
    Der Wirklichkeitsbegriff 200
    Das Denken in zwei Räumen 208
    Die vier Mandate 220

VI

DIE GESCHICHTE UND DAS GUTE 227
    Das Gute und das Leben 227
Die Struktur des verantwortlichen Lebens . . . 238
    Stellvertretung 238
    Wirklichkeitsgemäßheit 241
    Welt der Dinge — Sachgemäßheit — Staatskunst . . 250
    Schuldübernahme 255
    Das Gewissen 257
    Freiheit 264
Der Ort der Verantwortung 270
    Der Beruf 270

VII
Das „Ethische" und das „Christliche" als Thema 279
Die Ermächtigung zum ethischen Reden 279
Das Gebot Gottes 293
Das konkrete Gebot und die göttlichen Mandate . . 303
Der Mandatsbegriff 304
Das Gebot Gottes in der Kirche 309

ANHANG

I
Die Lehre vom primus usus legis nach den Lutherischen Bekenntnisschriften und ihre Kritik 323
1. Der Begriff und seine Zweckmäßigkeit . . . 323
2. Die Frage der theologischen Berechtigung . . . 324
3. Das Interesse am Begriff 326
4. Definition 326
5. Sein Inhalt 327
6. Sein Zweck 328
7. Die Mittel zur Durchführung 329
8. Der Verkündiger 331
9. Der Hörer 331
10. Der primus usus und das Evangelium . . . 332
11. Einige Folgerungen und Fragen 335
12. Kritik der usus-Lehre der lutherischen Bekenntnisschriften 339

II
„Personal"- und „Sach"-Ethos 341
1. Personal- oder Sach-Ethos? 341
2. Das Neue Testament 342
3. Bekenntnisschriften 346
4. Kritisches zu Dilschneiders These 347
5. Systematisches über die möglichen Aussagen christlicher Ethik über die weltliche Ordnung . . . 348

III

STAAT UND KIRCHE 353
  1. Begriffliches 353
  2. Die Begründung der Obrigkeit 354
    A. Aus der Natur des Menschen . . . 354
    B. Aus der Sünde 356
    C. Von Christus her 357
  3. Der göttliche Charakter der Obrigkeit . . . 360
    A. In ihrem Sein 360
    B. In ihrem Auftrag 361
    C. In ihrem Anspruch 364
  4. Die Obrigkeit und die göttlichen Ordnungen in der Welt 365
  5. Obrigkeit und Kirche 368
    A. Der Anspruch der Obrigkeit an die Kirche . . 368
    B. Der Anspruch der Kirche an die Obrigkeit . . 369
    C. Die kirchliche Verantwortung der Obrigkeit . 370
    D. Die politische Verantwortung der Kirche . . 371
    E. Folgerungen 373
  6. Staatsform und Kirche 374

IV

ÜBER DIE MÖGLICHKEIT DES WORTES DER KIRCHE AN DIE WELT 376

V

WAS HEISST: DIE WAHRHEIT SAGEN? 385

REGISTER 397
  Bibelstellen 397
  Bekenntnisschriften 399
  Sachen 399
  Namen 405

Appendix B: 1940 Outline Manuscript

38a   58

Grundlagen

Ethik als Gestaltung.   (Christentum und die anderen Religionen)

Erbe und Verfall   Erfolgsethik, Militarismus-Heorismus, Bedarfs-
                     versorgung, Heimatlosigkeit (Gegenwartsphiloso-
                     phi) Vergessen, Nihilismus, Todesverachtung.
                     Vitalismus, Verlust von:

                     Glaube, Persönlichem, Gemeinschaft (Liebe).
                     Spannung (Hoffnung).

Arbeit, Extreme.   Unbeseeltheit, Menschsein, Würde. Geschichte,
                     Wert des Leidens. Überzeugungen. Das Wort,
) das Geheimnis,
Urteilslosigkeit) das Wunder - man lebt von den Mitteln, den
     der Menge   )   Methoden, nicht vom Gegenstand
                     Bestandaufnahme des Christlichen Glaubens und
                     Lebens
                     (Problematik einer "Bestandaufnahme")

Schuld und Rechtfertigung (abendländische Schuld. Geschichtsproblem.
                           Glaube, nicht hinter die Schuld zurück-
                           kommen.

Erneuerung und Heiligung   Kirche und Welt(gestaltung) usus primus
                           Christus und die Gebote, die Gesetze und
                           die Gnade.

Erneuerung des Handelns

                     Die vorletzten und die letzten Dinge
                           (Tragödie, Werte, Psyche)
                                Tugenden   Pflichten
                     Der neue Mensch (
                                        Christus Antriebe
                                        Leben im Leib Christi

"Lieber dogt als Sklave" - "lieber Sklave als tot"

            das geknechtete Deutschland

II

BIOGRAPHICAL CONTEXT

Robin W. Lovin

When Dietrich Bonhoeffer took pen in hand in the Spring of 1940 and began to write his Ethics he fulfilled the expectations of some and surprised many others, including, perhaps, himself. Although the seminar papers he wrote as a student and the classes he taught in his brief career as a lecturer show an interest in the problems of ethics,[1] Bonhoeffer's own theological development after the summer of 1932 pushed him more and more to think about the church as the place of authentic Christian morality and to mistrust abstract and systematic ethics, which often seemed out of touch with the realities of Christian life.

Events outside the classroom and study reinforced this tendency, for they removed Bonhoeffer from the university and cast his lot decisively with the church. After Hitler came to power, Bonhoeffer could no longer work comfortably in the academic centers which had close ties to the state. He embarked on a career as a pastor and teacher in the Confessing Church, the German Protestant effort to maintain the historic freedom of the church and to resist the nazification of religious organizations. With war on the horizon in 1939, Bonhoeffer chose to remain in his country and with his church,

---

1. DB, 115-19; 257-67. Bethge's biography is the indispensable source for the narrative of Bonhoeffer's activities during 1940-43. In general, I have confined explicit references to DB to specific points the interested reader may want to check.

rejecting the opportunities which he briefly sampled for a new teaching career in the United States.

The Confessing Church was not the only claim on Bonhoeffer's loyalty. He was a member of a well-placed and active family. His brother, Klaus, his brother-in-law, Hans von Dohnanyi, and other family members held important posts in the civil service or the military. At the outbreak of World War II, several of them had already joined a circle of conspirators who would eventually attempt to assassinate Hitler. In the years ahead, Dietrich Bonhoeffer himself would be drawn into this resistance, and the problems it would pose for all the participants would become for him the starting point for a new understanding of responsible action.[2]

The manuscript hidden in the attic of his parents' home in Berlin before his arrest on 5 April 1943 bears the marks of all these influences, though not usually in a way that allows us to identify them neatly. The Ethics as we have it is unfinished. It consists of essays written under the pressure of events, of false starts and second thoughts, of pages in which Bonhoeffer was obliged for security reasons to obscure his meaning, and of passages which burn with the white-hot lucidity of one who knew he was risking his life for the ideas he expressed. Even more than with most books, we must read this one with an understanding of the man who wrote it and the times in which he lived. Taken alone, an essay on success[3] or words of praise for Bismarck's politics[4] are confusing elements to find in a book on Christian ethics. To understand them, we must see them against the events of the time and recognize the alternatives against which Bonhoeffer had to argue.

This essay is an attempt to understand the Ethics in relation to

---

2. Heinrich Ott, Reality and Faith: The Theological Legacy of Dietrich Bonhoeffer, trans. Alex A. Morrison (Philadelphia: Fortress Press, 1972), 251-257.

3. E, 75-78.

4. E, 240.

Bonhoeffer's background and the events which shaped his life as he wrote. We cannot, of course, reduce the normative claims of the Ethics to a set of facts about its author. When he says that responsible action includes readiness to accept guilt,[5] we cannot escape the implications that has for our own lives by inquiring more closely into the guilt that Bonhoeffer felt for the particular involvements that his wartime experiences forced upon him. Still less can we understand the Ethics by attempting simple causal explanations of its parts, saying that event A led to paragraph B. Nevertheless, to understand this work, we must treat it as more than a set of ideas. We must make the book a window onto Bonhoeffer's world, and we must use every resource we have available to enter the world in which this text emerged. Only when we have understood the historical and biographical influences on the Ethics can we begin to understand the ethical system Bonhoeffer developed and the claims it makes on us today.

I. THE PROBLEM OF A CHRISTIAN ETHICS

It could not have been easy for Bonhoeffer to write about Christian ethics, even without the disturbances of the early months of the Second World War. Bonhoeffer read widely in moral theology in preparation for his writing,[6] but for Protestants of his generation the history of that careful, systematic thinking about ethics had been radically interrupted by the work of Karl Barth.

The revolution in Protestant theology which began with Barth's Epistle to the Romans in 1921 placed its emphasis on God's initiative and action.[7] What can be said about God must proceed from God's own speaking, not by any analogies drawn from human experience.

---

5. E, 240.

6. DB, 303.

7. Karl Barth, The Epistle to the Romans, trans. Edwin Hoskyns (London: Oxford University Press, 1933).

This emphasis particularly called into question the usual ideas about ethics, for the secure knowledge of good and evil on which moral choices seem to rest is simply not available in a situation in which everything depends immediately on God's will. In the political disorders and cultural confusion that followed World War I, Barth insisted that Christians could not recreate a good society out of their own moral resources. They must respond obediently to the Word of God as they encounter it, recognizing that God is the chief moral actor in all situations and steadfastly refusing to generalize their specific responses to God's initiatives into moral rules that might apply to all people and to other situations. This did not stop Barth from writing a good bit on ethics,[8] but everything he said sharply differentiated Christian obedience from the search for knowledge of the good that had previously marked both theological and philosphical ethics.

Bonhoeffer had spoken out for Barth both among the skeptical representatives of the older liberalism in Berlin and before the largely uninitiated American theologians at Union Seminary during his studies there in 1930-31. For the Americans, Bonhoeffer tried to evoke the radicalism of Barth's theological starting point:

> I confess that I do not see any other possible way for getting you into real contact with his thinking than by forgetting for at least this one hour everything you have learned before concerning the problem. We have in Barth's theology not one of the countless variations of the solution to this problem from the Scholastics via Kant to Bergson or Dewey, but here we stand on an entirely different and new point of departure. We stand in the tradition of Paul, Luther, Kierkegaard, in the tradition of genuine Christian thinking.[9]

---

8. Some of Barth's lectures of 1928-29 are now available in English as Karl Barth, Ethics, trans. G. W. Bromiley (Grand Rapids, Mich.: Eerdmanns, 1981).

9. GS III, 111. The "problem" under discussion in this passage is the relationship between philosophy and theology.

Bonhoeffer's admiration for Barth's new beginning is clear. As a German and a resident of Berlin, he knew firsthand the social crisis that undid the liberal tradition of the nineteenth century, and he was thoroughly familiar with the new existentialist literature that raised these fundamental questions for philosophy as well. Heidegger's <u>Being and Time</u>, published in 1927, attempted to demolish the whole history of ontology from ancient Greece to the present in order to open the way for a new conception of being as experiential and temporal, rather than a timeless metaphysical reality. Bonhoeffer promptly incorporated some of Heidegger's basic ideas into <u>Act and Being</u>, which he wrote in 1931.

So Bonhoeffer was a theologian of the new generation, but he was never simply a Barthian. In a letter written to his friend Erwin Sutz, he lamented his inability to apprentice himself to a single teacher, as many of his contemporaries had attached themselves to Barth or to Emil Brunner. Then he wondered candidly, "Or wouldn't I have been able to stand it?"[10] The truth of the matter is that he probably would not. If "discipleship" was at the center of his early theology, apprenticeship was nevertheless incompatible with his personality.

The initial problem for Bonhoeffer's ethics was to find a plausible alternative to Barth's rejection of the traditional questions of ethics. Bonhoeffer read widely in Roman Catholic moral theology, and in the work of contemporary Catholics, including Max Scheler and Nikolai Hartmann. What distinguished Scheler and Hartmann from their Protestant counterparts was their insistence on the objective reality of moral values, so that the good could be known and sought by persons apart from direct reliance on the will of God. The Catholic ethics Bonhoeffer read thus attempted to restate in phenomenological terms the tradition that fundamental moral truths are part of a natural order than can be known everywhere and by all persons, without regard to religious faith. This emphasis on "the natural" would

---

10. NRS, 118.

become more important for Bonhoeffer as he developed his own thinking on ethics.

In 1940, however, no Protestant theologian could simply substitute knowledge of natural law for the radical obedience that Barth demanded.

Emil Brunner provided a Protestant alternative to Barth's ethics. He agreed that Christian ethics depends on the will of God, and he rejected philosophical attempts to establish an autonomous ethics based on reason or on objective values. Nevertheless, Brunner argued, God's will can be known in part from the patterns apparent in God's work. Marriage, family, religion, state and the worlds of work and culture everywhere establish some stable relationships to each other and require some of the same conditions in order to function well. Christians cannot be indifferent to these "orders of creation," and they can join forces on moral issues with others who understand the orders, even if these persons do not always acknowledge the Creator on whom the orders depend.[11]

Bonhoeffer appreciated the importance of God's creative action for the ordering of human life, as his 1932-33 lectures on creation at the University of Berlin make clear. His reliance on creation is sharply limited, however, by his emphasis on the Fall and the cosmic effects of human sin. The persistent orders of human life are not the order of creation God intended. They are at best "orders of preservation" that mercifully protect us from the worst consequences of our sinful separation from God.[12] Bonhoeffer's reservation has important roots in the history of Protestant theology, but his hesitation about the "orders of creation" language also marked his awareness that the Nazis regarded race and nation as basic human realities, and they used the language of the orders of creation to defend their nationalist and anti-Semitic policies. Faced with this, Barth

---

11. Emil Brunner, The Divine Imperative, trans. Olive Wyon (Philadelphia: Westminster Press, 1947).

12. CF/T, 88.

eliminated all language about the orders from his own theology and denounced Brunner for providing the opening for Nazi exploitation.[13]

Bonhoeffer understood the problem. Like the rest of his family, he rejected Hitler's vision of Germany's national salvation, and he used every opportunity to contrast the young leadership of the churches with the Nazi youth movement and to reinterpret the Nazi concepts of the Leader (Führer) and self-assertion (Selbstbehauptung) along lines more appropriate to the Christian faith.[14] Nevertheless, the fundamental Christian concern for the right ordering of the world which is God's creation seemed to Bonhoeffer too important to sacrifice to a terminological dispute with the Nazis. As he worked out his Ethics, he sought a way to speak about the concrete structures of state, work, family and church in which the Christian receives the commandment of God. He argued that the Christian concern to preserve these structures and direct them toward their proper function is also a way of working in the world and sharing responsibility with others.

On one level, then, Bonhoeffer's Ethics is an attempt to resolve the problem of Christian ethics that Barth posed for that generation of theologians. The immediacy of the Word of God, God's freedom to address each situation in a unique way, and the Christian's unconditional response to obey the Word as heard captured the imagination of European theologians and revived the study of theology, which was weary of adaptations from philosophy and confused by the collapse of a familiar culture; but the Word that renewed theology seemed to render ethical reflection impossible. Bonhoeffer's initial concern to make Christian action once again a legitimate subject for practical reflection shaped the Ethics, as it shaped his first teaching in Berlin.[15]

---

13. Karl Barth, "No!" in John Baillie, ed., Natural Theology (London: Geoffrey Bles, 1946).

14. GS II, 22-38; GS III, 258-69; 292-93.

15. GS III, 162-164.

The result is more than an intellectual compromise between Barth and Brunner. It presents Bonhoeffer's interpretation of the larger course of Western history in which his nation and his own life were caught. Above all, by 1940, Christian ethics had to include a Christian obedience clear enough about its directions to share its work with others, and an obedience sure enough of God's grace to risk the compromises, deceits and conspiracies that opposition to Hitler required. "Is there a Christian ethic?" Bonhoeffer had asked in a seminar title for the summer of 1933. Seven years later the question had become urgent for both the theologian and his church.

II. ECHOES OF FINKENWALDE

[Chapter I: Probably written spring and summer 1940, chiefly in Berlin.]

The first pages for the Ethics were probably written in Berlin, where Bonhoeffer could observe first hand the upsurge of patriotism that accompanied the beginning of the War, and where he contemplated his own narrowing options. His work since 1935 had been to train ordination candidates for the Confessing Church, first at a small seminary in the town of Finkenwalde, and then in a series of "collective pastorates" that allowed the ordinands to study and work in the less conspicuous setting of rural vicarages. Wartime restrictions ended that work early in 1940, and Bonhoeffer faced the likelihood of his own call-up for military service in the near future.

He did not, however, begin the Ethics with immediate attention to the moral dilemmas of his new situation. Bonhoeffer wrote by giving intense concentration to what he was prepared to put quickly into finished form. What he was prepared to write at that point in 1940 was a reflection on the era of his own life that had just ended, when his work had been dominated by the experience of the Confessing Church.

At Finkenwalde, Bonhoeffer had tried to give visible form to Barth's ethics of obedience. That discipline seemed best to prepare his students for the difficult work of pastors in the Confessing Church. Set in that context, Christian ethics must begin with a radical distinction between the life of faith and the values of the world. These lines are drawn not to exclude others from the Christian community's truth, but to protect the disciple from delusions and easy compromises with a value system that is in fact totally alien to the Christian faith. Finkenwalde was not a place of retreat from the challenges of Nazism. Christian faith could not afford the luxury of such isolation from the world. "Luther did not return to the world because he had arrived at a more positive attitude toward it.... By recalling Christians into the world he called them paradoxically out of it all the more."[16]

That Lutheran summons which dominated The Cost of Discipleship resounds too in Bonhoeffer's first attempt at a chapter for the Ethics. "The knowledge of good and evil seems to be the aim of all ethical reflection. The first task of Christian ethics is to invalidate this knowledge."[17] Christians must know the demanding path on which they are set, so the "hard sayings" of Jesus and the requirements of the Sermon on the Mount pervade this picture of the Christian life, and point up its contrast with the convoluted, legalistic discipleship of the pharisee. Christians, moreover, must not transmute active discipleship into a reflective knowledge of the good. The point of Christian ethics, if it is possible at all after Barth's devastating dialectical negations, must be to eliminate the reflective distance between hearing the Word of God and doing what it requires. The aim is to sketch a unity of the Christian life in which one's identity as a follower of Jesus, the hearing of his demand on one's life and the doing of his will are not separated by any space into which purely human values may intrude. "Obedience," as Bonhoeffer put it already in 1932, "is belonging in the form of hearing."[18]

---

16. CD, 298.

17. E, 17.

18. GS III, 162.

As a foundation for the systematic work of Christian ethics, this emphasis on the simple, natural unity of obedient Christian life seemed at first the appropriate place for Bonhoeffer to begin. It was a continuation of the work he had begun at Finkenwalde and carried on in The Cost of Discipleship. It was consistent with his first academic treatment of ethics during his teaching in Berlin, and in its emphasis on immediate responsiveness to the Word of God, it represented perhaps the only form of Christian ethics compatible with the theology of Karl Barth. Above all, it replaced intellectual perplexity and divided loyalties with the simplicity of honest action. In the New Testament, "the life and activity of men is not at all problematic or tormented or dark: it is self-evident, joyful, sure and clear."[19] That, as we shall see, remained an important theme in Bonhoeffer's ethics.

The problem was that while this clear witness and uncompromising obedience fit the idea of the Confessing Church for which he had worked at Finkenwalde, it fit less and less the reality of the Confessing Church in wartime, nor did it make much sense of his own ambiguous position. Sporadic arrests of the Confessing Church leaders and increasing restrictions on their activities made it more and more difficult for the church to do its work, while a growing sentiment of national unity led numbers of Confessing pastors to legalize their status by compromising with the pro-Nazi Reich Church Government. Bonhoeffer himself had been forbidden to visit Berlin on business since January 1938, though his visits to his family had allowed him to accomplish most of his purposes. Others in the Confessing Church, including some of the graduates of the Finkenwalde seminary, had suffered much worse. The radical distinction between the life of faith and the values of the world offered little guidance to Confessing pastors who, like Bonhoeffer, were faced with the prospect of a military call-up, nor did the distinction fully explain the persons of much integrity, but sometimes of little faith, who were beginning to gather around Admiral Canaris and Colonel

---

19. E, 26.

Oster, forming a center of anti-Nazi conspiracy in the Abwehr, the German military intelligence service. After writing about the "total and exclusive claim of Christ," Bonhoeffer also penned an unusual appreciation of the good "in the citizen-like sense," which had been needlessly ridiculed by the theologians' insistence on invalidating ordinary human knowledge of good and evil.[20] These sentences, which form the end of what we now have as Chapter II, indicate an appreciation of the humanist opposition to Nazism which was already growing in Bonhoeffer's experience as he wrote the theological affirmations of Chapter I.

III. HISTORY AND NATURE

[Chapter II: Probably written November 1940 in Berlin; Chapter III: Written fall 1940 at Klein-Krössin; Chapter IV: Written winter 1940-41 at the monastery of Ettal.]

Bonhoeffer began again on his Ethics in the fall of 1940. Whether he intended to incorporate the present Chapter I in the reconceived volume, we cannot be sure; but he certainly rethought the structure of the whole. An outline[21] divides the work into "foundations" and "structures," with some of the elements of the "foundations" outline corresponding to sections of the present Chapter III, "Ethics as Formation," and Chapter IV, "The Last Things and the Things Before the Last."

These chapters were written during a time when Bonhoeffer's intellectual energies could be largely devoted to his writing, before the disruptions of the War and his travels as a courier for the Abwehr conspirators. They are, then, the most complete chapters we have in hand, but they do not follow an altogether smooth line of development. In Chapters III and IV, Bonhoeffer lays his foundations

---

20. E, 60-63.

21. E, 8. Clifford Green's essay in this volume discusses this outline in greater detail.

both in history and in nature. This creates problems which will become apparent later when he tries to raise the "structure" on this split "foundation."

In the summer of 1940, Bonhoeffer travelled throughout East Prussia as an official "visitor" to Confessing congregations from the Confessing Church leadership. In August, he made arrangements to avert a military call-up and to escape the increasing restrictions the Gestapo were putting on his activities by accepting a position as an unpaid special agent of the Abwehr. This ostensible contribution to the military effort protected him in some measure from the jurisdiction of the civilian secret police, and in reality, of course, it put him in close contact with the military conspiracy against the Hitler regime. For the moment, his assignments would be limited, and he was able to spend some weeks in September and October at Klein-Krössin on the estate of Ruth von Kleist-Retzow, one of several wealthy supporters who had befriended him and assisted his work in the seminary at Finkenwalde. She now undertook to provide Bonhoeffer with a place where he could occasionally rest, and she assisted his work by collecting supplies of writing paper, which during the war became quite scarce.

It is tempting to attribute some of the social conservatism of Bonhoeffer's Ethics to his ties to these rural aristocrats on whose estates he felt so much at home and among whom, indeed, he eventually found his fiancée. Certainly there was a cultural affinity between the intellectual leaders from whom Bonhoeffer came and the older aristocracy. They shared a common commitment to personal honor, and they rejected the acquisitive values that marked the new entrepreneurs of Germany's industrial cities.[22]

In 1940, however, neither Bonhoeffer nor his supporters were thinking about the values of the good old days. Their minds were very much on current events in the West, where Hitler's armies won a

---

22. For a general discussion of these relationships, see Ernest K. Bramsted, Aristocracy and the Middle-Classes in Germany (Chicago: University of Chicago Press, 1964).

series of stunning victories that culminated in the fall of France and appeared to impose a new order on European history. Against this triumphalist presumption that German power had reversed the disgrace of 1919 and assumed at last its rightful dominance of European civilization, Bonhoeffer began his revised Ethics with the idea of "ethics as formation."

It quickly becomes clear that this concept owes little to traditional ideas of "Christian formation," the shaping of individual character according to Christian models of virtue and sanctity. Bonhoeffer may have borrowed the terminology from Catholic moral theology texts he collected in preparation for his writing,[23] and he may have noted parallel concerns in his lessons in discipleship for the seminarians at Finkenwalde, but his use of the concept in Ethics involves an ironic reversal. Just as Karl Barth once upended Catholic analogical theology by replacing the argument from human reality to the nature of God with an analogia fidei that argues from God's self-revelation to the nature of humanity,[24] Bonhoeffer now suggests that the important formation is not our conformity to Christ, but Christ's taking form in us, in the concrete events of history and in the historical life of the church.

> Ethics as formation, then, means the bold endeavour to speak about the way in which the form of Jesus Christ takes form in our world, in a manner which is neither abstract nor casuistic, neither programmatic nor purely speculative. Concrete judgements and decisions will have to be ventured here.[25]

Bonhoeffer offers an interpretation of Western history which is

---

23. DB, 619-120.

24. Karl Barth, Anselm: Fides Quarens Intellectum (London: SCM Press, 1960). Also see Robin W. Lovin, Christian Faith and Public Choices: The Social Ethics of Barth, Brunner, and Bonhoeffer (Philadelphia: Fortress Press, 1984), 30-42.

25. E, 88.

both concrete and comprehensive. He does not evade the brute fact of Hitler's success, but neither does he allow it to determine his reading of events. What we find in the history of the modern West is a record of defection from the reality of Christ to which the origins and the rise of the West are intimately bound. "What the west is doing is to refuse to accept its historical inheritance for what it is. The west is becoming hostile toward Christ. This is the peculiar situation of our time, and it is genuine decay."[26]

Bonhoeffer's interpretative framework is explicitly theological, but the content of his reading of history owes much to the great historians at Berlin, to Friedrich Meinecke and Hans Delbrück, as well as to Adolf von Harnack.[27] What the historians view as the emergence of a secular politics emancipated from dogmatic constraints, Bonhoeffer treats as the decay of an original unity of the West in the form of Christ.[28] Nevertheless, his history of the West is, like that of his mentors, also German history: the Reformation is the key event that shatters the unity of Christendom, and the rise of the Prussian state is a vital counter to the dehumanizing forces of nationalism and technology.[29] There is in these pages a faint but unmistakable echo of the young theology student who went off to Union Theological Seminary in 1930 with a notebook of answers for American assertions about Germany's guilt for the First World War. Bonhoeffer never wavers in his conviction of 1939 that Christians in Germany must will "the defeat of their nation in order that Christian civilization may survive."[30] At the same time, however, he sounds a

---

26. E, 108.

27. DB, 16, 52.

28. Compare especially Bonhoeffer's treatment of secularization (E, 95-108) with Meinecke's view in Friedrich Meinecke, <u>Machiavellism</u>, trans. Douglas Scott (New Haven: Yale University Press, 1951).

29. E, 101.

30. DB, 559.

sober warning to other parties in the War.

> The guilt of the apostasy from Christ is a guilt which is shared in common by the entire western world, however greatly the degree of the offense may vary. The justification and renewal must therefore likewise be shared in common by the whole of the west. No attempt can succeed which aims at saving the west while excluding one of the western nations.[31]

Bonhoeffer's theological account of Christ's taking form in the West, then, is closely bound to the events of current history. On close inspection, these pages from his wartime work curiously resemble the more public anticipations of the postwar world written about the same time by the English churchmen George Bell and William Paton.[32] Bonhoeffer already knew Bishop Bell, especially, from ecumenical meetings, and Bell would play an important role in Bonhoeffer's clandestine work in 1942. When Bonhoeffer wrote "Ethics as Formation," he could not have seen either Bell's book or Paton's. He did read both of them on a later journey to Switzerland, and in a response to Paton that he wrote in 1941, he offers the same sort of warning against punitive war aims that closes "Ethics as Formation."[33]

The convergence of concerns between Bonhoeffer's work and those of his English counterparts is all the more striking because direct influence seems impossible. It is rather the case that on both sides, at the beginning of what seemed destined to be a long war, theologians were already concerned to specify the elements of the Western, Christian heritage that might more successfully order the next peace. The fact that Bonhoeffer considered titling his book "The

---

31. E, 119.

32. See George K. A. Bell, <u>Christianity and World Order</u> (London: Hodder and Stoughton, 1940); and William Paton, <u>The Church and the New Order</u> (New York: Macmillan, 1941).

33. GS I, 356-71.

Foundations and Structure of a United West"[34] shows us that though he was prepared to see Germany defeated, he did not intend to see the Germans excluded from shaping the world after Hitler.

Bonhoeffer's appreciation of Christ's formative power in Western history perhaps gave him a new appreciation of those persons who were awakening, now too late, to the barbarities of the National Socialist regime. Among his family and their friends in Berlin, German victories brought despair, rather than patriotic joy. The humane values of personal honor, respect for culture and civilized treatment of enemies were being destroyed by a state which demanded unlimited loyalty and wrought unlimited destruction on those who opposed it.

The failure of cultural values pointed up the success, however limited, of the Confessing Church's resistance to Nazi Gleichschaltung, which pressured every institution to subordinate its own truth to the new order proclaimed by Adolf Hitler. While visiting his parents in Berlin in November 1940, Bonhoeffer was struck by the respect for the church's role among many persons who previously had maintained at best a distant tolerance for Christian institutions. As a theologian, he had long been an anomaly in a family of intellectuals who moved in Germany's most sophisticated circles. Now, as other alternatives to Hitler's dreamworld faded away one by one, he watched as the lawyers, officers and aristocrats sought to understand the liberating power of faith.

In this context, Bonhoeffer thought of a story by V. S. Soloviev, a Russian author and philosopher who wrote at the end of the nineteenth century. His story of the persecution of Christians by a megalomaniac emperor at some point in a fictional future enjoyed a certain popularity among German intellectuals in the 1930's.[35] In the face of the ultimate temptation to betrayal, Bonhoeffer recounts, the

---

34. E, 8.

35. See Vladimir Soloviev, War, Progress, and the End of History (London: University of London Press, 1915), 180-228.

leaders of the churches realize that the one important truth that must be preserved in Christianity is Jesus Christ himself. "That is to say that in the face of the Antichrist only one thing has force and permanence, and that is Christ himself."[36] Bonhoeffer never fully identified his church's struggle with the eschatological conflict, but he appropriated Soloviev's insight to explain both the persistence of the Confessing Church and the new attraction of the faith for the humanists whose opposition to Nazism was only now becoming really serious.

It was probably at this point, though it may have been earlier,[37] that Bonhoeffer wrote the little essay on Christ and good people that now appears as Chapter II in the Ethics. If the main current of Western history has become hostile to Christ, there are, nonetheless, those who perceive the decay and who, without fully understanding why, seek refuge with the people who have tried to maintain their formative relationship with "the one thing that has force and permanence" in history--Christ himself.

> Precisely through this concentration on the essential, the Church acquired an inward freedom and breadth which preserved her against any timid impulse to draw narrow limits, and there gathers around her men to whom she could not refuse her fellowship and protection: injured justice, oppressed truth, vilified humanity and violated freedom all sought for her, or rather for her Master, Jesus Christ.[38]

Bonhoeffer's work on the Ethics continued with little disruption, despite a shift in his personal circumstances. In mid-

---

36. E, 56.

37. See Clifford Green's essay in this volume for an account of the evidence that suggests that Chapter II was actually written to fill in part of the outline that Bonhoeffer drew up in the fall of 1940.

38. E, 58.

November 1940, he moved to the vicinity of Munich, where he was to wait for a further assignment from the Abwehr. In the meantime, he was protected from military call-up and from the increasingly suspicious attentions of the Gestapo. To appearances, of course, he was simply a pastor of the Confessing Church freed from regular assignments to pursue his theological studies.[39]

For a time, at least, the cover story was close to the truth. Bonhoeffer took up residence in the Benedictine monastery at Ettal, southeast of Munich. There he worked through most of the winter of 1940-41 on the themes he had sketched out that autumn at Klein-Krössin. The work of these months is Chapter IV in the present edition of the Ethics.

"Die vorletzten und die letzten Dinge," now well known in English translation as the tension between the "penultimate" and the "ultimate," continues the discussion of world history and Western culture that began in Chapter III, but with a new emphasis on the divine act of forgiveness that is the goal and terminus of all history. Characteristically, Bonhoeffer invokes this eschatological concept, not to deprive human choices of their importance, but precisely to give them their proper value in themselves. They are not the instruments of our justification before God, as though we could choose and do things simply to insure our own ultimate salvation. They must have value in themselves, or they will have none at all. "A way must be traversed, even though, in fact, there is no way that leads to this goal; this way must be pursued to the end, that is to say, to the point at which God sets an end to it. The penultimate, therefore, remains, even though the ultimate entirely annuls and invalidates it."[40]

Bonhoeffer's work at Ettal initially follows the plan set out at Klein-Krössin, but conversation with the monks and with Catholic opposition leaders in Munich doubtless reminded him of other traditions alongside his Protestant emphasis on justification by faith.

---

[39]. DB, 603-606.

[40]. E, 124-25.

Biographical Context

Set in that context of Bonhoeffer's experience, the abrupt transition to a discussion of "the natural"--precisely where the outline would lead us to expect a section on "the new man"--begins to make sense.[41]

"The concept of the natural has fallen into discredit in Protestant ethics," Bonhoeffer begins.[42] Yet two ideas from the Catholic natural law tradition aptly expressed what Bonhoeffer needed to say about the moral judgments that persons must make in the penultimate reality that precedes God's final judgment. Natural law theories suggest that despite the changes that human institutions undergo in history, there are rational grounds for evaluating these changes, and distorted forms of human institutions can be identified. The natural law also puts a heavy emphasis on the ability of each rational person to make these judgments, rather than relying solely on obedience to a superior authority.

Bonhoeffer's illustrations of the unnatural--"It is possible, for example, to organize the undermining of children's respect for their parents"[43]--leave no doubt that he was principally interested in a moral concept that would allow criticism of the Hitler regime. Where this new appreciation of the natural might have led is unclear. In a later essay, Bonhoeffer refers to the Protestant rediscovery of the natural, but he draws back from the suggestion that moral imperatives can easily be read in the requirements of nature. "The natural" serves him less as a way to identify what the limits on human action are than as a crucial reminder that the limits *do* exist.[44]

---

41. Bonhoeffer was, of course, familiar with natural law thinking from his earlier reading in Catholic moral theology, and while "the natural" does not appear in the outline written at Klein-Krössin, Clifford Green reports that there are notes on "das naturliche Leben" written on paper from Klein-Krössin. So it is possible that the discussion of the natural which now dominates Chapter IV was in some way in Bonhoeffer's thinking before he came to Ettal.

42. E, 143.

43. E, 148.

44. LPP, 10-11. For a further discussion of Bonhoeffer's relation to natural law thinking, see Lovin, <u>Christian Faith and Public Choices</u>, 152-55.

Only a few notes suggest how Bonhoeffer might have finished this chapter had he had time in 1941. What is clear is that alongside the historical account of the decay of Western culture, Bonhoeffer includes an immanent principle for the criticism of culture. The penultimate reality includes both history and nature, and these two are, sometimes at least, in conflict. Bonhoeffer's resolution of this tension, and perhaps even his recognition that this problem exists in the text, were forestalled by a journey to Switzerland that marked the beginning of extensive travels for the Abwehr that lasted until midsummer of 1942.

IV. REALITY

[Chapters V and VI: Written primarily summer and fall 1941 at Berlin, Klein-Krössin and perhaps elsewhere.]

During the breaks between his travels, Bonhoeffer continued to work on the intellectual problems of his Ethics, and he doubtless reflected on the particular moral problems of the conspiracy as well. The writings of this period are more fragmentary, though Bonhoeffer numbered the pages of the manuscript in ways that suggest he thought of them as a continuous work.

The most theoretical treatment of the problems of ethics comes in the pages that are now Chapter V, "Christ, Reality, and the Good." Here Bonhoeffer offers the principle of "reality" to join the "two spheres" often separated in Protestant ethics. "Reality" here is primarily a force for unity, an underlying oneness that belies the intellectual abstractions that separate church from world, the ideal from the real, or--may we add?--history from nature. This chapter serves thus to summarize and firm up the discussion of "foundations" that Bonhoeffer began in Chapter III. While he does not advert to the earlier discussion of the natural, the effect is to place that standard, like all other ideals, in the same christocentric perspective that governed his treatment of Western history.

It is possible, too, that Bonhoeffer conceived this chapter as the transition from "foundations" to "structures" in the outline of 1940. He introduces here the notion of *divine mandates* as the framework of experience in which our human encounters with christocentric reality take place. *Four* mandates--"labor, marriage, government, and the Church"--may seem an odd resolution to the problem of "thinking in *two* spheres," but it reflects his growing conviction that the concrete commandment of God can be found neither in the bare existential encounter of the person and the Word, nor in an abstract and universal principle that claims to apply to all times and places. "The ethical... already in itself... implies a definite structure of human society."[45] Bonhoeffer will say this more clearly in his second treatment of the mandates, written before his arrest in 1943 and now found as Chapter VII of the Ethics. What is important for the moment is that the theme is present from his first attempt to deal with the structures of life formed by Christ's presence in history.

The clear statement of "Christ, Reality, and the Good" was followed by an unusual number of hesitations and false starts. An attempt to follow up the present Chapter V with a chapter on "history and the good"[46] was interrupted by a second visit to Switzerland in September 1941, followed by a bout of pneumonia. When Bonhoeffer was able to return to work, probably at the very end of 1941, he seems to have scrapped the draft in favor of a new version, now Chapter VI of the Ethics, which employs many of the same themes, but conveys even more clearly the political ramifications of the ideas.

The Ethics text seems little affected by the momentous task that occasioned his travels. His role as an agent of the Abwehr conspiracy was to use ecumenical channels in a desperate and ultimately futile attempt to elicit Allied readiness to negotiate with an anti-Nazi government that would be established by coup d'etat. Apart from the fact that it would hardly have been wise to write about these contacts explicitly, Bonhoeffer had already laid the intellectual groundwork for

---

45. E, 272.

46. GS III, 455-77.

the appeal for a peace that would reunite Europe in his earlier essay on Western history. His response to Paton's The Church and the New Order, written on this second Swiss visit, is a case of the Ethics influencing his political work, and not the other way around.

His new thoughts in this period were drawn more and more beyond the conspirators' preparations to the deed itself. Once the deportations of the Jews began in October 1941, there could no longer be any question of the need to stop the regime of death and terror by whatever means were necessary.[47] But how could one understand that necessity as anything other than the brutal suppression of one violence by another? How could the conspirators claim to restore the rule of law by an essentially lawless act?

That was an important question for this group of conspirators, who not only shared an aristocratic preference for order and stability, but also understood that the success of their plan to terminate the War would depend on their ability to seize and retain control of Germany's political processes. A repetition of the socialist upheavals of 1919 or a drift toward anarchy would make the elimination of Hitler pointless.

Bonhoeffer's particular contribution to the conspiracy seems to have been his ability to cut through the reservations based on patriotism and the sanctity of military oaths to provide understandable grounds for action that the conspirators generally could share. Not all of them were Christians, but all were acquainted with the powers of command that go with high position among civil and military authorities. Bonhoeffer's first move, therefore, was to identify a form of "responsibility" (Verantwortung) which goes with position and reflects a natural authority like that of the parent in the home.[48] When this concrete responsibility is understood, appeals to a general obligation of obedience that treats the individual in isolation can be seen for the evasions they are, but the differentiated forms of responsibility also preclude just anyone from taking matters into one's

---

47. Eberhard Bethge, "Dietrich Bonhoeffer and the Jews," in 81-82.

48. GS III, 456.

own hands.

Bonhoeffer initially attempts an interpretation of the Sermon on the Mount to show that this differentiated, particularized understanding of responsibility is consistent with the christocentric account of reality, while it overturns the doctrinaire "realism" that would sacrifice all proximate structures of responsibility to "the unconditional self-assertion that subordinates everything to itself."[49] A principal change in the second draft of "History and the Good" is the introduction of a number of specifically political ideas that provide a more nuanced transition from the responsibility of the paterfamilias to that genuine Christian responsibility that "encompasses the whole of worldly affairs."[50]

Bonhoeffer seems to think first of political responsibility in the British sense of "responsible government," in which actions may be taken only by those who are accountable to the elected representatives of the people. Gladstone and Stanley Baldwin are cited for their respect for the rule of law. At the same time, Bonhoeffer recognizes that such direct accountability to the people and the law had not been a part of the German political tradition.

> The greatness of British statesmen, and I am thinking here, for example, of Gladstone, is that they acknowledge the law as the ultimate authority; and the greatness of German statesmen--I am thinking now of Bismarck--is that they come before God in free responsibility. In this neither one can claim to be superior to the other.[51]

The German idea of responsibility places on the politician a demand for responsiveness to a variety of forces and a prudent adjustment of objectives to the limits imposed by reality. Precisely

---

49. GS III, 473.

50. Ibid.

51. E, 240.

because he cannot be reined in by a representative body, the German politician may risk everything in singleminded pursuit of a goal. It is just that unconstrained subordination of facts to principle, reality to ideals, that Bonhoeffer found characteristic of Nazi politics. Hitler's goals were, of course, horribly wrong, but the pursuit of them was doubly evil because it was undertaken with the zeal of enthusiasts instead of the restraint of statesmen.

Bonhoeffer's notion of political responsibility thus comes very close to that of Max Weber, who himself admired Bismarck's political genius as much as he mistrusted the Iron Chancellor's tendency toward unlimited opposition to political and cultural forces who stood in his way. Weber's famous essay on "Politics as a Vocation" contrasts an "ethic of responsibility" with an "ethic of ultimate ends." The best politician, of course, is the responsible person who understands the compromises that are required of one in authority in a way that one who is not held responsible never can.[52] Reality for Weber, as for Bonhoeffer, is a force that bears more heavily on the one whose position requires decisions on behalf of others than it does on the theorists and ideologues who demand achievement of their objectives without regard for other consequences.

When Bonhoeffer tries to elaborate an initially theological concept of responsibility, then, he finds the basic framework for a political application already at hand. What the theologian contributes is not a fundamentally different idea, but a demand that the political responsiveness to reality be adequate to the whole of reality that is unified in Christ. "In this way we invest the concept of responsibility with a fullness of meaning that it does not acquire in everyday usage, even when it is placed extremely high on the scale of ethical values, as it was, for example, by Bismarck and Max Weber."[53]

Bonhoeffer's theological account of responsibility incorporates

---

52. See Hans Gerth and C. Wright Mills, eds., From Max Weber (New York: Oxford University Press, 1946), 77-128.

53. E, 222.

many values that would be familiar in the political discussions of his fellow-conspirators and among the class of leaders from whom they were drawn. The true politician for them was neither the speaker for a mass following nor the mere servant of the law. The true politician was responsible in a broad sense, as one having authority to make decisions which could not be challenged by mere majorities, but which had to stand the test of reality. To that extent, Weber's "ethic of responsibility" corresponds politically to the theological critique of general moral principles enunciated by Barth and Brunner and carried forward by Bonhoeffer.

Bonhoeffer's "structure of the responsible life" includes, however, the element of "deputyship" alongside the requirement of "correspondence to reality."[54] By that, he intends to rule out any exploitation of one's authority for personal gain, and he also warns against any optimistic anticipation that events will yield an obvious reward for virtue. True political responsibility, like the responsibility of the parent in the home, can only be exercised on behalf of others, and when that responsibility is taken in the context of a christocentric reality, it demands a commitment of self that risks everything for those for whom one is responsible. "In the face of the life which confronts us in Jesus Christ... partial responses are not enough and nothing less can suffice than the entire and single response of our life. Responsibility means, therefore, that the totality of our life is pledged and that our action becomes a matter of life and death."[55]

Late in 1941, Bonhoeffer already knew exactly what those lines had to mean for himself and his friends. His account of responsibility deftly wove their aristocratic code of authority and service into the fabric of his own moral theology, and the result will remain important as long as Christians in positions of authority and access to power confront the problem of evil in high places. What had been lost, however, was the stress on the moral significance of the structures of

---

54. E, 224.

55. E, 222.

everyday life and the New Testament emphasis on free, joyful and uncomplicated obedience. To turn his treatise on resistance into a comprehensive study of ethics, Bonhoeffer needed to integrate his account of the responsible life into the structure of the divine mandates and to relate both to the commandments of God. For this, he found inspiration in a new work by Karl Barth.

V. THE COMMAND OF GOD

[Chapter VII: Written from summer 1942 until Bonhoeffer's arrest in April 1943; chiefly in Berlin].

Bonhoeffer's ecumenical connections not only provided important channels of communication through which the Abwehr conspirators could reach the Allied governments; they were for him contacts with the wider world, and he valued their intellectual stimulation at least as much as their potential contributions to the conspiracy. Among the theologians he visited on his six trips abroad during 1941-42, probably only Bishop Bell fully knew his purposes. Many of the others were left to wonder how this pastor found it possible to travel so freely in wartime, and his repeated visits aroused some suspicions that he had perhaps gone over to the Nazi side.

One imagines, then, that some of the theological conversations were a bit strained, but Bonhoeffer seemed largely unaware of this, and he expressed real distress in a letter he wrote to Barth when, during his third Swiss journey, in May 1942, he learned what was being said behind his back.[56]

Political misunderstandings aside, Bonhoeffer entered eagerly into theological discussion during his visits to Switzerland, and there is some evidence that he hoped his colleagues there could attend to the systematic issues that eluded the overworked pastor-theologians of the

---

56. A collection of Bonhoeffer's correspondence with Barth during his wartime visits to Switzerland was found in Barth's archives in June 1981. The texts of these letters have been privately circulated by Christian Kaiser Verlag, Munich. An English translation has been prepared by John Godsey.

Biographical Context 93

Confessing Church. He tried to arrange a book of essays that would be a kind of Christmas present from the Swiss to their German co-religionists in 1941. The themes he assigned included history and eschatology, the forgiveness of sins and, significantly, a request that Barth write an essay on "Christian Responsibility."[57]

When Bonhoeffer sought to systematize his successive drafts on ethics, Barth's influence would be particularly important. In May 1942 he wrote Barth that he had obtained galley proofs of "your new volume of the Dogmatics" and that he had ahead of him about eight days of "complete peace and quiet in a boarding house on the Lake of Geneva.... There I want to try to work through at least the second half of your volume."[58]

The new volume that Bonhoeffer took with him for his holiday was Church Dogmatics II/2. The second half of that volume treats precisely the question, What sort of ethics is possible within the framework of Christian theology. Here, as he did before, Barth decisively rejects an apologetic ethics that accommodates itself to the wisdom of the culture. The church must without any compromise at all proclaim the Word it hears from God as authoritative. Theologians can enter the realm of general human ethics "only as the Israelites did or should have done on their entry into Canaan."[59]

> When they enter the field of ethical reflection and interpretation, they must not be surprised at the contradiction of the so-called (but only so-called) original inhabiants of the land. They cannot regard

---

57. These plans are detailed in a letter by Barth's assistant, Charlotte von Kirschbaum, in which she reports Bonhoeffer's requests to one of the Swiss contributors. This letter, dated 22 September 1941, was included with the Barth-Bonhoeffer correspondence discovered in 1981. It appears that the projected collection of essays was never produced.

58. Bonhoeffer to Barth, 13 May 1942. This letter from the collection in Barth's archives provides the first confirmation that Bonhoeffer had in fact seen Barth's Church Dogmatics II/2 before he wrote what is now Chapter VII of the Ethics.

59. Karl Barth, Church Dogmatics II/2 (Edinburgh: T. & T. Clark, 1957), 522.

them as an authority before which they have to exculpate themselves, and to whose arrangements they must in some way conform. The temptation to behave as if they were required or even permitted to do this is one which must be recognized for what it is and avoided.[60]

Christian ethics, Barth insists, is the study and proclamation of the command of God. Where popular morality implicitly acknowledges this source and follows it, Christian ethics can perhaps accept it, "for explicit theological principle is not everyone's concern."[61] But no secular form of ethical *reflection* can be admitted. "In the last analysis, therefore, the only strict answer to our question is to say that in a scientific form there is only one ethics, theological ethics."[62]

From a perspective of forty years' distance, we may say that Bonhoeffer's quiet days with the proofs of Barth's book were more productive than all the rest of his wartime travels. The sad fact is that the Abwehr conspirators failed not only in their attempts to assassinate Hitler, but also in their approaches to the Allied powers. In particular, Bonhoeffer's ecumenical contacts were unable to impress their political leaders with the possibility of an anti-Hitler coup led by responsible parties highly placed in the German government. Allied policy treated Germany and the Hitler regime as identical and insisted that only an unconditional surrender could bring hostilities to a close.

By the spring of 1942, Bonhoeffer wanted urgently to soften that Allied position. Change was important for the short-term success of the conspiracy, of course, but Bonhoeffer had also indicated in the Ethics drafts of 1940 his own fear that a punitive and exclusionary

---

60. Ibid., 520.

61. Ibid., 542.

62. Ibid.

Biographical Context

settlement would destroy the possibility for a lasting peace. He was aware that his 1941 reply to Paton's The Church and the New Order had received no definite response, and he now sought more direct lines of communication. When he learned while still in Switzerland in May 1942 that Bishop Bell would be spending three weeks in neutral Sweden, he made hasty arrangements to meet him there. The two met at Sigtuna, north of Stockholm, on 31 May. Hans Schönfeld, an ecumenical leader who also had contacts with German resistance groups, had preceded Bonhoeffer to Sweden and also took part in these discussions with Bell.[63] Bell was deeply impressed by what he learned of the preparations for the overthrow of the German government. He spent several months trying to convince first the British government and then American representatives in London that these particular plotters had to be taken very seriously, but in the end his efforts came to nothing. No government was willing to make contact with the conspirators, and the Allied policy remained implacable. The German people could not dissociate themselves from Hitler, and only an unconditional surrender would bring an end to the fighting.

Bonhoeffer, of course, could not know how Bell's efforts were faring. He carried out several more Abwehr commissions, including a brief trip to Italy, but by mid-summer his personal involvement in the conspiracy seems to have slowed. Bonhoeffer was not a man to idle away his time between assignments. He turned again to concentrated writing on the Ethics. He worked both at his parents' home in Berlin and on the Kleist-Retzow estate in Pomerania.

In this chapter, which proved to be the last, the influence of Barth is most apparent. Bonhoeffer begins this manuscript as he began his first chapter in the spring of 1940, by sharply distinguishing Christian ethics from ordinary moral reflection. "The 'Ethical' and the 'Christian' as a Theme," he headed the chapter, though there is a

---

63. DB, 662-64.

question mark in the manuscript[64] which perhaps betrays some doubts about that disjunction.

Bonhoeffer takes unusual care here to limit the scope of ethical reflection. To be sure, he never treats ethics and ethicists quite as Israel "did or should have done" the Canaanites,[65] but his concern is primarily with the defects and limits of the discipline.

> We can begin more easily by saying what, in any case, an ethic and an ethicist cannot be. An ethic cannot be a book in which there is set out how everything in the world actually ought to be but unfortunately is not, and an ethicist cannot be a man who always knows better than others what is to be done and how it is to be done.[66]

The negative ground-clearing that puts the "ethical" in its place and distinguishes it from the "Christian" makes possible appropriate attention to the real object of Christian ethics, the commandment of God. As in Barth's volume, there is here in Bonhoeffer a new emphasis on the idea that not everyone is called to participate in moral reflection or the formulation of moral principles. Obedient action is incumbent on everyone, but moral discourse requires a "warrant" (Ermächtigung).[67] What is important now is to incorporate this ethics discourse into the larger structure of command and obedience.

> The commandment of God is something different from what we have so far referred to as the ethical. It embraces the whole of life. It is not only unconditional; it is also total. It does not only forbid and command; it also sets free; and it does this by binding. Yet the

---

64. I am grateful to Clifford Green for this information.

65. See Barth's comments on "general human ethics" above.

66. E, 269.

67. E, 269-76.

"ethical," in a sense which still has to be explained, is part of it. God's commandment is the only warrant for ethical discourse.[68]

Bonhoeffer's beginning in the seventh chapter of his Ethics is surprising because it seems to dismiss some of the major insights of the chapters just before it. The attention to "the natural" and especially to history, which grew from Bonhoeffer's wartime experience, here have no immediate systematic significance. The problems of "responsibility" and "correspondence to reality" have faded into the background. What counts in ethics is the commandment of God. Has Bonhoeffer simply abandoned the earlier chapters and started over with a more promising, Barthian theme?

Perhaps. We cannot be sure how Bonhoeffer intended the chapter we have to be related to the others, and we know that it had been several months since he was able to concentrate on the manuscript. How much of Chapter VII was for him a new start and how much a continuation of Chapter VI we will never know for sure. But the chapter we have is no simple imitation of Barth. For the commandment of God, while it is quite concrete and specific, does not speak in defiance of all the everyday orderings of human life. The commandment of God is heard in the structures of the divine mandates, and in those structures, the careful attention to history and nature again enters Christian ethics.

> In its unity which embraces the whole of human life and in its undivided claim to man and to the world through the reconciling love of God, God's commandment, revealed in Jesus Christ, confronts us concretely in four different forms which it alone unites: the Church, marriage and the family, culture and government.[69]

---

68. E, 277.

69. E, 286. Bonhoeffer's lists of the mandates differ slightly in different places in the manuscript.

These persistent structures of human life and their unity become the key to understanding God's commandment for Bonhoeffer. What God requires are what these institutions need to function as they should as parts of God's creation; what God permits are the actions that allow them to flourish by binding our lives and loyalties to them. Determining these requirements and permissions will no doubt require attention to history and nature, but that is not enough guidance. What God requires is that these mandates function as a unity which the commandment alone unites. Each institution must retain its own integrity and its own structure of authority. Violation of that requirement is what made the Nazi innovations so profoundly "unnatural." Yet all the institutions must function together. That precludes any of them, even the church, from claiming a monopoly on truth and righteousness.

This is already apparent in Bonhoeffer's brief treatment of "The Commandment of God in the Church."[70] Like Barth, Bonhoeffer rejects the "fallacious appeal to Christian liberty" that led liberal Protestantism to abandon its responsibility to proclaim God's commandment in its specificity to society.[71] However, he is equally concerned with the error, which he sees as a characteristic of Roman Catholicism, that takes the church for the ultimate end of social life. This leads Christians to confuse the internal discipline of the Christian community with a warrant to order the other institutions of society as well.

The commandment of Jesus Christ does indeed rule over Church, family, culture and government; but it does so while at the same time setting each of these mandates free for the fulfillment of its own allotted functions. Jesus' claim to lordship, which is proclaimed by the Church, means at the same time the emancipation of family, culture and government for the realization of their own

---

70. E, 292-302.

71. E, 292.

essential character which has its foundation in Christ.[72]

Bonhoeffer may be unfair in charging Catholicism with neglect of this instrumental role of the church. It seems equally an error of sectarian forms of Protestantism. It is, however, clear that his own normative vision encompasses forms of obedience that cannot be identified simply by their correspondence to the moral systems codified by the church. Bonhoeffer's reading of Barth's <u>Dogmatics</u> appears to have provided the foundation that was missing in his own insightful essays on history and "the natural." To develop these ideas into a systematic ethics, especially a theological ethics, he had to find a more specific source of moral authority, and Barth's rather exclusive emphasis on God's commandment provided it. We will not understand Bonhoeffer's distinctive position, however, unless we recognize that his understanding of God's commandment includes those ventures of responsibility which in extraordinary circumstances are required to restore the possibility of ordinary obedience.

VI. THE END

Responsible action was much on Bonhoeffer's mind at the turn of the year 1943. To outward appearances this was a quiet time, a time of study and writing marked chiefly by important personal events.

As a Christmas present to his family and close friends, Bonhoeffer wrote an essay that reflected on their ten years of opposition to Hitler. It included this significant passage.

> Civil courage, in fact, can only grow out of the free responsibility of free men. Only now are the Germans beginning to discover the meaning of free responsibility. It depends on a God who demands responsible action in a bold venture of faith, and who promises forgiveness and consolation to the man who

---

72. E, 98-99.

becomes a sinner in that venture.73

The reference to the conspiracy is obvious, but this formulation also shows that the old themes of responsible action and "good, in its citizen-like sense" were not absent from Bonhoeffer's thoughts at the time he was writing his chapter on the commandment of God.

On 17 January 1943 Bonhoeffer was engaged to Maria von Wedemeyer, a niece of Ruth von Kleist-Retzow. In March, the family was absorbed in preparations for celebration of the seventy-fifth birthday of Dietrich's father. Beneath this domestic surface, however, there was much activity and nervous anticipation. The leaders of the conspiracy had decided that Hitler must now be eliminated, with or without Allied concessions, before Germany's military and political position could deteriorate further. Meanwhile, unknown to them, the Gestapo's Reich Head Security Office had begun to suspect that something was amiss in the military intelligence operation run by Admiral Canaris.

As so often happens in real history, the drama that was playing itself out in early 1943 ended inconclusively. Plans to take Hitler's life failed on 13 March and again on 21 March, but the attempts went undetected. When the Gestapo arrested many of the conspirators at the beginning of April, it was not for their plot against Hitler, but for their use of the Abwehr to cover the escape of several Jews through Switzerland. Bonhoeffer's work on the Ethics concluded on 5 April, when investigators took him from his study in his parents' home. Material for the chapter on "The 'Ethical' and the 'Christian' as a Theme" remained on his desk.

In prison, Bonhoeffer fretted over his failure to finish the Ethics,[74] prepared his defense in anticipation of a trial that never came, found ways to communicate with his family through friendly guards, and tried his hand at writing fiction. When the final coup

---

73. LPP, 6.

74. LPP, 129, 163.

attempt was planned for 20 July 1944, Bonhoeffer knew about it, and when the day came and went, he knew it had failed. By that time, however, his intellectual energies were fully engaged by a new approach to theology and the problem of "secular interpretation."[75] Concern for the past begins to fade, and even the unfinished Ethics does not trouble him.[76] Nevertheless, in the future he anticipates there is clearly a place for the moral righteousness that was so problematic for his generation of theologians. In worldly Christianity, all thoughts of self-righteousness must be set aside, but there seems to be a place even in the Christian life for righteous action that everyone can recognize.

> Our church, which has been fighting in these years only for its own self-preservation, as though that were an end in itself, is incapable of taking the word of reconciliation and redemption to mankind and the world. Our earlier words are therefore bound to lose their force and cease, and our being Christians today will be limited to two things, prayer and righteous action among men. All Christian thinking, speaking, and organizing must be born anew out of this prayer and action.[77]

---

75. LPP, 361.

76. Bethge dates this decisive change of mood from April 1944. See DB, 762-65.

77. LPP, 300.

III

A QUESTION OF METHOD

Larry L. Rasmussen

Dietrich Bonhoeffer never wrote an ethic. As we know from the gratifying detail supplied by Clifford Green in this volume,[1] and the work of Eberhard Bethge earlier,[2] the posthumously published Ethics is constituted of different, and incomplete, approaches to the volume Bonhoeffer planned.

Each of these approaches contains penetrating themes for the subject of this chapter, Bonhoeffer's method. "Proving the will of God," "conformation," "the ultimate and the penultimate," "the command of God"--these represent different methodological entry points for writing an ethic. Any one of them would be worthy of study. This chapter chooses two of them--"conformation" and "command"--for comparison. The reasons are simple. Bonhoeffer is most explicit about method in these sections, and they carry the longest history in his writings. There are intimations of both themes in the Bonhoeffer corpus well before Ethics.

Hanfried Müller contends that these two--"Ethik als Gestalt"

---

1. See Clifford Green, "Chapter One" in this volume.
2. Eg, "Vorwort," 14-17.

and "Ethik als Gebot"[3]--constitute two clearly different methods in Bonhoeffer's ethics. But that remains to be demonstrated. That they are separate treatments of method by Bonhoeffer is clear. Yet they may be but different approaches to what in the end is a single method. Comparing these treatments, in order to arrive at a statement of Bonhoeffer's methods, or method, is the task here.

There is a major impediment--the fragmentary character of Bonhoeffer's Ethics. It is immediately obvious to any reader, since a number of chapters break off at clearly unfinished points. Too, we now know that no chapter was ever completed to Bonhoeffer's satisfaction. Only one was even reworked. Some finish with outlines of what is to come, once the author can return to his work. That, however, he was never able to do. And beyond the incomplete chapters Bonhoeffer did draft, much of the remaining material is in smaller segments still--pages of notes of varying length, on papers of varying size and sort, all awaiting the chance to get on with Ethics.

The fragmentary character applies in a larger sense. The book as a whole is assembled from four clearly different beginnings. These were undertaken off and on through the years 1939-1943, between assignments for the Army Intelligence Service and the resistance cell located there. To these beginnings Eberhard Bethge has added five other pieces by Bonhoeffer. While they are pertinent to any discussion of Christian ethics, they were not written explicitly for the volume Bonhoeffer conceived as his major work.[4]

Considering the difficulties of deciphering the almost illegible manuscripts, the problems of putting the various parts in order and dating the larger divisions, it is little wonder Bethge has referred to the Ethics as "an absolute fragment."[5] The Forward to the sixth German edition, like Green's careful reconstruction in the present

---

3. Von der Kirche zur Welt (Hamburg: Herbert Reich Evang. Verlag GMBH, 1961), 288-289.

4. Eg, 13.

5. Eberhard Bethge, Lecture at Union Theological Seminary, 7 February 1967.

volume, reads like an essay in Redactionsgeschichte.

Ethics is fragmentary in yet another way. It was Bonhoeffer's judgment that not only the manuscripts, but his ideas were unfinished.[6] In short, the student intent upon uncovering Bonhoeffer's method in ethics is greeted with both literary and intellectual fragmentation.

Still, there are two beginnings by Bonhoeffer which are explicit about method. The first is "Ethics as Formation" ("Ethik als Gestaltung"),[7] written in the fall of 1940. The second is entitled "The 'Ethical' and the 'Christian' as a Theme,"[8] written the winter of 1942-43. The methodological motif in the latter is ethics as command. To these we turn.

I. ETHICS AS FORMATION

A. CHRISTOLOGY AND ETHICS AS FORMATION

In the christology lectures of 1933 Bonhoeffer spoke of Christ as the center of humanity, nature and history. "The one who is present in Word, sacrament and community is in the centre of human existence, history and nature. It is part of the structure of his person that he stands at the centre."[9]

The full elucidation of this was foreshortened by the semester's end. But we have sufficient indication of the line to ethics as formation. "The character of the statement about his centrality is not psychological, but ontological-theological."[10]

Christ as the center of humanity, history and nature means

---

6. LPP, 129.

7. Eg, 68-119.

8. Eg, 279-302.

9. CC, 62.

10. CC, 62.

"Christology is *logology*."[11] "Christology is *the* science, because it is concerned with the Logos."[12]

The point is that Bonhoeffer holds an ontology he understands christologically. His conceptualization of reality is a christological one. Reality has a christocratic structure. This is most clearly drawn out in Ethics, where Christ's taking up the world into himself establishes an *ontological coherence* of God's reality with the reality of the world.

> Whoever sees Jesus Christ does indeed see God and the world in one. He can no longer see God without the world or the world without God.[13].... In Jesus Christ the reality of God entered into the reality of this world. The place where the answer is given, both to the question concerning the reality of God and to the question concerning the reality of the world, is designated solely and alone by the name Jesus Christ. God and the world are comprised in this name. In Him all things consist (Col. 1:17). Henceforward one can speak neither of God nor the world without speaking of Jesus Christ. All concepts of reality which do not take account of Him are abstractions.[14]

The ontological coherence of God's reality and the world's in Christ leads Bonhoeffer to discuss moral action in two ways. In the end, they are the same--"conformation to Christ" (Gleichgestaltung)[15] and action "in accordance with reality" or "with due regard to reality"

---

11. CC, 28. Emphasis in the original.

12. CC, 28. Emphasis in the original.

13. E, 70.

14. E, 194.

15. Eg, 85.

(Wirklichkeitsgemässheit).16 After discussing the relation of Jesus Christ to reality, he makes the point straightforwardly. "Our conclusion from this must be that action which is in accordance with Christ is action which is in accordance with reality."17 Ethics as formation rests in the ontological coherence in Christ of God's reality and the world's.

If the student judges ethics as formation to be the heart of Bonhoeffer's entire ethic, then Heinrich Ott's thesis can be affirmed as the key to Bonhoeffer's method.

> Bonhoeffer's ethic as a whole is the attempt to make these thoughts about conformation to Christ into *the* principle of the Christian ethic and to work out the whole ethic from this standpoint.18

Accepting this judgment for the moment, we could construct Bonhoeffer's methodological procedure along these lines. The Christian answers the question "what am I to do?" by first answering the question "how is Christ taking form in the world?" or, as it is put in <u>Letters and Papers from Prison</u>, "who is Christ for us today?".19 Or it could be stated as well in the following way. The first question is, "what is the real?"; the second is "what action on my part would be in accordance with reality?".20 In this scheme moral action,

---

16. Eg, 241.

17. E, 229.

18. <u>Wirklichkeit und Glaube</u> (Zurich: Vandenhoeck und Ruprecht, 1966), 241-242. Translation and emphasis mine. The emphasis is warranted by the preceding sentence. There Ott calls conformation to Christ the "oberstes materielles Prinzip dieser Ethik," 241.

19. LPP, 279.

20. One attraction of this method is its applicability for both the Christian and the non-Christian. In the above set, the first is for the Christian, the second for the non-Christian. Yet both are the same because of Bonhoeffer's identification of the world-in-Christ with reality. The problematic arises at the point of epistemology. Can one know the real apart from knowing Christ?

methodologically considered, is action that is in conformity to Christ (in accord with reality); immoral action is action that deviates from Christ's form (from reality). Moral discernment is discerning the presence in our world of "the cosmic reality given in Christ."

> In Christ we are offered the possibility of partaking in the reality of God and in the reality of the world, but not in the one without the other. The reality of God discloses itself only by setting me entirely in the reality of the world, and when I encounter the reality of the world it is always already sustained, accepted and reconciled in the reality of God. This is the inner meaning of the revelation of God in the man Jesus Christ. Christian ethics enquires about the realization in our world of this divine and cosmic reality which is given in Christ.[21]

B. ETHICS AS FORMATION--A RELATIONAL, CONTEXTUAL ETHIC

Reality is one. But reality has a history. Christ is the same yesterday, today and forever. Yet the ways Christ wins Gestalt vary through time. "Who is Christ for us today?" Christian ethics must be contextual ethics. Ethics is "a matter of history" and "a child of the earth."[22] "The 'ethical' as a theme is tied to a definite time and a definite place."[23]

The historical character of reality and the polyphonic character of Christ's Gestalt results, for Bonhoeffer, in a relational, contextual ethic. It is contextual for the reason given--who Christ is for us today may not be who Christ was for us or others yesterday. "What can and must be said is not what is good once and for all, but the way in which

---

21. E, 195.

22. GS III, 48. The lecture was given in February 1929.

23. E, 85.

Method

Christ takes form among us here and now."[24] It is relational because it is *Christ* winning Gestalt. Here "the direction of action is shaped by the sense of excitement or gratitude which arises from a live, dynamic, and compelling encounter with the source of moral guidance."[25] Indeed, Bonhoeffer uses not only relational but intensely personalist language in his discourse on ethics. Yet that corresponds to the very nature of reality. "Reality is first and last not lifeless; but it is the real man, the incarnate God."[26] "[R]eality consists ultimately in the personal."[27] Christian ethics can only be relational when the actions emerge from a "live, dynamic and compelling encounter" with "the real man, the incarnate God," "the source of moral guidance."

> Whenever [the Scriptures] speak of forming they are concerned only with the one form which has overcome the world, the form of Jesus Christ. Formation can come only from this form. But here again it is not a question of applying directly to the world the teachings of Christ or what are referred to as Christian principles, so that the world might be formed in accordance with these. On the contrary, formation comes only by being drawn into the form of Jesus Christ. It comes only as formation in His likeness, as *conformation* with the unique form of Him who was made man, was crucified, and rose again.[28]

An important, logical question for any relational, contextual ethic is whether it bends toward atomism and relativism. Is the "here

---

24. E, 85.

25. Edward L. Long, Jr., A Survey of Christian Ethics (New York: Oxford University Press, 1967), 117. This is Long's description of relational ethics.

26. E, 228.

27. E, 228, note.

28. E, 80.

and now" so separated from the "there and then" and the present situation so unique that each ethical decision is a case unto itself? In an atomistic contextual ethic, each case must be approached *methodologically* as sui generis. If not, damage is done to the very integrity of the ethical. Bonhoeffer's 1929 Barcelona lecture presents just such an ethic.

> From all this it now follows that the content of ethical problems can never be discussed in a Christian light; the possibility of erecting generally valid principles simply does not exist, because each moment, lived in God's sight, can bring an unexpected decision. Thus only one thing can be repeated again and again, also in our time: in ethical decisions man must consider his action sub specie aeternitatis and then, no matter how it proceeds, it will proceed rightly.... The decision which is really required must be made freely in the concrete situation.[29]

The significance of this passage, for this study, is that it was written before Bonhoeffer took up the Gestalt Christi in his ethics. After he does so, the ethic loses its atomism while carrying its contextualism. It even develops a kind of christocentric natural law, or, more precisely, a christocentric alternative to natural law. "Natural life is formed life"[30] bearing universal rights, duties and relationships.[31] Natural life is formed life because Christ Himself entered into the natural life, and it is only through the incarnation of Christ that the natural life becomes the penultimate which is directed towards the ultimate. Only through the incarnation of Christ do we have the right to call others to the natural life and to live the natural

---

29. NRS, 45-47. Author's correction of translation. See GS III, 55-56.

30. E, 149.

31. See Bonhoeffer's discussion of "The Natural," 143-151 and "The Four Mandates," 207-213 and 186-187.

life ourselves.32

With the christological treatment of the natural, the penultimate and the mandates, considerable moral content becomes part of Bonhoeffer's contextual ethic. Christ has taken form in the world; reality has a discernible structure; and because Christ is the same yesterday, today and tomorrow, there is coherence and continuity in his winning Gestalt. Methodologically, Bonhoeffer's remains a relational contextual ethic of reality and its realization. But the atomistic character recedes as Bonhoeffer draws out the full force of the Incarnation and expands the arena and content of conformation. As the elaboration of universal laws, rights, duties and relationships occurs, the method of deciding, still done contextually, takes the form of something approaching casuistic reasoning.

These points--and some others--can be made by surveying the Bonhoeffer corpus.

C. THE PATH OF ETHICS AS FORMATION

The Communion of Saints (1927) is not a book on ethics. Its key term, however, is a critical notion for Bonhoeffer's ethics: "Christus als Gemeinde existierend"--"Christ existing as community."33 The intimacy of christology and sociology is worked out as the social character of revelation. The Incarnate God, existing "in, with and under" social relations, is the only one we know. For us no other God exists than the incarnate, present one. Bethge's sentence, summarizing Bonhoeffer's discussion, is succinct: "All we know, and this is breath-taking, is that the incarnated concreteness is *the* attribute as far as we can think."34

---

32. E, 145.

33. Author's translation; see CS, 136. The translation of Gemeinde is a notorious problem. Bethge sometimes translates the above as "Christ existing as church." See Eberhard Bethge, "The Challenge of Dietrich Bonhoeffer's Life and Theology," The Chicago Theological Seminary Review, LI, No. 2 (February, 1961), 9.

34. Bethge, Ibid., 8. Emphasis in the original.

In <u>Act and Being</u> we again meet the concrete Gestalt Christi. As in <u>The Communion of Saints</u>, Christ's form is in the ecclesial community.

> God is not free *of* man but *for* man. Christ is the Word of his freedom. God *is there*, which is to say: not in eternal non-objectivity but (looking ahead for the moment) 'haveable', graspable in his Word within the Church.[35]

More explicit discussion of the meaning of the Gestalt Christi for ethics emerges as conditions worsen in Germany and Bonhoeffer becomes involved in the first stirrings of the church struggle. In the 1932 seminar "Gibt es eine christliche Ethik?," student manuscripts share the following.

> The possibility of judging whether our action is good lies alone in Christ, the present and future One. All other "secure" possibilities, which appear to give continuity to the action, are to be rejected: 1. the orders of creation; 2. conscience; 3. a Christian principle of love; 4. the situation itself; 5. laying claim to the forgiveness of sins; 6. the Law, even in the form of the Sermon on the Mount.[36]

Another passage reads:

> Action is based in the coming Christ; therein consists its continuity. We stride into the future and our action must be determined through the Christ coming to us, from this Thou.[37]

It is questionable whether the student notes are entirely faithful

---

35. AB, 90-91. <u>Act and Being</u> was written in 1931.

36. DBg, 1075. The material "Gibt es eine christliche Ethik?" is an appendix.

37. DBg, 1075.

Method

in stressing the coming Christ even more than Christus praesens. At least Bonhoeffer's concentration is upon the latter in the christology lectures given that winter and in a major theological address delivered during the time the seminar was conducted.[38] Yet the salient item is Bonhoeffer's rejection of any basis for Christian moral judgment outside Christ.

Ethics as formation in christology is even more clearly present in The Cost of Discipleship.

> To be conformed to the image of Christ is not an ideal to be striven after. It is not as though we had to imitate him as well as we could. We cannot transform ourselves into his image; it is rather the form of Christ which seeks to be formed in us (Gal. 4.19), and to be manifested in us.... We must be assimilated to the form of Christ in its entirety, the form of Christ incarnate, crucified and glorified. Christ took upon himself this human form of ours. He became Man even as we are men.... He has become like a man, so that men should be like him. And in the Incarnation the whole human race recovers the dignity of the image of God.... Through fellowship and communion with the incarnate Lord, we recover our true humanity.[39]

This is language striking in its virtual identity with the section "Ethics as Formation" written in the fall of 1940.[40] But a difference does exist, and it is of momentous importance for ethics as formation. The difference is the expanded arena of conformation. The expansion is, in fact, key for Bonhoeffer's move from The Cost of Discipleship to Letters and Papers from Prison. The theological expression of this is given in Bonhoeffer's formula:

---

38. CC, passim, and NRS, 157-173.

39. CD, 341. Initial publication was in 1937.

40. E, 64-119.

> The more exclusively we acknowledge and confess Christ as our Lord, the more fully the wide range of His dominion will be disclosed to us.[41]

In both cases (Ethics and The Cost of Discipleship) the ethics of formation strike a clear tone. But in The Cost of Discipleship ethics as formation is predominantly a churchly ethic. In Ethics it is the expanded ethic of the Christian in the world. The "wide range of His dominion" has been uncovered. Bethge's summary is again succinct:

> The exclusiveness of the Lordship of Christ--that is the message of The Cost of Discipleship. The expansiveness of Christ's totality--that is the new accent of the Ethics.[42]

In the section on formation in Ethics we first encounter the notion of the mandates. Not so much *which* mandates are discussed[43] is of ranking importance; rather, that they are Bonhoeffer's attempt to treat the christological unity in a concrete, even empirical fashion, as well as a theological one. The mandates are the media of conformation.

In summary, the Gestalt Christi, as a moral category, has taken on theocratic breadth. With that, method has moved away from a wholly atomistic contextual ethic to a contextual ethic which speaks easily of universal rights, duties and relationships. These may indeed vary through time and be imbedded in the movement of cultures and history. But they share the coherence and continuity of Christ's own form in the world.

The last mention of this motif leaves the reader with whetted

---

41. E, 58. It is intriguing, but not coincidental, that this change occurred in tandem with Bonhoeffer's move from churchly to political resistance.

42. DBg, 806. Translation mine.

43. Bonhoeffer was experimenting here in any case. One time he names four (E, 207); another time he substitutes one for another (E, 286); still another time he wonders where "friendship" belongs and if culture and education should not be added to marriage and family, work, state and church (LPP, 193).

appetite and a touch of frustration.

> The question how there can be a "natural piety" is at the same time the question of "unconscious Christianity," with which I am more and more concerned. Lutheran dogmatists distinguished between a fides directa and a fides reflexa. They related this to the so-called children's faith, at baptism. I wonder whether this does not raise a far-reaching problem. I hope we shall soon come back to it.[44]

> God is in the facts themselves.[45]

II. ETHICS AS COMMAND

A. THE PATH OF ETHICS AS COMMAND

The thesis of this section is that while ethics as command is a genuine methodological motif in Bonhoeffer, it is chiefly borrowed from Barth. To be sure, Bonhoeffer was himself an appreciative--though not uncritical--Barthian. We are saying, however, that where Bonhoeffer makes the most of ethics as command he is actually borrowing from Barth and appropriating this for uses of his own. How ethics as command is related to the original Bonhoeffer motif--ethics as formation--is the discussion following upon this one.

Without doubt ethics as command is a *genuine* and important motif for Bonhoeffer. But it is not an *original* one.

The Barcelona lecture serves again as a convenient starting-point. There is little mention of "command" as such, although there are some affinities in terms such as "being addressed," "God's call" and "claim." One passage must be cited at length. It carries

---

44. LPP, 373. In Lutheran dogmatics fides directa means unconscious response to God-in-Christ in contrast to fides reflexa, meaning reflective, conscious response.

45. LPP, 191.

premonitions of a theme later found under the rubric of ethics as command.

> Ethics is a matter of earth and of blood, but also of him who made both; the trouble arises from this duality. There can be ethics only in the framework of history, in the concrete situation, at the moment of the divine call, the moment of being addressed, of the claim made by the concrete need and the situation for decision, of the claim which I have to answer and for which I have to make myself responsible. Thus there cannot be ethics in a vacuum, as a principle; there cannot be good and evil as general ideas, but only as qualities of will making a decision. These can be only good and evil as done in freedom; by contrast, principles are binding under the law. Bound up in the concrete situation, through God and in God the Christian acts in the power of a man who has become free. He is under no judgment but his own and that of God.[46]

The address entitled "A Theological Basis for the World Alliance" was given three years later in July 1932. It contains theme after theme found in later writing; for example, reality and command. That most amazing statement is here: "What the command is for the preaching of the Gospel, the knowledge of firm reality is for the preaching of the command. *Reality is the sacrament of command.*[47] Bonhoeffer insists:

> The word of the church to the world must... encounter the world in all its present reality from the deepest knowledge of the world, if it is to be authoritative. The

---

46. NRS, 46-47. Translation corrected; see GS III, 56-57.

47. GS I, 147. Translation mine. The emphasis is Bonhoeffer's. The translation, NRS, 164, is very bad. It reads "for the preaching of the sacrament" instead of "for the preaching of the command" (Gebot).

church must be able to say the Word of God, the word of authority, here and now, in the most concrete way possible, from knowledge of the situation. The church may not therefore preach timeless principles, however true, but only commandments which are true today. God is "always" *God* to us "*today.*"[48]

The example is timely.

> In the event of taking a stand on war the church cannot just say, "there should really be no war, but there are necessary wars" and leave the application of this principle to each individual; it should be able to say quite definitely: "engage in this war" or "do not engage in this war."[49]

The conclusion is this.

> But, if the church really has a commandment of God, it must proclaim it in the most definite form possible, from the fullest knowledge of the matter, and it must utter a summons to obedience. A commandment must be definite, otherwise it is not a commandment. God's commandment now requires something quite definite from us. And the church should proclaim this to the community.[50]

"Today God's commandment for us is the order of *international peace.*"[51] On a page that parallels discussion of the 1932 seminar on ethics[52] we again find Bonhoeffer addressing christology and ethics.

---

48. NRS, 161-162. Emphasis in the original.

49. GS I, 146. Author's translation. See NRS, 162-163.

50. NRS, 163.

51. NRS, 167. Emphasis in the original.

52. See notes 36 and 37, citing the essay "Gibt es eine christliche Ethik?"

This time there is explicit reference to the command of God.

> The command can come from nowhere else than the origin of promise and fulfillment, from Christ. From Christ alone we must know what we must do. But not from him as the preaching prophet of the Sermon on the Mount, but from him as the one who gives us life and forgiveness, as the one who has fulfilled the commandment of God in our place, as the one who brings and promises the new world. We can only perceive the commandment where the law is fulfilled, where the new world of the new order of God is established. Thus we are completely directed toward Christ. Now with this we also understand the whole order of fallen creation as directed solely towards Christ, towards the new creation.[53]

At least this much can be said about ethics as command: the command is a specific, prophetic word to the concrete situation, or it is not God's command; its center is in Christ; and the command itself, if it is truly God's command, corresponds with reality.

Before leaving the 1932 address we should take cognizance of Bonhoeffer's growing interest in ethics. From this juncture onward, it never left him, and culminated in his consideration of Ethics as his major life project.[54] In August 1932 he wrote a friend:

> I gave an address in Czechoslovakia on the theological foundation of this work [that of the World Alliance] and attempted in so doing to quiet my theological

---

53. GS I, 150. Author's translation; see NRS, 166. The last line anticipates the mandates, the natural and the penultimate as discussed in Ethics. It is worth mentioning, however, that this line and those which speak of "reality" should not lead us to conclude that Ethics are here in nuce. Whatever the anticipation, "reality" in this address is not yet the full-blown christocratic understanding of it that Bonhoeffer presents in the Ethics. There is much in this address that points to, but is not yet Bonhoeffer's grand Christo-universal vision of this world.

54. LPP, 163.

Method

conscience, but there are still many questions to bring up. At bottom everything hangs on the problem of ethics, that is, actually in the question of the possibility of the proclamation of the concrete command by the church.⁵⁵

There is no gainsaying that The Cost of Discipleship is a wholly "ethical" book punctuated with the concrete commands of Christ to his disciples. While it is a passionate moral tract for the times and a call to battle, it lacks an explicit hermeneutic of ethics as command. Reflection on method is simply missing, despite the important formula that "*only he who believes is obedient, and only he who is obedient believes.*"⁵⁶

In fact, it is only in the fourth approach of Ethics that we find a prolonged reflective effort on the method of ethics as command.

Here is the borrowed Barth. This is striking for several reasons. Barth's name is not mentioned. In fact, it is mentioned nowhere in Ethics! Secondly, Bethge does not mention Barth in the long list of books he records as Bonhoeffer's reading during the time Bonhoeffer wrote materials for Ethics.⁵⁷ Bethge does list Church Dogmatics II/2 as Bonhoeffer's reading in Tegel in December 1943-January 1944. Bonhoeffer requested II/2 in a letter to Bethge near Christmas time 1943.⁵⁸ He fails to mention, however, whether he has or has not seen parts or all of it before. But, we now know,⁵⁹ Bonhoeffer did use it

---

55. GS I, 33. Author's translation.

56. CD, 69.

57. DBg, 803-804. Bethge does say, however, that the list is incomplete.

58. LPP, 171.

59. At the time this paper was written, the June 1981 discovery of letters from Bonhoeffer to Barth hadn't yet happened. The letter of 13 May 1942 includes the following: "I have been in Zurich for a few days, since yesterday with the Pestalozzis. Now, armed with the galley-proofs of your new volume of the Dogmatics which Mr. Frey has procured for me, I want to spend about eight days on the way to Geneva in complete peace and quiet in a boarding house on the lake

the winter before when the portions of Ethics on "The Command of God" took form. It is a little curious, furthermore, that Barth himself does not mention the coincidence of this portion of Bonhoeffer's ethics in his own, even though he commented at length on Bonhoeffer's ethics.[60]

If Bonhoeffer, Bethge and Barth do not mention the coincidence of ethics as command in Ethics and ethics as command in Church Dogmatics II/2, can it in fact be so? The parallels are clear.

The sections in question in Bonhoeffer are "The Commandment of God"[61] and "The Commandment of God in the Church."[62] The portion of Church Dogmatics II/2 under scrutiny is "The Command of God."[63]

Bonhoeffer writes:

> The commandment of God is permission. It differs from all human laws in that it commands freedom.[64]

Barth writes:

> The form by which the command of God is distinguished from all other commands, the special form . . . consists in the fact that it is permission--the

---

of Geneva recommended to me by the Pestalozzis. There I want to try to work through at least the second half of your volume." Bonhoeffer's reference is to II/2 of the Kirchliche Dogmatik; the second half is "The Command of God." I am using a translation of the letters provided by John Godsey.

60. See Karl Barth, Church Dogmatics II/4, trans. by A. T. Mackay and others (Edinburgh: T. and T. Clark, 1961), 258-267. This is fascinating. Barth criticizes Bonhoeffer extensively on one point only--the concrete command in the mandates. This is the one place in all the sections in Ethics on the Command of God where Bonhoeffer deviates from Barth.

61. E, 277-285.
62. E, 292-302. Between these comes "The Concrete Commandment and the Divine Mandates."

63. Karl Barth, Church Dogmatics II/2, trans. by G. W. Bromiley and others (Edinburgh: T. and T. Clark, 1957), 509-782. The space used to treat this same subject is typical of each!

64. E, 281.

Method   *121*

> granting of a very definite freedom.⁶⁵

The original texts are as follows.

> Das Gebot Gottes ist *Erlaubnis*. Darin unterscheidet es sich von allen menschlichen Gesetzen, dass es die *Freiheit--gebietet*.⁶⁶

> Die Form, durch die das Gebot Gottes sich von allen anderen Geboten unterscheidet, die besondere Form... besteht darin, dass es *Erlaubnis* ist: *Gewahrung einer ganz bestimmten Freiheit*.⁶⁷

Barth makes this point again and again.

> The command of God orders us to be free.... This is what characterizes the command of God, distinguishes it from all other commands.⁶⁸.... The command of God sets man free. The command of God permits. It is only in this way that it commands.⁶⁹

From Bonhoeffer we hear: "The commandment of God permits man to live as man before God."⁷⁰

On another matter Barth enters this paragraph.

> It is this definiteness that the command is unconditional, leaving us no other choice than that between obedience and disobedience. Its unconditional character consists

---

65. Church Dogmatics II/2, 285.

66. Eg, 298. Emphasis in the original.

67. Karl Barth, Kirchliche Dogmatik II/2 (Zuerich: Evangelischer Verlag A. G. Zollikon, 1946), 650. Emphasis in the original. This is the second edition. The portions of Bonhoeffer being compared were probably written the winter of 1942-43.

68. Church Dogmatics II/2, 588.

69. Church Dogmatics II/2, 586.

70. E, 282.

in the fact that, independently of our views, always and in every relationship in which I find myself placed, it has the particular form that God demands from me in all seriousness, this or that concrete thing.[71]

A few pages later Barth, illustrating the definiteness of the command, weaves his way through the Old and New Testaments. He finds multiple examples of God's concrete speech to humanity. These include Abraham, Jacob, Moses, Jesus Christ, the disciples and Paul.[72]

Now note Bonhoeffer's paragraph on the definiteness of the command and the examples which follow.

> God's commandment is the speech of God to man. Both in its contents and in its form it is concrete speech to the concrete man. God's command leaves man no room for application or interpretation. It leaves room only for obedience or disobedience. God's command cannot be found and known in detachment from time and place; it can only be heard in a local and temporal context. If God's commandment is not clear, definite and concrete to the last detail, then it is not God's commandment. Either God does not speak at all or else He speaks to us as definitely as He spoke to Abraham and Jacob and Moses and as definitely as in Jesus Christ He spoke to the disciples and through His apostles to the Gentiles.[73]

Another time Bonhoeffer says:

> God's commandment... is always concrete speech *to* somebody. It is never abstract speech *about* something or *about* somebody. It is always an address, a claim,

---

71. Church Dogmatics II/2, 669.

72. Church Dogmatics II/2, 673-674.

73. E, 278.

and it is so comprehensive and at the same time so definite that it leaves no freedom for interpretation or application, but only the freedom to obey or to disobey.[74]

Another time Barth says:

The command of God... is a claim addressed to man in such a way that it is given integrally, so that he cannot control its content or decide its concrete application.... It comes to us with a specific content, embracing the whole outer and inner substance of each momentary decision and epitomising the totality of each momentary requirement. It does not need any interpretation, for even to the smallest details it is self-interpreting.[75]

On still another aspect of the command Bonhoeffer writes of its effects.

The commandment of God becomes the element in which one lives without always being conscious of it, and, thus it implies freedom of movement and of action, freedom from the fear of decision, freedom from fear to act, it implies certainty, quietude, confidence, balance and peace.[76]

No single passage in Barth contains the compactness of the foregoing paragraph. But an entire section, entitled "The Goodness of the Divine Decision,"[77] contains *every single one* of these elements at one point or another.

In the chapter on the command of God in the Church

---

74. E, 279-280.

75. Church Dogmatics II/2, 665.

76. E, 280.

77. Church Dogmatics II/2, 708-732.

Bonhoeffer discusses, over several pages, the command as proclamation. Then follows a section on christology. Hardly surprising in its subject matter, it *is* surprising in its length and in its relative disconnectedness from the preceding and succeeding portions. These three pages are among the finest and, in some ways, the most original in Bonhoeffer. There are path-finding, liberating passages under the headings "Jesus, the eternal Son with the Father from all eternity." "Jesus Christ, the crucified Redeemer" and "Jesus Christ, the risen and ascended Lord." Yet what is striking are the similarities to the three pages of intense christological reflection in Church Dogmatics II/2, in the section "The Presupposition of the Divine Judgment."[78] Both are too lengthy to quote in full here. Nor are excerpts as telling as the whole, since the distinctive stamp of each author is evident throughout. But the reader is referred to this comparison as further evidence of the influence of Church Dogmatics II/2 on Bonhoeffer's fourth approach to an ethic.

What is to be made of all this?

First, the portions on the command of God apparently received no revision. They were part of the last writings of Bonhoeffer for the present Ethics, and were on his desk at the time of his arrest. Certainly they were never intended by him for publication in their present form.[79] Thus, an innocent borrowing occurs here and there. But what may have been only raw material for Bonhoeffer himself later emerged as the end product when the editor patched pieces together for publication. Bethge knows, of course, that these are not, in any event, the polished pieces Bonhoeffer would have produced, were publication at hand for him.

Second, the content here *is* genuine Bonhoeffer, though not original. The themes of the concreteness and specificity of the command, the emphasis given obedience, the christocentricity of the

---

78. Church Dogmatics II/2, 738-741.

79. See the letters of 18 November 1943 and 15 December 1943, LPP, 129, 163.

Method 125

command, the embrace of all of life by the command and the conferring of freedom--all these have genuine and strong antecedents pre-dating Bonhoeffer's study of Church Dogmatics II/2. There is no doubt whatsoever this last approach to an ethic is authentic Bonhoeffer, albeit Bonhoeffer as the student of Barth.

Third, there are changes in, and additions to, the material used from II/2. These show the *difference* of Bonhoeffer from Barth. For example, whereas Barth usually writes that the command of God confers a permission, a freedom, to do this or that, Bonhoeffer drops the article! Bonhoeffer's strongest emphasis is not Barth's--Barth's theme of constant accountability before God. Bonhoeffer's, rather, is God's permission of man to live "as man, and not merely as a taker of ethical decisions."[80]

> The commandment of God permits man to be man before God. It allows the flood of life to flow freely. It lets man eat, drink, sleep, work, rest and play. It does not interrupt him. It does not continually ask whether he ought to be sleeping, eating, working or playing, or whether he has some more urgent duties.[81]

This would not be denied by Barth. But it does not carry the emphasis with him it does for Bonhoeffer. Lehmann rightly judges this subtle change in Bonhoeffer from Barth: the attempt to break from any "formal and concrete rigidities" of the conception of command while yet holding onto the command of God. After Lehmann quotes Bonhoeffer's definition of the command as permission to live as man, he concludes: "To put the matter this way has the two-fold advantage of emphasizing in Christian ethics the personal relations between God and man established by God's action and *will*, rather than the *command* of God."[82]

---

80. E, 282.

81. E, 283.

82. Paul Lehmann, "The Foundation and Pattern of Christian Behavior," Christian

An important addition to the material from Barth is Bonhoeffer's concretizing the command in the mandates.

The mandates are solely dependent upon the one command,[83] but no *single* mandate can claim to embody the one command of God or even claim a position of superiority over any other mandate. They are conjoined so that only by cooperation and coordination do they properly function in fulfillment of the one command.[84] They exist *for* one another, and one cannot replace another. In fact, mutual limitation is an aspect of their activity as *God's* mandates.[85]

> The supremacy of the commandment of God is shown precisely by the fact that it juxtaposes and coordinates these authorities in a relation of mutual opposition and complementarity and that it is only in this multiplicity of concrete correlations and limitations that the commandment of God takes effect as the commandment which is manifest in Jesus Christ.[86]

The mandates are definite historical forms of the command of God.[87] In fulfilling duties within the mandates (as a husband or wife, for example, or father or mother, as breadwinner, citizen or church member) we do God's will, whether we are cognizant of it, intend it or

---

Faith and Social Action (New York: Charles Scribner's Sons, 1953), 101. Emphasis in the original. There is a scale of freedom as increasing permissiveness as one moves from Barth's ethics to Bonhoeffer's to Lehmann's. The place held by obedience to God and service to neighbor in Barth becomes responsibility to God and neighbor in Bonhoeffer and freedom before God and neighbor in Lehmann. This parallels the weight of emphasis on the indicative over the imperative as one moves from Barth to Bonhoeffer to Lehmann. The subtle changes in the material Bonhoeffer takes from Barth illustrate these shifts of emphasis away from Barth's strong tones.

83. E, 288.

84. E, 291.

85. E, 291.

86. E, 279.

87. E, 278.

not. Here the "flood of life flows freely." Bonhoeffer regards this normal discharge of moral responsibilities as *pre-ethical*.[88] For him, the rather self-evident nature of duties in marriage and family, state, church and work is certainly a matter of morality, but not ethics in a technical sense. The ethical arises only when the moral course itself is brought into question.

> There are, of course, undoubtedly occasions and situations in which the moral course is not self-evident, either because it is not, in fact, followed or because it has become questionable from the point of view of its contents. It is at such time that the ethical becomes a theme.

On an immediately previous page Bonhoeffer had concluded that the ethical is "tied to a definite time and a definite place."[89] It is a matter only when the "shall" and "should" impinge from the periphery of existence because a particular, assumed moral course has been rendered questionable.

Such a conception of the ethical yields two methodological results for Bonhoeffer. First, it makes ethics contextual. Bonhoeffer's ethics are contextual on other grounds as well, but here the conclusion is derived from the fact that the mandates structure life in such a way that the "ethical" only arises at exceptional times. It arises when the duties and obligations required by the mandates are *not* clear. At those times, Bonhoeffer insists that discovering the proper course can only come about through the link with the particular persons, times and places of this "pre-ethical" environment and its characteristically "built-in" responsibilities. Ethics must be done contextually.[90]

Bonhoeffer's conception of the ethical also serves, as he

---

88. E, 283.

89. E, 267, 264.

90. E, 272-273.

expresses it, "to prevent a pathological overburdening of life by the ethical," "to prevent... abnormal fanaticization and total moralization of life."[91]

The conclusion is this: the ethical is *part* of the command of God. It is far from the whole. The command comprises the ethical. But the reverse is not true.[92] Indeed, the command first of all "sets free for *unreflected* doing"[93] by forming life in the mandates. Only when this divinely warranted life process goes astray does its rectification take the form of God's command as the concrete "ethical."

On the subject of the mandates Bonhoeffer's discussions of ethics as formation and ethics as command are arranged precisely alike. For ethics as formation the mandates are historical forms of the Gestalt Christi which embody and direct the normal processes of life. The ethical as a theme arises when "who Christ is for us today" is in question as that engages our behavioral responses to his changing forms. The ethical arises in these exceptional times and can be answered only with an eye to these times, i.e., contextually.

In ethics as command the mandates are historical forms of the command of God. This command first of all sets humanity free, in the mandates, for unreflected doing, for "the free-flowing flood of life." But when the "shalls" and "shoulds" are not clear, "the fixed place and the fixed time of the ethical"[94] arises and the command of God takes the form of the specifically ethical. Decision-making is again done contextually and reflectively.

In both cases, Bonhoeffer's contextual ethic has become increasingly "filled" with moral, but "pre-ethical," content. The "ethical" is increasingly marked off as a vital, but "peripheral," event.

---

[91]. E, 265.

[92]. E, 285.

[93]. E, 280. Emphasis mine.

[94]. E, 270.

Method

> To confine the ethical phenomenon to its proper place and time is not to invalidate it; it is, on the contrary, to render it fully operative. Big guns are not the right weapons for shooting sparrows. In respect of its contents as well as of its character as an experience the ethical phenomenon is a peripheral event.[95]

In both cases the outcome of the "filled" contextual ethic is the same, an increased emphasis upon a kind of natural law. Creation is so formed in Jesus Christ that moral continuities span time and space. We cited this earlier for ethics as formation. Now we note it for ethics as command.

> The commandment of Jesus Christ, the living Lord, sets creation free for the fulfilment of the law which is its own, that is to say, the law which is inherent in it by virtue of its having its origin, its goal and its essence in Jesus Christ.[96]

So we have done more than note Bonhoeffer's addition to the material taken from Barth. We have seen the mandates as forms of the one command and observed the parallel outcome in Bonhoeffer's separate treatments of the mandates.

But the original purpose was to make a judgment on Bonhoeffer's use of Barth for the ultimate reason of clarifying

---

95. E, 265-266. The German for "peripheral event" is "Grenzereignis." This does not connote "unimportance" as "peripheral" does in English. It means a particular location, as we have described above. Occupying "a fixed time and a fixed place" does not thereby make the ethical a matter of less importance for Bonhoeffer. On the contrary, it is a matter of "big guns."

96. E, 298. Perhaps this is the place to refer the reader to the methodological move to near casuistry as Bonhoeffer wrests moral directives from the innate laws that result from the forming of the command (or the forming of Christ). Particularly the sections, albeit unfinished, on "natural rights" show this. Bonhoeffer discusses euthanasia, abortion and suicide in this manner. See Ethics, 149-172. It is more than methodological coincidence that the same pattern occurs in Barth's ethics. For some illustrations, see Church Dogmatics III/4, on "Respect for Life," 324-397, and "Protection of Life," 397-470.

Bonhoeffer's own method. He went beyond borrowing. He altered the material in accord with his own emphases and used it in connection with an original theme, the mandates.

While Bonhoeffer's distinctive emphases and theme cannot be compared with Barth's in detail, note should be made of considerable contrast. Bonhoeffer chooses to focus theologically on the *human* pole of God's command and say how the living of life proceeds under the command. How we live fully, precisely *as* humanity, occupies Bonhoeffer's attention. The mandates and, in other sections, the natural and the penultimate, are his categories for explicating this. Yet in the Barth galleys Bonhoeffer read, the human dimensions of the command of God are engaged only to give expression to how the gracious command, as *God's*, dominates and shapes those dimensions. Bonhoeffer, but not Barth, chooses to focus on "the temporal character of human life, its fulness and its frailty."[97] This is Bonhoeffer's own mark, not that of Church Dogmatics II/2. There are, incidentally, intimations here of the Letters and Papers from Prison theme that the Christian life is one of genuine and complete "worldliness" (Weltlichkeit).[98]

B. THE PLACE OF ETHICS AS COMMAND

The final question is whether this methodological motif, ethics as command, holds the same rank for Bonhoeffer as does ethics as formation. There are clearly elements with a pedigree in Bonhoeffer's writings. Its genuineness and importance are thus not to be doubted. But does it carry the load, and the interest, that ethics as formation does? I think not. Letters and Papers from Prison gives good indications to that effect, if not conclusive ones.

The theological letters contain little that is explicit about method. But they show direct lines between theology and ethics[99] (if

---

97. E, 282.

98. See, for instance, LPP, 361.

99. This holds for the following: LPP, 169-173; 278-282; 285; 302-303; 315-

such a distinction is even meaningful in Bonhoeffer's later writings). In *all* instances, the concern is who Christ is for us today. For Bonhoeffer, this is the same question as how Christ takes form in a world-come-of-age. Only once is the command of God even mentioned. And that is only a passing remark about an explanation to the Ten Commandments Bonhoeffer was writing at the time. The remark itself has little to do with method. It is quite significant, in short, that for every passage bearing on the Christian life, the starting point is a discussion about the Gestalt Christi and/or the world-come-of-age.

That ethics as formation is the motif foremost in Bonhoeffer's latest thought is perhaps best illustrated from the outline of the book he planned and on which he had begun work. (A book usually represents a stronger commitment to the ideas than do occasional letters.) In this outline the impressive factor is the unity of theology, ecclesiology and ethics. The movement is from Jesus as "the man for others" to the Church as only Church when it "exists for others," to a new life in the world as "existence for others," a new life "through the participation in the being of Jesus," interpreted non-religiously.[100] The vita Christiana is not spoken of in a way that even hints of the command of God. The focus is simply "participation in the being of Jesus" (Sein Jesu).

The piece that does speak of the command of God is, as mentioned, the Ten Commandments assignment done on request in 1944. The few comments which might be construed to bear upon method are in line with those in Ethics. There are none Bonhoeffer has not expressed earlier, and there are none he felt of sufficient excitement to share with Bethge.[101] The clear excitement in the prison literature is christological discernment and formation in a

---

316; 332-333; 335-337; 357-361; 361-363; 369-370; 373.

100. LPP, 380-383.

101. Dietrich Bonhoeffer, "The First Table of the Ten Commandments," in John D. Godsey, Preface to Bonhoeffer (Philadelphia: Fortress Press, 1965), 50-67.

world-come-of-age.

If we conclude from this that ethics as formation is not only the more original methodological motif in Bonhoeffer but also the one that captures his most intense interest, are there further available reasons for such a conclusion?

Here again the judgments must be acknowledged as inconclusive. They are offered tentatively.

Bonhoeffer claimed a new appreciation of the nineteenth century and of liberalism in theology. He stated his desire to combine the trends of liberalism and neo-orthodoxy.[102] This high evaluation of the heritage of liberalism and of the nineteenth century can be interpreted as amiable to the christological content and method of ethics as formation. It is far less friendly to ethics as command, with its heavy Barthian bases.

> The question is: Christ and the world that has come of age. The weakness of liberal theology was that it conceded to the world the right to determine Christ's place in the world; in the conflict between the Church and the world it accepted the comparatively easy terms of peace that the world dictated. Its strength was that it did not try to put the clock back, and that it genuinely accepted the battle (Troeltsch), even though this ended with its defeat.[103]

Secondly, Bonhoeffer took obvious delight in his "discovery" of the world-come-of-age. It stands to the fore in letter after letter. He immediately sought to relate his christology to this analysis. "Let me just summarize briefly what I am concerned about--how to claim for Jesus Christ a world that has come of age."[104] The result was an even heavier emphasis on Bonhoeffer's already strong theologia

---

102. LPP, 378.

103. LPP, 327.

104. LPP, 342.

Method 133

crucis.

> He [God] is weak and powerless in the world, and that is precisely the way, the only way, in which he is with us and helps us. Matt. 8:17 makes it quite clear that Christ helps us, not by virtue of omnipotence, but by virtue of his weakness and suffering.... The Bible directs man to God's powerlessness and suffering; only the suffering God can help. To that extent we may say that the development towards the world's coming of age outlined above... opens up a way of seeing the God of the Bible, who wins power and space in the world by his weakness. This will probably be the starting-point for our "secular interpretation."[105]

Because Bonhoeffer sees the "Mundigkeit" (adulthood) of the world as the occasion for proclaiming the utter "Weltlichkeit" (worldliness) of God, it would appear that ethics as formation would be the more conducive to proceeding, methodologically. This is underscored with Bonhoeffer's view of the world's "Mundigkeit" as itself a result of Christ's taking shape among humans and that it is God who compels us to recognize that we live in the world etsi deus non daretur.[106]

This does not of itself exclude the motif of ethics as command, of course. Yet not only is it absent as a subject of discussion; apparently it fits less well than ethics as formation. Certainly the theological and "ethical" excitement of the letters rotates about the form of Christ in a world-come-of-age.

The last reason is equally remote from truly hard data but it merits consideration.

> It was not in ethics, as is often said, that [Barth] subsequently failed--his ethical observations, as far as

---

105. LPP, 360-361.

106. LPP, 360-361.

> they exist, are just as important as his dogmatic ones--; it was that in the non-religious interpretation of theological concepts he gave no concrete guidance, either in dogmatics *or in ethics*.[107]

How serious is this deficiency, this lack of non-religious interpretation with guidance in dogmatics and ethics? For Bonhoeffer, it was as serious as "claiming for Jesus Christ the world-come-of-age"!

> What is bothering me incessantly is the question what Christianity really is, or indeed who Christ really is for us today.[108] If our final judgment must be that the western form of Christianity, too, was only a preliminary stage to a complete absence of religion, what kind of situation emerges for us, for the Church? How can Christ become the Lord of the religionless as well? Are there religionless Christians? If religion is only a garment of Christianity--and even this garment has looked very different at different times--then what is a religionless Christianity? Barth, who is the only one to have started along this line of thought, did not carry it to completion, but arrived at a positivism of revelation, which in the last analysis is essentially a restoration. For the religionless working man (or any other man) nothing decisive is gained here.[109]

If Barth does not offer concrete guidance for non-religious interpretation in ethics, as Bonhoeffer says, is Bonhoeffer finished with Barth's ethics? That would be concluding too much. Still less can it be concluded that Bonhoeffer would be finished with ethics as

---

107. LPP, 328. Emphasis mine.

108. LPP, 279.

109. LPP, 280.

command, which in any case is authentic Bonhoeffer. What *can* be concluded, however, is that Bonhoeffer wants an ethic which can be given expression in a non-religious interpretation of theological concepts. It is also clear he does not find that ethic in Barth's writings. He finds it in "participation in the being of Jesus, 'the man for others'"! "The man for others" is Bonhoeffer's own non-religious christological title and for him it is pregnant with the stuff of ethics. Bonhoeffer is on the trail of what he regards as essential--a Christian ethic that can be expressed non-religiously; and this ethic is closer to ethics as formation than ethics as command. At least Bonhoeffer pursues it wholly in the mode of ethics as formation.

With hesitation due an incomplete corpus, I conclude that ethics as formation is not only the more original methodological motif in Bonhoeffer; in the end it is also the reigning one. Had Bonhoeffer's ethics had a future of his own crafting, I think it would have developed along this line, with less mention of the command of God and more of the discernment of Christ's form in a world-come-of-age, and the shape of the Christian life appropriate to that form.

III. ONE METHOD OR TWO?

The fragmentary nature of Bonhoeffer's most provocative writings sets us upon the course of pursuing dual methodological motifs. Now the question is: are there in fact two methods? Assuming for the moment there are, how do they compare, if we place them side by side?

In both, the overriding thrust is toward concreteness.

In both, the ethic is an ethic of reality and realization. The Gestalt Christi and the command of God both have correspondence with reality. They bring to concrete expression in this world the cosmic reality given in Christ.

In both, ethics is done contextually. The ways Christ takes form among human beings vary through time. God's concrete command can only be heard in a local and temporal context.

In both, ethics is relational. The supreme importance of the command of God is that it is the command of Jesus Christ, true humanity. The supreme importance of the Gestalt of reality is that it is Christ's form. The Christian moral life is an ongoing, dynamic relationship with its center, God-in-Christ.

In both, the relational, contextual ethic becomes increasingly "filled." Both methods move from an atomistic ethic to an ethic emphasizing the coherence and continuity of the Gestalt Christi, or the command of God. The outcome in both is a large place for the "natural" and for the mandates and their innate laws.

In both, the mandates play an indispensable role. In one, they are the media of conformation; in the other, the media of obedience. In both, they compose the pre-ethical, though moral, environment, and they prevent life from an overburdening by the ethical.

In both, the ethical occupies a "peripheral" location. It has a fixed time and place. The ethical arises when the structured flow of life in the mandates has been subjected to disruption and/or severe questioning; when "who Christ is for us today" is in doubt; or what the command of God is concretely is itself problematic.

In both, moral action is the same. Obedience to the command of God is, for moral content, identical with conformation to Christ.[110] (Here is a resolution of the two methods, if there are two.)

For both motifs, all the faculties of the self are employed in ethical discernment: in the one case, in order to discover the present concrete command; in the other, to discern the current, specific form of Christ.[111]

In both, the methodological direction is from the question and answer about the indicative to the question and answer about the imperative. From: "how is Christ taking form among us here and now?" to: "what action on my part conforms to his action?" From: "what is God-in-Christ commanding here and now?" to: "what action

---

110. E, 299.

111. E, 37-43.

Method 137

on my part is action in keeping with this command?" In both, the weight is clearly on the imperative. It is permissive, authorizing life.

In both, the underlying assumption for Christian ethics is reconciliation, i.e., the recovered unity of God and the world in Christ.[112] In both, the point of departure for Christian ethics is the Body of Christ.[113] Christian ethics, on these counts, stands alone in relation to all other ethics.

In both, deputyship or vicarious action has an ontological base and the supreme ethical deed is the deed of free responsibility.[114] This deed is the breakthrough to reality at the particular time and place of the "ethical." In both, however, the final judgment of the deed lies in the hands of God. Both are ethics firmly grounded in justification by grace alone.[115]

What are the differences, if these are two methods?

Methodologically considered, there are probably none of great consequence. Müller is correct in pointing to the "Roman Catholic" *tone* in ethics as formation, in contrast to a classically Protestant one in ethics as command.[116] But he is wrong in characterizing the former as a Lutheran brand of gratia non tollit, sed perficit naturam.[117] This underestimates the methodological importance of the *dialectic* of the natural and the unnatural, the ultimate and the penultimate, and the "Yes" and "No" to the world within the Gestalt Christi--Incarnation, Crucifixion and Resurrection. Ott's comparison of Bonhoeffer with Teilhard de Chardin and Thomas Aquinas suffers the same error.

Is there one method or two?

---

112. E, 70; 298.

113. E, 85; 299.

114. E, 222; 224; 291; 284-285.

115. E, 120-121.

116. Müller, 289-292.

117. Ibid., 290.

The safest answer would be that this remains an open question because Bonhoeffer's theology and ethic remain open-ended. Continuities are very strong, but his method is not complete.

The more precise, if riskier, conclusion is that Bonhoeffer's is an ethic of reality and realization which finds methodological expression in two basic motifs, one of which is the more original and the more enduring. In the end, ethics as command should be regarded as a genuine motif, but a subordinate one. Both are authentic but the latter is in better tune with Bonhoeffer's christocratic vision of humanity, nature and history. Its "fit" is better. Yet it would be an unwarranted projection backwards from <u>Letters and Papers from Prison</u> to name ethics as formation *the* method of Bonhoeffer's ethics. By his own testimony, his ideas were unfinished. That holds for matters of method, as for others.

PART TWO: STUDIES IN THE <u>ETHICS</u>

IV

THE EUTHANASIA TEXT

William J. Peck

I. THE IMPACT OF PERSECUTION ON WRITING.

While in retrospect Dietrich Bonhoeffer's life was profoundly dramatic, some of his writings exude an air of scholarly calm which seems, at least during World War II, to conflict with his external circumstances. An example of such calm philosophical writing was a fragment he composed in 1941 as a part of his Ethics--the discussion of euthanasia. It bears scrutiny.

I propose to analyze that piece of writing in order to throw light on the question of text and context in a setting of persecution.[1] The purpose is exploratory, in keeping with the implication that the title of our volume really means not simply "more studies" but "new studies" or studies at a new level of detail and complexity. Just as "Chapter

---

1. This presupposes the whole discussion about the definition of a text. For important contributions to the efforts in textlinguistics see such authors as János Petöfi, T.A. van Dijk, and I. Bellert; the positions of Paul Ricoeur and the explorations of Clifford Geertz represent another relevant level. Floyd Merrell, A Semiotic Theory of Texts, (Berlin, New York, Amsterdam: Mouton de Gruyter, 1985), 1-10, usefully summarizes the status of the question. My essay approaches the issues inductively, contributing materials and problems, but not (consciously) moving from a prior theoretical orientation.

One" offers a thorough review of the textual problems, this chapter seeks to illustrate how much more there is in a given passage than at first meets the eye. Thematic studies of Bonhoeffer's thought easily overlook the nooks and crannies and too readily interpret abstractly this master of concrete particularity. But there is nothing abstract about living and writing during a war.

Leo Strauss, in his Persecution and the Art of Writing[2] distinguishes between writing in an age of prevailing liberalism and writing in most other periods. In a comment which could well apply also to Bonhoeffer he notes that the death of Socrates itself is evidence that classical Greece must be counted with the times of persecution:

> Socrates was... confronted with the alternative, whether he should choose security and life, and thus conform with the false opinions and the wrong way of life of his fellow-citizens, or else non-conformity and death.[3]

We know that ultimately Bonhoeffer chose the alternative which led to death, but we also know that he was eminently practical and, as a writer, careful, with an eye for the censor, in his choice of words.[4] He tended to avoid careless risks even in his private writings, especially after he began to participate in the political conspiracy

---

2. (Glencoe, Ill.: The Free Press, 1952), 22, 29.

3. Ibid., 16. Strauss even goes so far as to suggest that Plato's use of Socrates as a foil, a partially fictionalized speaker who could utter the unorthodox and dangerous opinion, was no mere playful writing device but a necessary means by which to avoid persecution himself. As a writer in a situation of persecution, Bonhoeffer's practice resembles that of Plato; as an ethicist his story, in part, parallels that of Socrates.

4. DB, 503. For an illuminating psychohistorical study of the question of Bonhoeffer's special interest in the theme of death see Kenneth Earl Morris, Bonhoeffer's Ethic of Discipleship: a Study in Social Psychology, Political Thought, and Religion (University Park and London: Pennsylvania State University Press, 1986). See also DB, 530.

against Hitler. Indeed, failure to attend to this influence on his writing style in the Ethics has caused a number of critical commentators to overlook his references to the plight of Jewish victims in such veiled phrases as "the weakest and most defenceless brothers of Jesus Christ."[5]

The study of texts written under persecution raises the difficult question of "reading between the lines," difficult because ignoring it may lead to inadequate conclusions. Still, Strauss lays down firm criteria:

> The historian ...will follow such rules as these: Reading between the lines is strictly prohibited in all cases where it would be less exact than not doing so. Only such reading between the lines as starts from an exact consideration of the explicit statements of the author is legitimate. The context in which a statement occurs, and the literary character of the whole work as well as its plan, must be perfectly understood before an interpretation of the statement can reasonably claim to be adequate or even correct.[6]

The following analysis, conducted, by intention at least, in agreement with these provisos, pursues three approaches: (1) descriptive (a "surface reading"), (2) interpretive (a "depth reading"), and (3) comparative (of which more will be said below), to throw light on the euthanasia text segment and to argue that it indeed contains evidence of significant "writing between the lines."

---

5. E, 114; see Eberhard Bethge's balanced and profound discussion of this phrase in "Dietrich Bonhoeffer and the Jews," in ER, 80-81. Although Bethge is making a theological point, he does clearly identify the referent as "Jews." The fact that this was a confession designed for possible public use sufficiently explains the more intensive degree of veiling.

6. Strauss, Persecution and Writing, 6.

II. A PRELIMINARY OVERVIEW.

On the definition of a text the text-linguists can help us only by delimiting the text over against the sentence.[7] The relation of text to context is much more problematical. Gerald Guiness points to the problem of the receding context and illustrates the difficulty of arriving at viable boundaries. He sums the problem up in a helpful way however:

> My whole argument to this point has been devoted to defending the thesis that there is no solution to the problem of text and context in the abstract.[8]

This advice, so close to Bonhoeffer in its penchant for the concrete, will be followed here. The first task is to "locate" the text through a review of the immediate biographical and historical context of the euthanasia text segment.[9]

Bonhoeffer had recently been transferred to the Munich office of the Abwehr and, on November 17, 1940 became a guest at the Benedictine monastery at Ettal.[10] There, in mid-January 1941, he wrote the section in his Ethics on euthanasia. On January 20, he reported in a letter to Eberhard Bethge that he was just then working on the question of euthanasia and that he was finding Catholic ethics

---

7. García-Berrio, Antonio, "Text and Sentence," in Petöfi, János S., ed., Text vs Sentence: Basic Questions of Text Linguistics, First Part (Hamburg: Helmut Buske Verlag, 1979), 26, says that, "referring to the 'expressed text' rather than text taken as a whole..., to distinguish text from sentence, we study the varying complexity of their deep structures." That is, just as phonemes and morphemes are the first two levels of linguistic reality, so 'sentence' is the third and 'text' is the fourth.

8. Gerald Guiness, "How Much Context?", in Forastiori-Braschi, Eduardo, etal. eds., On Text and Context: Methodological Approaches to the Contexts of Literature (Editorial Universitaria: Universidad de Puerto Rico, 1980), 153.

9. This review presupposes Lovin's contextual study in Chapter II and carries it forward through a more detailed concentration on a narrower field.

10. GS II, 381.

The Euthanasia Text

both instructive and practical, especially for the topic at hand.[11] In the same letter he mentioned that he had just completed a piece for Weckerling of the Bädermission, a brief discussion of theology and medicine entitled "The Best Physician."[12]

In a letter to Bethge, dated January 15, Bonhoeffer alluded to Exodus 23:7, in which the killing of innocent life is forbidden.[13] Since this biblical quotation plays a decisive role in his argument he clearly was already working on the euthanasia issue on January 15. Both of these pieces composed in mid-January were done in the larger setting of the discussion of "the natural," which Bonhoeffer began to write on December 10, 1940, in other words, not long after his arrival at Ettal.[14]

This preliminary sketch of the immediate context "locates" the text biographically and prepares for the analysis of the euthanasia fragment itself, both as a puzzle and as a source of insight into the composition of the Ethics. After digging into the problematics of surface and depth, a method which attends to the details of the text as a self-contained object, the analysis shifts to a comparative mode.

This has two parts. First one needs to study those aspects of Bonhoeffer's situation which do not emerge overtly in the euthanasia text but which do become apparent through the brief theological essay, "The Best Physician."[15] It is important to read this essay in close connection with the question of Bonhoeffer's being incognito at that time, a time when he was unable to reveal his political thinking (let alone his activities) to his fellow churchmen and former students. Because it was written concurrently or at least within a few days of the writing of the euthanasia passage, it yields revealing insights into

---

11. GS II, 394; E, 159-166.

12. "Der beste Artzt," GS II, 395; see GS III, 426-430.

13. GS II, 392.

14. GS II, 389.

15. GS III, 426-430.

the complex state of his mind at that juncture. It rounds out our picture of his whole situation; in a certain sense it is more than a mere contrast, it is part of a larger "text", consisting of all his writings (including letters) penned during January, 1940. These writings reveal the concrete architectonic or structure of his situation at that time, which in turn supplements the interpreter's resources for an accurate reading of each of the individual texts.

In a second form of comparison, one can go outside an author's work altogether, and by examining a parallel text on the same theme, from the same culture, and written contemporaneously, one can discover unforeseen characteristics of the original text. A memorandum on euthanasia which Bishop Theophil Wurm addressed to high party officials in October 1940 will serve as the parallel document. Bishop Wurm engaged in an eloquent, cunning, and effective struggle against the "secret" killing of by then already more than 100,000 patients from church and state institutions who were classified as incurably sick, insane, crippled, or otherwise possessed of lives deemed "not worth living."[16] The task is to describe the contrast between Wurm's and Bonhoeffer's strategies and statements in order to illuminate the Bonhoeffer text from an external vantage point after it has first been subjected to intense and formal internal analysis. This will further clarify the issue of "writing between the lines."

III. DESCRIPTION: A "SURFACE READING"

The difference between surface and depth, long important in the interpretation of texts,[17] may seem to some readers too obvious and

---

16. Gerhard Schäfer, ed., <u>Landesbischof D. Wurm und der Nationalsozialistische Staat: 1940-1945, Eine Dokumentation</u> (Stuttgart: Calwer Verlag, 1968), 113-146.

17. One thinks of Chomsky, Freud, and Ricoeur as offering modern ways in which to make this distinction, but also of older ways such as the Book of Job, the Gospel of Mark, and the tragedies of Aeschylus. The method used here is derived directly from the struggle with the text fragment itself.

labored. But the metaphor of layers in a text is a useful aid in sorting its contents and observing its structure. The intention here is, first, to arrive at a "surface reading," the reading which an educated person might make in the absence of special knowledge about dates and local circumstances, and to draw up an inventory of the resulting issues. The next section is a "depth reading" which interprets those clues in the text which force the reader to search beneath the surface and which, eventually, justify a "reading between the lines."

For the "surface reading" the logical place to start, because it opens the discussion of euthanasia, is the sentence: "The first right of natural life consists in the safeguarding of the life of the body against arbitrary killing."[18] For Bonhoeffer killing is arbitrary whenever it involves deliberate destruction of innocent life, that is, "life which does not engage in a conscious attack on the life of another." He excludes capital punishment and war from this prohibition on the grounds that guilt, either individual or collective, is involved. He then notes that this principle has been challenged by a quite different philosophical view, summed up in the term euthanasia, which holds that an innocent life when adjudged "no longer worth living" may be destroyed. The proviso is that the killing be done painlessly. Next he formulates his own guiding principle, namely, "that the decision about the right to destroy human life can never be based upon the concurrence of a number of different contributory factors." He explicitly refers to the requirement of *unconditional necessity* and adds that in the presence of such a necessity the killing not only may but "must be performed." However, one is obligated to avoid this outcome if there is even the slightest possibility of doing so, an argument which he grounds on the work of the Creator and Preserver of life.

Next he replies seriatim to two groups of arguments favoring euthanasia, those based on the interests of the patient and those

---

18. E, 159, and 159-166 for the entire segment under discussion. The following paragraphs are a precis of this segment; citations are avoided even in the case of direct quotations.

invoked for the sake of the healthy. He repudiates each argument, essentially on the grounds of our limited ability to know and therefore to judge. Also he considers that attributing different degrees of value to human lives leads to impossible consequences, for it would rule out the risking of life by the strong on behalf of the weak. He adds that in the position which argues from social utility "it is not perceived that life, created and preserved by God, possesses an inherent right..." God is the source of the ultimate value of life; other sources, like the subjective will to live, are not trustworthy. Indeed the consequence of the distinction between lives that are and are not worth living is the progressive extermination of one group after another.

Conversely, the absence of that distinction leads to heroic efforts by medical personnel and creates social value. Reasons of health and economics adduced in favor of euthanasia in cases of incurable hereditary diseases Bonhoeffer rejects because less absolute measures are adequate and the standard of living of society as a whole will hardly be threatened. Care for the sick may also be motivated by the quite natural reason that one might oneself fall into that condition. Moreover, quarantine is a sufficient protection against the danger of epidemics, except perhaps when plague breaks out on board ship, in which case "the decision would have to remain open." The real source of the euthanasia thesis, Bonhoeffer contends, is a philosophical view which seeks by superhuman effort to wipe out what appears to be meaningless disease. It struggles against the "essential character of the fallen world itself." This unlimited biologization and rationalization of life threatens its continued existence. He concludes that the question whether euthanasia is permissible must therefore be answered in the negative, summing up his case with the biblical quote: "The innocent...slay thou not."[19]

On the surface, this is a rather traditional and straightforward, though powerful, piece of ethical reasoning. It is a "text" with a clear topic and based on a coherent plan. It is conservative in the sense that

---

19. E, 166 (Exodus 23:7, RSV).

it is informed with a distrust of rationalistic innovation. On the other hand its theological references are muted and phrased in the language of general culture rather than with technical precision. That is to say, he feels quite free to omit specifically christological language, though the larger context, namely, the relation of the ultimate and the penultimate, from which this fragment emerges, is clearly christocentric. To sum up, this "surface reading," discloses a general ethical statement which, if considered valid at all, would be equally valid any time and anywhere.

IV. INTERPRETATION: A "DEPTH READING."

What are the clues in this "surface reading" which, nevertheless, press the scholar toward a "depth reading"? There are a number of features which present problems, features which in one way or another seem not to fit. For example, anyone accustomed to think of Bonhoeffer as being a "contextual" ethicist will have been surprised by the frank employment of principles and consequences in his argument.[20] How is this, for some people unexpected, phenomenon to be explained? Again, what is to be made of the concessions to war and capital punishment? How do such concessions accord with Bonhoeffer's thought elsewhere on the subject of war and with his personal history? However, these are rather minor and peripheral issues compared to the central puzzle which haunts this text immediately below the surface. Indeed, the central argument seems to contain a direct contradiction. On the one hand, in discussing arguments favoring euthanasia, he finds no instance in which the destruction of an innocent life would be permissible and ends by rejecting euthanasia altogether. On the other hand, he insists on including in the discussion the proposition that there *are* cases of final necessity for killing. It is no accident that exactly at this point in the

---

20. See, for an example of his expected views, E, 192, "An ethic of motives or of mental attitudes is as superficial as an ethic of practical consequences."

text he omits the term "innocent." Why, then, mention the guilty at all, since all the issues related to euthanasia per se come under the heading of "not slaying the innocent"?

The prominence of the theme of permissible circumstances for killing the guilty, then, is the main clue that the text contains more than a simple discussion of euthanasia. This contradiction or ambiguity in the argument culminates in the illustration about the ship on which some persons catch the plague and might have to be eliminated for the sake of the survival of the rest of the passengers. At the "surface level" Bonhoeffer leaves the question open. In other words he has chosen an illustration which introduces an ambiguity. But on closer inspection that ambiguity turns out to be pivotal for the basic structure of the whole segment. Neither the segment nor the illustration are allowed to rest in the dictum that euthanasia is always impermissible; the text seems almost constrained to add that a single absolutely unavoidable reason (of state ?) might require the taking of a life.

If the illustration is read as an allegory for the sinking German ship of state, a possible reading on the assumption that final reasons of state are in fact alluded to as a theme, the illustration becomes a call for courageous action to redress the situation. When the "hidden text" is read in this way, what at first appears to be a contradiction in the structure of his argument becomes in reality the means for conveying a very precise yet veiled communication: one may (in extremely exceptional situations), if one must, and one must if one may, slay the guilty.

Several considerations weigh in favor of the likelihood that there is an allusion here to the ethical validity of a highly specific goal of the resistance movement, the assassination of Adolf Hitler. While an unfinished manuscript might well be expected to contain minor discrepancies, this is more, a genuine and surprising "surplus" of elements within the text. To reiterate, the primary reason for seeing something "between the lines" here is the contradictory argument within the text itself. A close reading shows that everything

Bonhoeffer says about euthanasia proper is covered by the injunction: do not slay the innocent. At the same time, he insists on listing several cases in which it is not arbitrary to kill those who are guilty of a conscious attack on the life of another. The list includes the criminal, "the enemy in war," even the inadvertent victim in war, who is guilty by virtue of membership in the aggressor nation. Pointedly, the list does *not* include the option of tyrannicide.

Yet we know that Bonhoeffer had only recently been assigned to the Munich post of the Abwehr, and must just at that time have been intensely occupied with the ethical questions posed by membership in the resistance movement not only as they bore upon his own case as an ordained Lutheran pastor but also as they impinged on the conscience of each one of the conspirators. But he could not directly discuss the ethics of the resistance movement without imperiling its members and aims. Therefore, as Bethge puts it: "Anyone who looks in his Ethics for a direct justification of a coup d'etat, and detailed instructions for it will be disappointed."[21]

If we come to the Ethics text, then, with the question whether cryptic allusions to the conspiracy are to be found there, just as there are many documented instances in his letters--one, indeed, in a letter to his mother dated December 28, 1940, two and a half weeks prior to his working on the euthanasia segment[22]--we discover many unequivocal examples. Most of them are tied up with the call to free responsibility and the acceptance of guilt.[23] One lies within the euthanasia passage itself in the comment on "the socially valuable man...who will be ready to risk his life,"[24] for surely this statement exactly describes the members of the conspiracy. Another instance of

---

21. DB, 625.

22. GS II, 398.

23. E, 236-254, see also Larry L. Rasmussen, Dietrich Bonhoeffer: Reality and Resistance (Nashville: Abingdon Press, 1972), 51-57.

24. E, 163.

a reference "between the lines" to the conspiracy is, then, precisely the one under discussion, now adducible because already established on other grounds. With a twist not devoid of irony, if one thinks for a moment of the possibilities in the term "mercy killing," Bonhoeffer has kept open the option of an ethically permissible, because absolutely unavoidable, taking of a human life. We know from other sources that this was his position on the question of assassination in the particular case of Adolf Hitler.[25]

Finally, the conception of an ultima ratio or of reasons of state lies close to the surface in the requirement, put forward in the very next paragraph after the listing of examples of the guilty, that there be *a single, sufficient, and inescapable reason* if a given instance of killing is to be permitted; (elsewhere in the Ethics the term necessità is discussed more directly, although still in a well-disguised fashion).[26] Tyrannicide, one must therefore concede, is, for Bonhoeffer, just such a case as well as the only such case, and is therefore the essence of what is being alluded to "between the lines."

Now a text is more than a group of words on paper; it is a pattern of meanings which arise out of a social situation. Consequently, a "depth reading" of a text will examine the role of reference communities to which the author is known to have belonged. During the Ettal period Bonhoeffer's Roman Catholic hosts constituted the most immediate of these communities. His appreciation for their contribution has already been noted.[27] Indeed, the contents as well as the style of the text as perceived through the "surface reading" were clearly influenced by the dialogues which he had been enjoying with the Abbot and the Benedictine Friars at Ettal.[28] The calm and methodical style of thinking, along the lines of the natural law

---

25. DB, 627.

26. E, 238-239.

27. See footnote # 11.

28. GS II, 394.

tradition in Catholic ethics, replete with deductions from principles and weighing of consequences, certainly reflects the impact of this reference group.

Because of Bonhoeffer's statements about hesitating to use the name of God, especially when he was talking to Christians,[29] we may take the instances in the euthanasia text segment in which he names the deity, almost commonplace in their simplicity, as a record of the sort of thing he might have said from time to time in the circles of the resistance, a second reference group, though by no means second in importance.

The use of reason, understood as the limited organ of knowing, that is, as the noetic aspect of the natural, as opposed to the Kantian understanding of the sovereign spontaneity of reason, also belongs to the scientific style and ethos of his family and the group of "good people" in the conspiracy. Some of his father's sober medical empiricism constitutes a facet of this reference group's influence.

Among authors as a reference group, one of the clearest influences on his language about the natural was Schlatter's Ethics, Bonhoeffer's copy of which was part of the "theological library" at Finkenwalde. Nature, joy and concreteness are prominent themes in that book, often set off by the owner's lines in the margins.[30] The fact that he seems comfortable to be speaking of principles and consequences may, in addition to the Ettal context, reflect the wide reading he had been doing in the field of ethics, and it certainly illustrates his own stated method of "assessing possibilities and consequences...and the whole apparatus of human powers."[31]

---

29. E, 126.

30. Adolf Schlatter, Die Christliche Ethik, Zweite Auflage (Stuttgart: Calwer Vereinsbuchhandlung, 1924), 4, 17, 25, 27, 111, and especially "because we honor nature as God's creation, we also require that joy which arises out of natural events,"[my translation, ed.] 307. Bonhoeffer's personal copy of this book is in the possession of Eberhard and Renate Bethge.

31. E, 40.

But, a critic could well be asking at this point in the interpretation, was he not also a theologian, and a rather strict one of the Barthian persuasion? What had become of this reference group comprised of the Confessing Church leadership and his theological colleagues? Had he really lost or suppressed his theology when he came to writing about the subject of euthanasia? The answer is to be derived from two sources: 1. the text itself, and 2. the concurrent piece, "The Best Physician." Taking the text first, one notes that two features of his argument, both decisive for understanding the entire exercise, contain the full weight of his christological theology as we know it from elsewhere in the Ethics. Both are expressions of the benign limits to which the Christian faith subjects human arrogance. One of these expressions takes the form of Bonhoeffer's critique of the limitless process of rationalization and biologization at the root of the National Socialist euthanasia program, which, he says, is directed "against the essential character of the fallen world."[32] Here is an exceedingly deft use of the doctrine of original sin, completely integrated into and pivotal for his argument, and yet not stated in such a way as to turn away his peer-group of modern and worldly fellow-conspirators.

The other piece of vintage theology is the theme of "not knowing good and evil." That this is not only the theme of the first chapter of the Ethics but pervades it through and through, and that this is not only the chief preoccupation of Creation and Fall, and to a large extent, The Cost of Discipleship, but also appears already in the category of the actus directus in Act and Being, is well known to students of Bonhoeffer. In the euthanasia fragment it takes the form of "not knowing," that is, not knowing enough to rule on the reasons offered in favor of destroying innocent life. Frequently he asks, "who is to judge...?" and "who can tell...?"[33] Indeed, when he rules out the aggregating of arguments for euthanasia, requiring instead a single

---

32. E, 165.

33. E, 161.

The Euthanasia Text

absolutely cogent reason, he is in practice, displaying "the courage not to know."

The ability and the courage "not to know" is a central feature of Bonhoeffer's ethics.[34] Such an ability presupposes strenuous attention to all available facts and requires those hard decisions, infused with responsibility and insight, which alone enable a person "not to judge."[35] His ethics appear here in their essential depth; for the core and structure of his ethics consists in the fact that they are a critique of all ordinary ethics whether philosophical or otherwise. Indeed, the opening lines of the Ethics make the point resoundingly.

> The knowledge of good and evil seems to be the aim of all ethical reflection. The first task of Christian ethics is to invalidate this knowledge.... Christian ethics claims to discuss the whole problem of ethics, and thus professes to be a critique of all ethics simply as ethics.[36]

V. COMPARATIVE: "THE BEST PHYSICIAN"

While this struggle over the problem of euthanasia was going on in Bonhoeffer's mind and in his discussions at Ettal, he was writing the brief piece, "The Best Physician." On the surface it is a thoroughly traditional homiletical exposition of the statement in Exodus 15:26 "I am the Lord, your healer."[37] It begins:

> In the midst of nature's beauty we see a child being rolled along in a wheel chair. Whoever has a heart which has not grown insensitive to a neighbor's plight, will see in this a sign that all is not in order in our

---

34. E, 28-37.

35. E, 30-31.

36. E, 17.

37. GS II, 395.

world. A world in which this picture of torment and affliction is possible is not the original creation of God. The world has fallen away from its origin, authority has been usurped there by destructive forces.[38]

What are we to make of this evidently sentimental ejaculation which contrasts so sharply with the closely reasoned philosophical prose of the euthanasia segment?

In theory a person might write two texts concurrently and yet avoid any overlap. In Bonhoeffer's case, if one looks beneath the "surface," one finds significant and revealing overlap between his euthanasia piece and "The Best Physician." Because the latter exists, the historian does not need to guess what Bonhoeffer might have said, in mid-January, 1941, to that reference group which had largely been omitted from the euthanasia text. We have his exact words. Structurally, then, the piece for Weckerling completes the picture of Bonhoeffer's authorship during the composition of the euthanasia fragment. In "The Best Physician" the pastors and laity of the Confessing Church, indeed of the evangelical church generally, are addressed directly. These two texts, consequently, express and hold together two sides of Bonhoeffer's life which at the time had to exist in a relation of incognito."[39]

One can also discover hidden themes and issues in the text by comparing it to the companion text where the same themes may be explicit. For example, the theme of nature's beauty, with which "The Best Physician" opens, might appear platitudinous to the casual reader; when the dating sets this reference to nature into the context of Bonhoeffer's rediscovery of the natural in the Ethics, the passage acquires a fresh relevance. The clash between the natural harmony of the landscape and the suffering of the child in the wheel chair is now

---

38. GS III, 426.

39. DB, 661-669, and W.Peck, "The Role of the 'Enemy' in Bonhoeffer's Life and Thought," in A.J. Klassen, ed., A Bonhoeffer Legacy: Essays in Understanding (Grand Rapids, Michigan: William B. Eerdmans, 1981), 346.

The Euthanasia Text

understood to embody the fundamental opposition between the natural and the unnatural as these themes are developed in the <u>Ethics</u>.[40] Now the child is no longer a mere child-in-general, but rather becomes one of the crippled children who were currently being dragged away from their institutional homes and put to death.

When Bonhoeffer asks whether there are still people whose hearts are sensitive to their neighbors' plight, he is not so much registering a jejune complaint as reflecting his exhausting and discouraging struggle against the pressures of National Socialism. When he uses the phrase "this picture of torment and affliction," he is not slipping toward melodrama as the casual reader might suppose, but is coldly sober. At this point in the war almost half of his Finkenwalde students had been killed in action.[41] Moreover, through his brother-in-law, Hans von Dohnanyi, he had access to inside information about the crimes of the regime. It was therefore no exaggeration, but rather an instance of those occasions when theological statements carry political meaning, for Bonhoeffer to say: "The world has fallen away from its origin; authority has been usurped there by destructive forces."[42]

Of course, on the "surface" this is a strictly traditional theological statement, but the circumstances of its timing in relation to the euthanasia piece strongly suggest that Bonhoeffer also has in mind that usurpation of authority which not only permits but requires drastic and final measures. In this way, unexpectedly, "The Best Physician" supports the thesis that the euthanasia segment contains provisions for the slaying of the guilty; further, it points to the nature

---

40. E, 147-148.

41. DB, 595, by the summer of 1941, "out of about 150 Finkenwalde students more than 80 were killed in action."

42. GS III, 426. See Kenneth Earl Morris, <u>Bonhoeffer's Ethic of Discipleship: a Study in Social Psychology, Political Thought, and Religion</u> (University Park and London: The Pennsylvania University Press, 1986) 11-16, on the concepts of authority, authenticity, and nihilism.

of the crime: usurpation of authority.[43]

Our method, valid for the historian who wishes to coax a text toward "self-disclosure," has, of course, drawn together many strands of evidence, *not any one of which alone would have been decisive.* That is as it should be. The method is cumulative; it amasses small and apparently trivial details until they produce a critical turning point so that a text which was perceived in one way now reveals unexpected contents and connections. While the full significance of our "depth reading" of the euthanasia fragment will not disclose itself without the help of the comparison with Bishop Wurm's corresponding "text," several details are nevertheless now close enough to the surface for comment.

For example, there is a quite moving detail, already mentioned above, namely, the fact that he tacitly approves of capital punishment. It is, after all, the way he would die. But his mentioning the issue here, apart from its logically necessary role in the "surface reading," is not entirely accidental. There is a socio-cultural aspect, a sense of belonging to an aristocratic and conservative group which accepted war and capital punishment simply as a matter of course. One could raise the question whether these were strategic concessions, necessary for effective communication with military men. But there is a fine line between strategy and simply belonging to one's culture. The likelihood is that in the best sense of these words he was a German patriot and a Lutheran preacher right to the end.

But there is a profound theological fit too in his being executed under a charge of treason, for he understood from the outset that the "deed of free responsibility" (advocating tyrannicide), which we have judged to be central to the euthanasia fragment, would entail guilt before the law. In a final creative transmutation Bonhoeffer was able to accept this guilt as valid at two further levels. First, he interpreted

---

43. This usurpation is the very danger against which Bonhoeffer had warned in his radio speech, "Der Führer und der Einzelne in der jungen Generation," GS II, 22-38.

the political conspiracy per se as an act of repentance.[44] Second, at the highest level he was also able, when the end came, to accept the thought of his own manner of death as a sharing in the suffering of God.[45]

But that is not the last thing to be said in interpretation of this passage, because it also contains a reference to the plight of the Jews. To whom if not to them could he be referring when he says: "one group of human beings after another would in this way be condemned to extermination."?[46] A modern historian draws the conclusion eloquently: "the undertaking to exterminate the Jews was in a way only a radical extension of the euthanasia program."[47]

Bonhoeffer objected strenuously to the euthanasia program in its full significance, not only through formulating the argument analysed here, but through risking and then giving his life in solidarity with the victims.[48]

VI. WURM'S STRUGGLE AGAINST EUTHANASIA

Comparison can sometimes provide insights that are not available in any other way. An example is to be found in the considerable help afforded by the comparative method in completing the "depth reading" of Bonhoeffer's text fragment on euthanasia. Here is the background. Under the cover of the invasion of Poland and the outbreak of war, Hitler, in a secret memorandum, post-dated to September 1, 1939, ordered his personal physician to give certain

---

44. Rasmussen, Reality and Resistance, 56.

45. DB, 790; LPP, Letter of July 21, 1944, 370.

46. E, 164.

47. Earnest Christian Helmreich, The German Churches under Hitler (Detroit: Wayne State U. Press, 1979), 313.

48. William Jay Peck, "From Cain to the Death Camps: an Essay on Bonhoeffer and Judaism," Union Seminary Quarterly Review, 28 (Winter, 1973), 172-173.

doctors, still to be appointed, an expansion of their authority so that they could provide mercy death for persons certified to be incurably ill.[49] That was the entire legal basis for a program which eventually killed over 100,000 persons.

Soon some of the church institutions for epileptics, the handicapped, and the mentally ill received orders to fill out information forms on their patients. Soon after that, with three days notice, thirteen persons were carried away on a gray bus from the Pfingstweide epileptic home in Württemberg.[50] Within a few days their families received death notices together with permission to apply for release of the ashes. The causes of death were obviously trumped up, taken from a standard list. The reasons for the sudden cremation, given out as danger of contagion, were hardly to be believed especially when, for example, a heart attack was the officially certified illness. The local communities were shocked; rumors spread rapidly. A large number of such reports began to filter in to the bishop of Württemberg, Theophil Wurm. Wurm and Bodelschwingh, both nationally known and respected church leaders, began to mount efforts to oppose the action of the state.[51] Dietrich Bonhoeffer cooperated by arranging for his father to give them technical advice on medical issues.[52] A number of pastors wrote carefully reasoned, and even more carefully worded, letters of protest.[53]

Against this background, at the end of October, 1940, Bishop

---

49. Schäfer, Wurm, 115.

50. Ibid.

51. Others, such as Bishop Galen, would have to be included in a more comprehensive study.

52. DB, 592.

53. Schäfer, Wurm, 118-134. See, for example, Pastor Sauter's letter of July 17, 1940, to Cuhorst, a high official, which ends with the moving and dramatic words: "Dixi et salvavi animam meam!" Ibid., 124.

Wurm sent a lengthy memorandum to appropriate high officials.[54] The memorandum was widely circulated and is known to have been received by Hitler.[55] Its every line is calculated for political effect. It establishes the known facts about this supposedly top-secret activity: that about 2000 persons in the "land" [state] of Württemberg have been killed so far and that 100,000 persons in a "land" of 3,000,000 inhabitants, including family members of the deceased as well as medical workers and maintenance staff, are affected. It describes the arrival of the transport buses, the patients' fear, the fact that victims include not only the hopelessly retarded but some who are capable of working and, definitely, of feeling. As a result of these happenings the care-givers are deeply shaken and the doctors become depressed upon having to obey orders which for the most part they inwardly reject. It is shocking, moreover, to see a wife, whose husband has faithfully visited her during her stay at the institution, torn away from him and taken to be killed; it is disquieting, too, that veterans wounded in the first world war are not exempted.

The argument that other families are sacrificing their sons in the war effort, the bishop continues, is not convincing to the families of these victims. The former are offering an accepted and honored gift of patriotic devotion freely given; some of the latter might even feel the same way were it not for the sinister untruthfulness which marks the whole procedure. The credibility of the government is being destroyed and distrust is even threatening to reach as far as the Führer himself. Think of the effect on the morale of the army if soldiers must fear such treatment for handicaps sustained during the fighting. To bring the whole laboring population to a state of paralysis hardly accords with the vital release of life energies to which National

---

54. Ibid., 134-139.

55. "Fraülein H" discovered this during her quite courageous interview with Hitler, sometime between November 30 and December 3, 1940. She warned him that his reputation was at stake among the populace and gave him copies of Wurm's correspondence condemning euthanasia. Hitler admitted that the euthanasia law existed and that he had signed it. Ibid., 142-143.

Socialism has dedicated itself. That is why so many faithful Party members are becoming downcast over this policy.

When the British bombers killed epileptic children at Bodelschwingh's institution at Bethel there was a public outcry and the press compared the atrocity to the slaughter of the innocents at Bethlehem, but on the same day hundreds of similar children were coldly picked up from their institutions and put to death. The whole thing becomes even more grotesque when one knows that Pastor Braune has been sitting in prison for months now on the charge that he wrote a letter protesting these doings. Are the whispered rumors in Party circles, that experiments are being conducted on new lethal gasses, true? The doors are wide open to the spread of every sort of destructive rumor and no threats of punishment will be able to stop the spreading infection of a deep mistrust.[56] Such, in brief compass, was Bishop Wurm's argument.

His conclusion was that, while the catastrophes of war are acceptable "to our brave population," the planned destruction of their handicapped neighbors goes against their deepest ethical and religious sensitivities. When the government puts the criminal to death or requires our lives to protect against an enemy who threatens our future, that is acceptable to Christian teachings. But the willful destruction of our innocent fellow citizens is an attack upon the magisterial rights of God Himself the like of which no morally self-respecting nation has hitherto dared to mount. In killing its weaker citizens, Germany sinks to the level of a primitive nation. Every German who cares about the honor and the future of his people urgently demands an end to the matter.

The above is an accurate "surface reading" of Wurm's text. The "depth reading" would probe the ways in which this protest fits into a web of national feelings and priorities. The document is a courageous public act with a realistic chance of success. Its argument is essentially a call for strengthening the government by ridding it of a

---

56. The above is a paraphrase of Bishop Wurm's Memorandum, Ibid., 134-139.

The Euthanasia Text

pestilential danger. In fact Wurm's efforts seem to have had a genuine impact. On August 24, 1941, Hitler issued an order through his personal physician to discontinue the euthanasia program.[57]

On the issue of secrecy there is deep irony in a comparison between the strategies and actions of Bonhoeffer and Wurm. While the former lived under multiple layers of secrecy, inevitable under the harsh rules of espionage which his understanding of necessity imposed, the latter made the government's policy of secrecy the prime object of attack. Both were patriots, but only Wurm could build his case on patriotic and religious sentiment. Both were attacking Hitler and National Socialist policies in deploring euthanasia, but Wurm had to make his case by pleading on behalf of ways to strengthen Hitler's position and enhance the people's trust in their Führer.

The contrast between the two strategies is rooted in the definition of the basic problem which each was in fact addressing. Wurm was taking direct action against measures which were threatening the community; he could elicit help from the community's increasing state of disquiet. His goal was to stop the euthanasia program. His arguments were structured in such a way that, eventually, Hitler had to listen.

Bonhoeffer on the contrary, did not perceive the euthanasia program as in itself the basic problem; for him the immediate political goal had to be to stop the war and end the policies of injustice toward the Jewish population. Therefore while he undoubtedly intended in

---

57. Kurt Nowak, 'Euthanasie' und Sterilisierung im 'Dritten Reich' (Göttingen: Vandenheock & Ruprecht, 1977), 85. This fact was apparently either not known to Bonhoeffer, in spite of his special sources of information, or otherwise his sources revealed that the practices were continuing, for he included the euthanasia policy among the active grievances which he listed in a briefing paper in November, 1941, for General Canaris on behalf of the evangelical churches. No distinction is made in this document between the official policy, which ended in August, and sporadic instances which continued afterwards and in retrospect have been called "wild euthanasia." GS II, 432; see DB, 594. Fredric Wertham, "The Geranium in the Window: The Euthanasia Murders," in Dennis J. Horan and David Mall, eds., Death, Dying, and Euthanasia (Frederick, Maryland: Aletheia Books, University Publications of America, Inc., 1980), 633, asserts that the killings did not stop but only became more hidden and more cruel.

the long run to contribute through his Ethics to the post-World War II discussion, the evidence shows that in the short run he was setting down a reflection, even to some extent containing an element of personal stock-taking, aimed at encouraging a small group of fellow-conspirators. He had decided that the way to contribute to the goal of abolishing euthanasia could not, at least in his own case, be the path of public protest. The sole alternative available to him was the infinitely more dangerous path toward tyrannicide. This finding confirms quite precisely the structure which our "depth reading" of his euthanasia text fragment disclosed on internal and biographical grounds.

VII. CONCLUSION

One conclusion to be drawn is that the question "what is a text?" cannot adequately be answered in general. Bonhoeffer's penchant for concreteness, once again, has found its confirmation. Of course, "difference" establishes the place of text between sentence and context; it is distinguishable from both. But as one moves step by step from "surface" description to "depth" interpretation, one leaves the sphere of the general and the timeless; one discovers again and in detail the importance of time and timing. He was writing during January, 1941, shortly before the fatal conference took place at Weissensee during which the Nazi leadership adopted plans for the "final solution." Therefore the euthanasia issue had not yet been eclipsed by the escalating scale of horror; there was still space for significant opposition. Bonhoeffer offered such opposition both by using his personal contacts and by writing a theoretical critique even though the latter had to remain essentially a private essay more offered to a few friends than, as in the case of Wurm, intended to produce a direct impact on public events.

Although he had already been forbidden to speak in public, he was not yet under the order not to publish. That came on March 27,

1941.[58] So he may have been intending to write for a larger audience and, in some way, to register a strong current protest against euthanasia. At the same time it is certain that the Ethics was meant too, for the coming generation. That feature of his text dominates the "surface" reading. But an investigation of clues, which at first reveal nothing, finally shows that there lurked, "between the lines," an argument favoring tyrannicide; at that level too, he was acting for the sake of the coming generation.

---

58. DB, 840.

V

WHO AM I? BONHOEFFER AND SUICIDE

Gerard Th. Rothuizen

I. BLACKMAIL?

In his Ethics (or rather what the exigencies of war left us of his notes, fragments and even some completed units) Dietrich Bonhoeffer includes a section on what he understands by 'suicide'[1] and what it means to him.

It is interesting from the point of view of morality that he does not condemn suicide as "unethical." Indeed, he even considers a rejection of suicide on such grounds impossible. That seems significant in the light of Christian and also more general attitudes in the past. At the same time we have to guard against an obvious misunderstanding, because Bonhoeffer also refuses to approve of suicide:

> If suicide must nevertheless be declared wrongful, it is to be arraigned not before the court of morality, or of

---

1. This chapter is a translation, by Edwin Robertson and William Peck, of G. Th. Rothuizen, "Wie ben ik? Dietrich Bonhoeffer en de suicide," Wijsgerig Perspectief 23 (1982/83) #6, 144-149. [Tr. note: Rothuizen observes that by using the German term "Selbstmord", Bonhoeffer stresses the idea of "self-murder," 144.]

men, but solely before God's court.[2]

He is saying that it must be condemned, not, however, as "unethical," but instead only as "untheological"; he rejects it not from the point of view of morality, but of faith. We can see that it is not the presence of so-called low motives that establish this "no" to suicide; a person may continue to *live*, for the lowest motives. Another person, Bonhoeffer emphasizes, may take his life for the highest motives. This conveys an entirely different tone than one finds in the pronouncement by Thomas Masaryk, a person with some "reputation" in the field of suicide, who stated that the motives are "very seldom moral."

Bonhoeffer continues: "It is not bodily life itself which possesses an ultimate right over man."[3] Nor can society, in his view, claim such an ultimate right in the way Aristotle spelled it out. Nor can one defend a "no" with the thought, long taught in the Christian Church, that the deed makes repentance and therefore forgiveness impossible. What an overrating of the last moments of life! Moreover, many Christians die without benefit of repentance.[4]

All of these arguments have a certain validity in a general sense, but Bonhoeffer finds them less than decisive. Convincing arguments do exist, but they are not to be sought in the sphere of morality, which deals with law and prohibitions including the command to repent. We are not, therefore, dealing with law, but grace, which speaks not of the "unethical," but of "sin" and "unbelief."

But now he deals with suicide (and with other subjects like contraception, sterilization, abortion, euthanasia, etc.) under the heading of "The Natural." One may well ask how this can be possible when we have heard so much about grace and so little about nature. Still we read:

---

2. Eg, 178-179. [Ed. note: the translation in E, 168 is incorrect.]

3. E, 168.

4. E, 168-169.

> It is... life itself that tends towards the natural and keeps turning against the unnatural to bring about its downfall. This, in the last analysis, is what underlies the maintenance and recovery of physical and mental health.[5]

This kind of language (which occurs, by the way, in the introduction to the section on "The Natural" and not in the paragraphs on suicide) smacks more of biology than theology. Or may it rightly be called grace that it happens so naturally in this way? I may presume this from what I read a little later on:

> And indeed in the rights of natural life it is not to the creature that honour is given, but to the Creator. It is the abundance of His gifts that is acknowledged.[6]

One could safely call the tackling of the problem mentioned above unorthodox, especially if we take into account the time when these notes were written (1940-1941). This is not to say that the religious responsibility has been ignored in the past; the Christian tradition up to that time always taught that a person who tried to commit suicide sinned against nature, himself, his neighbor and God. But the person in question was placed under the judgment of that God, not under his grace and that becomes different here, even if it still concerns the *judgment* of grace.

What one could ask oneself finally, that is if we--all in all-- are not once again thrown back into morality, is to what extent a person might experience all of this "religiosity" as a form of moral blackmail, rather than as a helpful message. I refer to the overtones in the following type of statement: "Daddy is not angry (because you did this or that), only terribly sad." In the meantime, beware! One could of course counter this entire line of reasoning with a "so what?" Since when are fathers not allowed either to be angry, on the one hand, or

---

5. E, 147.

6. E, 151.

sad on the other? What a burden to place on fathers!

II. BARTH AND BONHOEFFER

However original Bonhoeffer may have been, he also learned from others. He was (despite his obstinate independence) an enthusiastic disciple of Karl Barth, whom he visited in 1931 immediately upon his return from a study year in America, shortly before the summer vacation and in time to catch the last of Barth's lectures that semester in Bonn. We know that Barth had also lectured on ethics, first in Münster (1928-29) and then more recently in Bonn. Writing to his friend Erwin Sutz, Bonhoeffer said that he had read the last pages of the lecture notes from "Ethics II," which had been held in the winter semester.[7] That can be taken literally, but it is also possible that he finished reading the notes, all of them, and it even seems possible that he is also referring to "Ethics I" (held in 1930). That would be particularly interesting, because in that series of lectures, Barth dealt with suicide.

No matter when Bonhoeffer studied these lectures, he did not simply copy them. Barth wrestles with a question which for Bonhoeffer, ten years later, is no longer a question: "Whether we are not here dealing with a forbidden cowardice." At the same time there is a striking agreement when we read: "It is not the task of the church to define a doctrine of the rejection and condemnation of suicide nor to preach it." In that quote from Barth, we should read "doctrine" as "moral teaching." On one point, Barth goes further than Bonhoeffer, or appears to, when he says that he cannot agree with Adolf Schlatter, an authority both in New Testament and in ethics, when Schlatter states that the act is "a rejection of God's help, grasping at the possession of limitless power over ourselves." How can that be decided for someone else?[8] Bonhoeffer was also a disciple of

---

7. GS I, 18.

8. Karl Barth, Ethics, tr. Geoffrey W. Bromiley, (New York: Seabury Press,

Schlatter and the expression (indeed used by him also in quotation) comes in connection with the proper point of objection for him: the right to self-justification, to the point of putting oneself to death. Bonhoeffer says:

> Suicide is the ultimate and extreme self-justification of man as man, and is therefore--from the purely human standpoint--in a certain sense even the self-accomplished expiation for a life that has failed. This deed will usually take place in a state of despair, yet it is not the despair itself that is the actual originator of suicide, but rather a man's freedom to perform his supreme act of self-justification even in the midst of this despair. If a man cannot justify himself in his happiness and his success, he can still justify himself in his despair. If he cannot make good his right to live a human life in the life of his body, he can still do so by destroying his body. If he cannot compel the world to acknowledge his right, yet he can still assert this right, himself, in his last solitude. Suicide is a man's attempt to give a final human meaning to a life which has become humanly meaningless. The involuntary sense of horror which seizes us when we are faced with the fact of a suicide is not to be attributed to the iniquity of such a deed but to the terrible loneliness and freedom in which this deed is performed, a deed in which the positive attitude to life is reflected only in the destruction of life.[9]

It is this self-justification--not exactly an argument snatched out of the air, for, as Pavese put it, before his own suicide, "the great mission of life is to justify oneself"--which Bonhoeffer, once more, is able to accept when it transpires within the sphere of morality, but which

---

1981), 126-128.

9. E, 167-168.

from a religious point of view he is compelled to reject.

But we need not continue that now. We do not know for certain how far Bonhoeffer is following Barth in dealing with our theme; but we do have clear evidence of influence moving in the reverse direction, namely, in Barth's ethical writings published in Church Dogmatics III/4, during his lifetime as distinct from the earlier volumes mentioned above. Here Barth, commenting on what Bonhoeffer had written ten years before, described it as "the most cautious statement so far written on this matter."[10] Barth considers "escape" and "cowardice" no longer very impressive accusations and the same goes for other morality-based counter arguments, which we already found invalidated by Bonhoeffer. They are variants of Aristotle's view that the community has a prior claim or else of the argument from the impossibility of repentance. Moral arguments now no longer carry weight with Barth: he considers them abstract. Their veto power for him has disappeared. This, however, offers no open door any more than it does with Bonhoeffer. The suicide is not prevented by a command, "Thou shalt live," but by a "Thou mayest live," wording which all but borrows literally from Bonhoeffer's discussion:

> Man does not need to lay hands upon himself in order to justify his life. And because he does not need to do this it follows that it is not rightful for him to do so.[11]

But sin against the life one is permitted to live is also for Barth far more serious than sin against the life one is forced to live; Schlatter appears to come off better as much as twenty years before. This does not mean that suicide is unforgivable, on the contrary. The fact of forgiveness places this sin in a category with other sins, which beside it are often far more sinful. But the forgiveness makes the sin no less

---

10. Karl Barth, Church Dogmatics, III/ 4, 404.

11. E, 169.

Suicide 173

a sin.[12]

Barth did not only borrow from Bonhoeffer. Although in a sense he lagged behind, in another way it seems that he also moved further along the path from the lectures of 1930 (or 1928) than the later Bonhoeffer in mitigating his stand against suicide. That is, Barth went further even than to advocate the granting of forgiveness for the act. We will now try to go deeper into that matter and at the same time go back to Bonhoeffer, with whom we are still not done--not by a long shot.

III. ON THE GENERAL AND THE PARTICULAR

To begin with, we are not finished when we define his thought in terms of a moral "yes"; and a religious "no." He takes us further when he suddenly remarks:

> Far more difficult than the determining of this general principle is the judgment of particular cases. Since suicide is an act of solitude, the ultimate decisive motives almost always remain hidden.[13]

We gather, then, that not every "self-killing" is "self-murder" in the proper sense of the word.

We are curious to know what he means by these "particular cases," which do not fall under the initial judgment. Now, that is not difficult because he makes it perfectly clear. He includes the captured rebel, who fears that under torture he might betray his friends; or the statesman who only by his own free death can spare his country grievous harm; or the sufferer from incurable disease who sees that the expense of his care will bring about material and psychological ruin for his family. He thinks also of the church fathers who held that self-destruction was permissible when a woman was threatened with a

---

12. Barth, Church Dogmatics, III/4, 403-413.

13. E, 170.

fate worse than death, by rape (but he knew of the great exception: Augustine). Bonhoeffer also mentions leaving the last place in the boat to another when the ship is sinking or shielding the body of a friend from the bullet with one's own body.[14]

It is also clear that in these "particular cases," Bonhoeffer is not advocating a so-called "situational ethics" *in general* much less an "ethics of principles" (though Bonhoeffer was of course more sympathetic toward the former type of ethics than the latter). The "particular case" in question is a very special instance: the case in which one can and must clearly speak of a sacrifice. By means of such cases, he sought to make room for a distinction between "self-murder" and "self-killing." But when a decision about suicide does not entail a sacrifice of this kind, he must continue to say, "no." It is precisely the sacrifice which constitutes the difference between the one and the other.[15] Also in an essay on "The Right to Self-assertion" Bonhoeffer plays the idea of sacrifice off against suicide, because au fond my self-assertion is at the disposal of the other, who is my brother.[16]

Barth (with whom we have not yet finished) took over the difference between "self-murder" and "self-killing" from Bonhoeffer in 1951, a difference which in the lectures of 1928 and 1930 he did not yet know, or at least did not consider in so many words. However he made his contribution by spelling this distinction out in another way. As early as in Bonn (and two years before in Münster) he had also spoken of a "particular case," but this became--significantly enough--a case with absolute openness and it was not filled with the alibi of a sacrifice. Nor did this happen twenty years later in Church Dogmatics, III/4. There the "particular case" is above all a borderline case . The idea of a sacrifice--which Barth already knew in 1928 and

---

14. E, 172.

15. E, 170.

16. GS, III, 258-269.

which Bonhoeffer could have borrowed and worked out for himself--is elaborated to the extent that a self-surrender (Hingabe) is necessary, but this sacrifice (up to and including self-killing) can be directed not only toward our neighbor, but toward God as well. That would be a sacrifice acceptable to God, along the lines of Romans 12.1 and Colossians 3.5.17

IV. WHY DID BONHOEFFER GO BACK?

But now we turn back definitely to Bonhoeffer. In relation to him we can remark: someone who said "yes" to death, by deliberately sacrificing his own life for others in such a loyal way, has some right to say "no" when suicide is under consideration as a matter purely of "one's own self-interest."

That needs to be heard. It needs to be heard except when in some degree even this sacrifice is like suicide. This is precisely the resemblance Van den Berk has taken up in reference to the case of Bonhoeffer himself. He makes the point quite clearly in an article which he published in 1975 under the title, "Bonhoeffer and death."18 In that article we read that

> one at least is inclined to believe that Bonhoeffer's throwing himself into the war machine with the attendant danger to his life and the fact that he was arrested, imprisoned and ultimately executed was in the deepest sense related to his longing for death. *He simply was longing for the end to come.*19

This thought corresponds with Bonhoeffer's decision to return from America shortly before the outbreak of war and in the certain

---

17. Barth, Church Dogmatics, III/4, 411.

18. M. E. M. Van den Berk, "Bonhoeffer en de dood," in Tijdschrift voor Theologie, (Nijmegen, 1975), 158-181.

19. Ibid., 177-178 [author's emphasis].

knowledge that it would break out, a return which would inevitably involve him in illegal activities in Germany and would cost him his life. Van den Berk's article appears to recapitulate the argument in his dissertation, published a year earlier. In the opinion of a psychoanalyst (A. Hustinx), who read the dissertataion: "It is clear. Bonhoeffer looked for death; in the deepest sense he longed for the hangman's rope, in order that an end should be made to his life from without, because he could no longer endure it from within." [20]

Although the first of these suspicions advances ominously in the direction of the second, one needs to interject that feelings of self destruction are not exactly the same as suicide. Nevertheless, however impressive this suggestion appears ("clear" to the psychiatrist; "tended to believe" for the theologian) it is not true. Why then, in fact, did Bonhoeffer go back to Germany in 1939? The reason appears to be quite different: it is a question of "remaining true to." That can also contain something destructive. But it is the destructiveness of which John 15.13 speaks ("greater love has no man than this, that a man lay down his life for his friends") and that is not the destructiveness of suicide.

Furthermore, Van den Berk is disappointing in that he fails to mention the fact that Bonhoeffer strenuously tried to escape death. After his arrest he himself with great cunning and initial success, twisted and turned, trying in every possible way to ward off condemnation during his hearing. In prison he was sick with longing for the joys of the past in general and for his friends and fiancee in particular. In the poem "The Past" he wrote:

> I would inhale the fragrance of your being,
> absorb it, stay with it,
> as on hot summer days the heavy blossoms
> welcoming the bees

---

20. Ibid., 158.

intoxicate them,
as privet makes the hawk-moths drunken--[21]

(Reprinted with permission of Macmillan Publishing Company from *Letters and Papers From Prison*, Enlarged by Dietrich Bonhoeffer. Copyright © 1967 by SCM Press, Ltd.)

He ached to be free; he gave up a promising attempt at escape only because of his fear of reprisals against family members who were also under arrest. He continued to believe that he would survive; see, for example, his letter from prison on 15 December 1943, in which, in spite of wavering, he talks of finishing his <u>Ethics</u>, of marriage, of his longing to have a child and "not to vanish without a trace."[22]

Van den Berk's theory is clearly revealed in the title he gave to his thesis: "Bonhoeffer, captivating and captive." What he means by "captive" is that Bonhoeffer during his lifetime succeeded, to a degree, in becoming "free from," while failing, to the same degree, in becoming "free for."[23] But Sperna Weiland in his contribution to Eberhard Bethge's "Festschrift" rightly pointed out that for Bonhoeffer freedom always stood decisively "in relation to" and always was a synonym for "responsibility;" one may also add "love." All this does mean something, because the same author, without mentioning Van den Berk's name, clearly appreciates a psychological "contribution"; moreover he appears convinced that Bonhoeffer's hurried return from America also contained traces of feelings of homesickness--which one might call love for himself--and that they even played an excessive role.[24] That his return, indeed to the valley of death, had to do less with destruction than with solidarity may be

---

21. LPP, 321.

22. LPP, 163.

23. M.E.M. Van den Berk, <u>Bonhoeffer, boeiend en geboeid: de theologie van Dietrich Bonhoeffer in het licht van zijn persoonlijkheid,</u> (Boom Meppel, 1974), 314.

24. J. Sperna Weiland, "Ein Paar Gedanken über Freiheit" in <u>Wie eine Flaschenpost: Oekumenische Briefe und Beiträge für Eberhard Bethge</u>, eds. Heinz Eduard Tödt, et al. (München: Chr. Kaiser Verlag, 1979), 95-102.

judged from the letter he wrote to his American colleague Reinhold Niebuhr, once he had made up his mind to leave:

> I must live through this difficult period of our national history with the Christian people of Germany, I will have no right to participate in the reconstruction of Christian life in Germany after the war if I do not share the trials of this time with my people.... Christians in Germany will face the terrible alternative of either willing the defeat of their nation in order that Christian civilization may survive, or willing the victory of their nation and thereby destroying our civilization. I know which of these alternatives I must choose; but I cannot make that choice in security.[25]

The excessive feelings of guilt under which Bonhoeffer labored (rightly noted by Van den Berk), as expressed in the poem Jonah, can be interpreted as arising from his sense of solidarity with the sins of his people; here again a prophet, who in this case was not deserting, allowed himself to be thrown overboard as a sin offering.[26] These were the precise feelings that induced Bonhoeffer, long before the "Stuttgart Declaration of Guilt" (1945), to confess guilt (in his Ethics), in the name of the church in Germany, not least on behalf of "the weakest and most defenseless brothers of Jesus Christ," whom we are constrained to identify as the Jews.[27]

Meanwhile it is theologically intriguing (and not only theologically) to examine a fixation, which can certainly be found in Bonhoeffer, about the suffering of God, because this fixation can easily give occasion to (or be the consequence of) a deification of

---

25. GS I, 320. [Ed. note: This was Niebuhr's reconstruction and therefore not an exact quote.]

26. LPP, 398-399. [Ed. note: Jonah was written in October 1944 shortly after the danger to his family caused him to give up his plan to escape from prison.]

27. E, 114. See Eberhard Bethge, "Dietrich Bonhoeffer and the Jews," in ER, 80.

Suicide

suffering as such--an idolatry, from which indeed Bonhoeffer appears never to have been completely free. But this "basis" seems far too fragile to support the excessively bold assertions which Van den Berk permits himself.

V. THE HIGHEST FEAST?

With that we have not yet disposed of Van den Berk--nor of Bonhoeffer. For Bonhoeffer was not only preoccupied with suffering, but also with death. That is not only said by Van den Berk, but also by his closest friend, Bethge, who speaks of a Faszinosum which recurred throughout his life. Indeed as an eight-year-old, Bonhoeffer did not spare his twin sister an earnest discussion about death. We also read in his reminiscences that he "was eager at an early age to die a beautiful and pious death." And the title of the lectures which he planned to give in the University of Edinburgh in 1939 (the war prevented him from giving these) was to have been: "Death in the Christian Message." It must be noted that the reminiscence which we have just quoted was rounded off at the end with the words: "Now he kept silence over the beautiful and pious death and forgot it." But Van den Berk treats this as if it were an instance of repression, noting that the thought of death always came back.[28]

That sounds important indeed. But it is also significant that Van den Berk tends to underplay the fear of death, with which Bonhoeffer appears to be soaked from his youth and which surfaces again as an even more significant reminiscence, in his comment in the U.S.A. in 1931 ("The number of suicides mounted up in a frightful way" at the end of World War I)--or sublimates it by interpreting the fear or horror mentioned above, as a desire for death. The deepest explanation of it all is, according to him, that "Bonhoeffer suffered from a melancholy so deeply rooted that the idea that he might die

---

28. Van den Berk, "Bonhoeffer en de dood," 169. DB, 23-25.

terrified him far less than that he must remain alive."[29] Bonhoeffer was certainly not without melancholy (see below). But also he did not lack an opposing balance of hilaritas, of which the prison letters are as full as Van den Berk's article is empty. Likewise it is not to be denied that Bonhoeffer experienced strong feelings of desire for death. Van den Berk knows of this and takes strong examples from, among other places, the so-called "Fragment of a Drama."[30] It must be said of these feelings that they belonged precisely to his temptations. One may ask: who is not aware of such feelings? Besides, Bonhoeffer diagnosed those feelings, interrupted them and in that sense passed them by.

One text which Van den Berk mentions--but it is notable that he seems not to be prepared to consider it as central--attracts our attention in view of all this. I quote a verse from the well-known "Stations on the Way to Freedom," the one entitled, "<u>Death</u>":

<small>(Reprinted with permission of Macmillan Publishing Company from *Ethics* by Dietrich Bonhoeffer. Copyright 1955 by SCM Press, Ltd.)</small>

Come now, highest of feasts
On the way to freedom eternal,
Death, strike off the fetters,
Break down the walls that oppress us,
Our bedazzled soul and our ephemeral body,
That we may see at last
The sight which here was not vouchsafed us.
Freedom, we sought you long
In discipline, action, suffering.
Now as we die we see you
And know you at last,
Face to face.[31]

When this verse came into Bethge's hands he was troubled.

---

29. Ibid., 179.

30. Ibid., 174, and FP, 13-47.

31. E, 15.

And Sperna Weiland asked himself how far death as the highest feast fits in with freedom "in relation to."[32] For a moment, one is tempted to think of the Dutch poet Boutens: "Good Death, whose purest piping...." The difference is that this sentence can be understood only as pagan, while Bonhoeffer's poem can be read also as wholly Christian. Longing for death can be read here as longing for heaven, much in the manner of his last known words: "This is the end--but for me the beginning of life."[33] Moreover, freedom "in relation to" can here be read as "in relation to God." Be that as it may, one need not read a suicidal tendency into the verse. Otherwise, one would be obliged to interpret the Christian attitude per se as suicidal. But although Van den Berk explains the Christian faith of Bonhoeffer in masochistic terms, in such a way that one is led to ask if all the faithful are masochists, even for him the "Christian" attitude is not in itself fatal, let alone self-destructive.

VI. WHO AM I?

Yet it is not unthinkable that Bonhoeffer could have been animated with a very special passion for death. And that also owing to something, that produced a real desperation in his soul: a very special (he says it himself) acedia or tristitia, which, to use the words that Van den Berk has taken out of the mouth of Bethge, "pulled him down into the bleakest grey," so that "as it were, he stiffened in all his bones and no longer knew at all what was happening to him." He was in a state of hibernation.[34]

It was a deep state of depression, which of itself does not necessarily lead to suicide. It need not, but it could. Such states are known. The case of Luther is known and Bonhoeffer had felt this

---

32. Weiland, "Gedanken," 100.

33. DB, 830.

34. Van den Berk, Bonhoeffer, boeiend en geboeid, 100.

temptation, as we know from hints he left on a scrap of paper when he was first imprisoned: "Suicide, not out of a sense of guilt, but because basically I am already dead, balance sheet closed, finished."[35] Bonhoeffer was oppressed with the fear that he might betray someone and therefore was inclined to consider making an end to himself. But, leaving that motivation aside--for, after all, the interrogations, as a matter of fact, rather soon proved relatively innocuous and continued that way for a long time--he undoubtedly experienced the temptation to suicide and that during his life as a whole and not only in his cell. The issue is illuminated when one looks at the Bible study on "temptation," which he completed before the war. We were already thinking of that little book when we attributed to Bonhoeffer a certain desire for death in general. If we read that study very carefully, we are struck with the fact that these feelings can be understood with special reference to suicide, and also that this reveals its threat in combination with the acedia and tristitia, which afflicted him for many years. It was a combination which must have been felt on his pulses and in his bones.[36]

It is remarkable that all of this did not continue beyond the early days of his imprisonment. Bethge is very positive on this point[37] and has an explanation too.[38] One could say that this explanation amounts to the theory that for Bonhoeffer suicidal feelings do not absorb the idea of sacrifice, but on the contrary are themselves absorbed by that idea. This sacrifice changes the character of suicide. A sacrifice, if

---

35. DBg, 934, [Rothuizen's translation]. See DB, 736.

36. CF/T, 124. "The temptation to desperatio, to despair (acedia) , this despair drives him either into the sin of blasphemy or into self-destruction, to the extremity of despair, to suicide...."

37. DB, 736.

38. Eberhard Bethge, Am gegebenen Ort: Aufsätze und Reden, (München: Chr. Kaiser Verlag, 1979), 80. Bethge speaks about "Bonhoeffer's freedom for a few human partners in deadly peril," and draws the conclusion that "it is really true and not astonishing that he, Bonhoeffer , could precisely then announce that the tristitia and the acedia of earlier years had disappeared."

needed, is given in solidarity, not despair. It is as though Aristotle after all must still be taken seriously.

But we spoke of a very special acedia and tristitia and we did this because we see Bonhoeffer as prey to an extreme dejection, *not* (as Bethge expressly insists) out of weakness, but in the realization of an extraordinary strength which he displayed.[39] It is as if the strength created an almost deadly shyness in him, if not a fatal self-contempt; an unfathomable loneliness also. It is as though a person can no longer keep up the effort to become a kind of god and remain so-- rightly! Much if not all of this power was broken when he was imprisoned: or better, it was diminished by a half. In this connection, let us look at the famous verses in "Who am I?"[40] The verse with which the poem begins is,

> (Reprinted with permission of Macmillan Publishing Company from *Letters and Papers From Prison*, Enlarged by Dietrich Bonhoeffer. Copyright © 1967 by SCM Press, Ltd.)

> Who am I? They often tell me
> I would step from my cell's confinement
> Calmly, cheerfully, firmly,
> Like a squire from his country house ...

Following that verse, there comes a little later the verse that holds the question:

> Am I then really all that which other men tell of?
> Or am I only what I know of myself?
> Restless and longing, and sick,
> Like a bird in a cage,

---

39. DBg, 574: "These depressions.... were less the result of temptations which beset the weak than of the satiety and weariness of the extremely capable." See DB. 420.

40. LPP, 347-348.

Struggling for breath...

With these two accounts we can associate two characteristics: strength and weakness. We know that Bonhoeffer held out and that he conquered the temptation to commit suicide. How? We know from the Ethics that his answer is: not in one's own strength, but by grace.[41] When we take a closer look at the poem, "Who am I?", we want to say: that fits in, but only in part! As we come to the last letters (about the so-called "world-come-of-age") we realize that the contrasts between nature and grace, strength and weakness, no longer present him with a dilemma.

Bonhoeffer's ability to combine strength and weakness, nature and grace, is something always needed, something we can always use. He says in the Ethics, referring to suicide and the one contemplating it, among other things, the following:

> Such a man does not believe that God can again give a meaning and a right even to a ruined life, and indeed that it may be precisely through ruin that a life attains its true fulfillment.[42]

Is this the easy talk of one who happens to be exhibiting his own superb balance? Possibly, but there is more going on, because the man who wrote such things was himself also "ruined" and even would increasingly be "ruined" until the moment when nothing was left of him but dust on the ground and ashes in the wind. He is able to help us because he was the same man who wrote that the only thing that matters is that we be prepared to see in the fragment-and-no-more, that we all represent, the whole for which we are designed and created. In a shard he always saw the whole vase.

Who am I? That is a question he must also have thought of as,

---

41. E, 169.

42. E, 172.

Suicide

at the beginning of the war, he finished the paragraph about suicide in the Ethics, not only with the "prohibition" of suicide on the basis of grace, but also and finally with the humble question:

> But who would venture to say that God's grace and mercy cannot embrace and sustain even a man's failure to resist this hardest of all temptations?[43]

This embrace seems in Bonhoeffer's thought to encompass more than sheer pardon or remission of sins. It is a word written very near to an incident, which must have moved the author profoundly. It is a word written close to the departure from this life of a good acquaintance[44] along with his family. Before he and his immediate family committed suicide this acquaintance said like King David: "I would rather fall into the hands of the living God than into the hands of men." It was the artist Klepper who said it, married to a Jewess and father of two foster children, one of whom managed to emigrate to England just in time. Klepper's diary was published after the war. The title was: "Under the shadow of Thy wings." Speaking of embrace...

---

43. E, 172.

44. In English "acquaintance" implies that the persons concerned have met and this was not exactly the case. Bonhoeffer already knew a great deal about Klepper, but before being introduced to him (by Hammelsbeck) Klepper had died. See Oskar Hammelsbeck, "In Discussion with Bonhoeffer," in Wolf-Dieter Zimmermann and Ronald Gregor-Smith, eds., I Knew Dietrich Bonhoeffer, (London: E.T. Collins, and New York: Harper & Row, 1966), 181. DB, 618.

PART THREE: BONHOEFFER'S ETHICAL THEOLOGY

VI

BONHOEFFER'S DOCTRINE OF LOVE

John D. Godsey

I. INTRODUCTION

To speak of love in the theology of Dietrich Bonhoeffer is to go far beyond the word itself. The problem is not simply one of definition and usage, but the fact that, in one sense, "love" can be said to encompass the whole of God's creative and redeeming action toward and upon humanity and the whole of the Judaeo-Christian response to that action. The entire history of salvation can be placed under the overarching umbrella of love. Thus one must remain mindful in dealing with the concept "love" in Bonhoeffer's thought, as in the thought of most Christian theologians, that in reality this involves such broad subjects as God's grace, election, reconciliation, justification, and sanctification, on the one hand, and human gratitude, reverence, loyalty, and responsibility, on the other.

Because "love" can be seen to touch every point in the circumference of Christian theology, it will be necessary to limit this essay primarily to Bonhoeffer's own use of the term in his various writings. Even this itself is not an easy task, and no claim to an exhaustive treatment is being made here. Rather, what is attempted in the following is an introduction to the theme: tracing Bonhoeffer's understanding of both divine and human love during his theological career, indicating its general configuration and characteristics, and locating the center from which all flows and which holds everything together. Anticipating my conclusion, I believe that to an extraordinary degree all that Dietrich Bonhoeffer meant by *agape* love can be summed up in one name: Jesus Christ.

II. LOVE IN SOME RECENT THEOLOGY AND ETHICS

Before turning to Bonhoeffer, however, we shall better be able to appreciate and evaluate his contribution if we examine it against the background of some of the recent discussions of the subject. Most of these discussions are in one way or another dependent upon Anders Nygren's classic study entitled Agape and Eros,[1] the first part of which was published in original Swedish and German translation in 1930. It is interesting that in Bonhoeffer's Sanctorum Communio, his dissertation on The Communion of Saints which he presented at the University of Berlin in 1927 and published in modified form in 1930, he argues against the "fatal confusion of eros and *agape*"[2] and sets forth clearly his own interpretation of Christian love that avoids the confusion. In this work, and even in subsequent writings, Bonhoeffer seems to be unaware of Nygren, and the same is true of Heinrich

---

1. Anders Nygren, Agape and Eros: A Study of the Christian Idea of Love. Part I, trans. by A. G. Hebert (London: SPCK, 1932); Part II, Vol. I, trans. by Philip S. Watson (London: SPCK, 1938); Part II, Vol. II, trans. by P. S. Watson (London: SPCK, 1939); revised and partly retranslated in one volume by P. S. Watson (London: SPCK, 1953). The Swedish originals of Part I and Part II were published in 1930 and 1936, the German translations in 1930 and 1937. For English-language readers a convenient summary of Nygren's views is found in his article, "Eros and Agape," in A Handbook of Christian Theology (New York: Meridian Books, 1958). Critical essays, with a reply by Nygren, are found in Charles W. Kegley, ed., The Philosophy and Theology of Anders Nygren (Carbondale and Edwardsville: Southern Illinois University Press, 1970).

2. CS, 120.

Doctrine of Love 191

Scholz's significant monograph of 1929, Eros und Caritas,³ which differentiates between Platonic and Christian love. On the other hand, Bonhoeffer makes reference to Paul Althaus' Communio Sanctorum,⁴ a study of Luther's view of the Christian congregation in which Althaus contrasts eros and *agape* in his discussion of the concepts of love in Augustine and Luther. Since this book was published in 1929, Bonhoeffer states his regret that he could use it only sparingly but expresses delight in its support of his own views. Besides Althaus, Bonhoeffer gives evidence through the footnotes in his dissertation that he was in dialogue at this point with such authors as Augustine, Luther, Kierkegaard, Schleiermacher, Ritschl, Barth, Bultmann, Lohmeyer, Scheler and Seeberg.⁵

Nygren's Agape and Eros has been pivotal for all subsequent discussions about Christian love, because he so starkly contrasted the two types of love and formulated a theory of their relationship in the history of the church. *Agape*, a word unknown in classical Greek and used only sparingly in Hellenistic Greek, is deliberately chosen by the New Testament authors and the apostolic fathers to depict God's love revealed and given through Jesus Christ. According to Nygren, this divine love is not a human possibility, for it is the self-giving love, best seen in the cross of Christ, that forgives sins and binds us into one body--a selfless, serving and helping love.⁶ Nygren lists four features of the idea of *agape*: it is (1) spontaneous and "unmotivated," (2) "indifferent to value," (3) creative or, better, value-creating, and (4) the initiator of fellowship with God.⁷

---

3. Heinrich Scholz, Eros und Caritas (Halle [Saale]: Max Niemeyer Verlag, 1929).

4. Paul Althaus, Communio Sanctorum (Munich: Chr. Kaiser Verlag, 1929).

5. CS, 118-126, 226-228.

6. Nygren, "Eros and Agape," in A Handbook of Christian Theology, 97-98.

7. Nygren, Agape and Eros, 75-81. These four features are conveniently listed and cogently discussed in Gene Outka's Agape: An Ethical Analysis (New Haven and London: Yale University Press, 1972), 155-157.

Quite the contrary of this sacrificial and giving love, which depicts God's way to humanity, is eros: that egocentric, desiring kind of love which Nygren finds most favorably represented in Plato's "longing of the soul upward toward the world of ideas," but which in all of its forms is in the end a "wanting to have"--a grasping, taking, possessive love that is really self-love. For Nygren, these two loves are utterly incompatible, because they represent two entirely different orientations of life, two fundamental motifs that compete with each other. Eros is an egocentric love that entails self-affirmation, *agape* is a selfless love that involves self-surrender.[8] Eros is human love, *agape* divine. The word eros is avoided in the New Testament, but a third Greek word for love that is sometimes found in the New Testament is philia, which denotes friendship and affectionate feelings. However, philia is subsumed by Nygren under eros.

The history of the Christian idea of love, according to Nygren, is of how eros, stemming primarily from Greek Platonic thought, and *agape*, originating in the New Testament, were first joined together in Augustine's concept of caritas and then were sundered again in the Renaissance (primarily a revival of the eros-motif) and in the Reformation (primarily a revival of the *agape*-motif). Nygren interprets Augustine's view of love as the basic desire of humans to seek their own good; if that desire is directed toward worldly, perishable objects, it becomes cupiditas (false love), but if directed upward to God and the eternal, it is caritas or the right kind of love which alone satisfies their need for happiness. Love directed to God, then, becomes the right kind of self-love. The tension in the doctrine of caritas, with its mixture of eros and *agape*, is obvious: a love that is primarily desire, and thus egocentric, can hardly arrive at a genuinely selfless love of God.

In Nygren's judgment, it is Luther who returns the church to pure *agape*-love with his doctrine of justification by faith alone. In opposition to the dominant Catholic doctrine that what justifies us is

---

8. Nygren, Handbook, 99.

faith formed by love (fides caritate formata), Luther taught that humankind is justified sola fide. That is, it is God's *agape* in Christ alone and not our caritas that justifies. Thus our love, released from any possibility of merit with respect to salvation, is able to give itself freely out of sheer gratitude--"seeking not its own" and prepared to be, if necessary, a "lost love." With this, writes Nygren, Luther regained the New Testament understanding of "the *agape* of the cross."[9]

The responses to Nygren's view of the abyss between eros and *agape* have been many and varied.[10] As could be expected, Catholic theologians,[11] following the maxim that grace does not destroy but perfects nature, have attacked Nygren's "either/or" as being too sharp a division and have defended the "both/and" of Augustine's caritas. It is pointed out, for instance, that eros in its best Platonic sense is a love of highest devotion, even approaching *agape*, and not merely the self-

---

9. Ibid., 100-101.

10. The following are some of the most important works on love that have given detailed consideration to Nygren's views: John Burnaby, Amor Dei: A Study of St. Augustine's Teaching on the Love of God as the Motive of Christian Life (London: Hodder and Stoughton, 1938); M. C. D'Arcy, S.J., The Mind and Heart of Love: A Study in Eros and Agape (New York: Henry Holt, 1947); Victor Warnach, Agape: Die Liebe als Grundmotiv der neutestamentlichen Theologie (Düsseldorf: Patmos-Verlag, 1951); Paul Tillich, Love, Power and Justice (New York and London: Oxford University Press, 1954); Daniel Day Williams, The Spirit and the Forms of Love (New York and Evanston: Harper and Row, 1968); Gene Outka, Agape: An Ethical Analysis (New Haven and London: Yale University Press, 1972). See also Paul Tillich, Systematic Theology (Chicago: University of Chicago Press, 1951, 1957, 1963), Vol. I, 279-286, Vol. III, 129-138, 177-182; Reinhold Niebuhr, The Nature and Destiny of Man, 2 volumes (New York: Charles Scribner's Sons, 1941, 1943), Vol. II, 68-72, 81-87, 246-247; and Karl Barth, Church Dogmatics, IV/2 (Edinburgh: T. and T. Clark, 1958), 727-840. A writing which stems from the nineteenth century but which has played an important role in the modern discussion is Søren Kierkegaard, Works of Love (Princeton: Princeton University Press, 1946). Two significant biblical studies are James Moffatt, Love in The New Testament (London: Hodder and Stoughton, 1929) and Victor Paul Furnish, The Love Command in the New Testament (Nashville and New York: Abingdon Press, 1972).

11. See, for example, the discussion in D'Arcy, Mind and Heart, Ch. 2, especially in his appendix on caritas in Catholic tradition, 76-83. Discerning treatments of this and other issues are found in the essays by Victor Warnach, John M. Rist, John Burnaby, and Rudolf Johannesson in Kegley, ed., Philosophy and Theology.

assertive and acquisitive love characteristic of ancient religions and mystery cults. Even so Protestant a theologian as Karl Barth denies the incomparability of *agape* and eros, asserting that they have in common at least their point of departure in human beings. We love either in one way or the other. Neither is inherent in our nature, which itself is to be with God as our eternal Counterpart and, correspondingly, to be with our fellow humans--a structure chosen and willed and ordered by God. For Barth, *agape*-love is being free for God and our fellow humans, whereas eros-love is the new and absurd act of shutting ourselves off from this freedom. Unlike Nygren, who portrayed the history of the opposition between eros and *agape* as ending with Luther's destruction of the caritas-synthesis, Barth believes it is of the essence of this history that the opposition cannot be fully overcome this side of the eschaton. This does not mean, of course, that Christian *agape* is not superior, since it is grounded in God's love for humankind and not in our own self-love. Barth wants to assure us that God is on the side of erotic human beings, too.[12]

Barth's insistence that humans become liberated for *agape*-love, which according to him is always an act rather than an attitude, points to another difference with Nygren, who in a much-criticized passage depicted humans as mere instruments used to pass on God's love to their neighbors, "the tube, the channel, through which God's love flows."[13] For Nygren, then, God is also the subject of Christian love, a view which for Barth "effaces all clear contours and destroys all healthy distances."[14] Barth even prefers to speak of divine love as the *basis* or *ground* rather than the *origin* of human love. As such, he defines divine love as a love which is electing, purifying, and creative, that is, a love that is unmotivated except for God's own motivation, a

---

12. Barth, Church Dogmatics IV/2, 738-751.

13. Nygren, Agape and Eros, 735.

14. Ibid., 752.

Doctrine of Love

love that is grace(including judgment!) for sinners, and a love that causes those who are loved by God also to love.[15]

Jesus' "double command" to love God and to love one's neighbor as oneself (Matthew 22:34-40; Mark 12:28-34) has raised a number of issues that must be faced by interpreters of love. Are the two commands of equal importance? Are we really to love God, and if so, what does this mean? What is the content of neighbor-love, and who is our neighbor? Are we commanded to love ourselves, or does Jesus simply assume that we do this naturally? In any case, what is the content of "self-love"? And, finally, can love that is understood as *agape* be commanded at all?

Before addressing any of these issues, it should be pointed out that many commentators, Nygren among them, believe it is a fundamental mistake to begin one's interpretation of love in the New Testament with the "double commandment" rather than with God's act of justification by grace through faith. To do so, they contend, not only is likely to raise problems regarding the relationship between law and gospel, but also tends to beg the question as to whether *agape*-love can be commanded. Kierkegaard, who in his Works of Love centers his treatment of love around Jesus' two-fold commandment, insisted that love *must* be commanded; otherwise the sinful tendencies which linger on even in Christians would stifle obedience. This commandment is a "royal law" with divine authority, and only as such does it astonish and shock and offend. According to Kierkegaard, the command to love is not new, not to heathendom and certainly not to Judaism, but "the idea that love is a duty is an everlasting innovation--and everything has become new."[16]

But how can *agape*-love, which is free and spontaneous by its very nature, be commanded without turning it into spiritless legalism? Neither Nygren nor Barth believes that *agape* is well understood as something demanded. After all, God's love involves a self-giving

---

15. Ibid., 766-783.

16. Kierkegaard, Works of Love, 21.

which is liberating rather than demanding. In Barth's words, "If God's love as His free self-giving to and for man is the basis of man's love, it can have the character only of a liberation which man is given for an action which in correspondence to that of God can only be free and not one which is required or imposed from without, which he is constrained to fulfil."[17] Indeed, Barth believes "Thou shalt love" is a doubtful translation of Deuteronomy 6:5, which would be more accurately rendered "Thou *wilt* love."[18]

On the other side of this issue, however, we find Ernst Kinder, who in an article on "Agape in Luther" criticizes Nygren for disposing too quickly of the commandment of love by referring to its legal character. He claims that for Luther the commandment of love, which is the summary of the whole law, is not exhausted in its judging, condemning and death-dealing function but is also God's call to humans, inviting them to the life of salvation, helping them towards faith and helping faith transform itself into that love which is the fulfilment of humanity's created purpose.[19] In a similar vein, H. Richard Niebuhr considered the love commandment to be both demand and gift: "In the language of Christianity love of God and neighbor is both 'law' and 'gospel'; it is both the requirement laid on man by the Determiner of all things and the gift given, albeit in incompleteness, by the self-giving of the Beloved."[20] Niebuhr defines the purpose of the church to be "the increase among men of the love of God and neighbor."[21]

Another debated question regarding the double commandment

---

17. Barth, Church Dogmatics IV/2, 781.

18. Ibid., 782.

19. Kegley, Philosophy and Theology, 218-219.

20. H. Richard Niebuhr, The Purpose of the Church and Its Ministry (New York: Harper and Brothers, 1956), 32.

21. Ibid., 31. Cf. Victor Furnish, who emphasizes that the love command is the claim of God, not to the law but to the person and work of Christ. See The Love Command in the New Testament, 199-205.

Doctrine of Love 197

is whether there can be such a thing as "love for God." Nygren, who is chary of using *agape* to describe humankind's relation to God and prefers to use the term "faith" instead, points out that *agape* is spontaneous, unmotivated love, whereas in relation to God, human love can never be spontaneous and unmotivated but is always responsive. Paul, he contends, is reluctant to speak of humankind's "*agape* for God," since human love can never be of the same quality and magnitude as God's love for humanity.[22] Outka, who agrees that the meaning of "love" in "love for God" and "love for neighbor" cannot be altogether univocal, nevertheless denies that "faith" is an adequate substitute for "love." Faith as pure receptivity vis-à-vis God, he contends, does not exhaust the meaning of response, which includes love for God as the active element, the placing of the self at God's disposal. "Faith," says Outka, "is being grasped by God and love is adhering to Him."[23]

Other critics of Nygren on this point indicate that "love for God" is clearly to be found not only in the Synoptic Gospels but also in Paul. Victor Warnach refers to Romans 8:28, and First Corinthians 2:9, 8:3; and John Rist adds to this list Ephesians 6:24.[24] Barth, in an illuminating excursus in Church Dogmatics in which he recants his earlier "Puritanical" opposition to the notion of humankind's spontaneous love for God and Jesus, affirms unabashedly that we *can* love God and that this love for God, which means to be interested in God-in-Christ and to give ourselves to God, is the basis for our liberation for obedience to God and love for our neighbor.[25] Thus for Barth, with much of Catholic tradition and in contrast to Nygren, "love for God" cannot be translated without loss into either faith or

---

22. Nygren, Agape and Eros, 213.

23. Outka, Agape, 51.

24. Kegley, Philosophy and Theology, 149, 172.

25. Barth, Church Dogmatics IV/2, 795-798.

neighbor-love.[26]

Because Jesus himself linked so closely together the commandments to love God and to love your neighbor as yourself, virtually all interpreters consider the two commandments to be inseparable and interrelated. However, differences arise over the definition of neighbor and the content of neighbor-love. "Neighbor" can be viewed as the human being who, because of proximity and need, lays claim to our attention; but others emphasize that neighbor-love must be extended to all of humanity. Barth, unlike most interpreters, believes that in the Bible itself "neighbor" is generally restricted to "fellow Israelite" or later, in the New Testament, to the community of Jesus Christ. Thus he does not think Christian love for the neighbor should automatically be turned into a universal love of humanity, although he also would not restrict it to the baptized. According to him, we must be constantly open to God's leading in this matter, prepared to love tomorrow where we did not love today.[27] Perhaps no one has defined the neighbor more inclusively than H. Richard Niebuhr in the following statement:

> He is the near one and the far one; the one beside the road I travel here and now; the one removed from me by distances in time and space, in convictions and loyalties. He is my friend, the one who has shown compassion toward me; and my enemy, who fights against me. He is the one in need, in whose hunger, nakedness, imprisonment and illness I see or ought to see the universal suffering servant. He is the oppressed one who has not risen in rebellion against my oppression nor rewarded me according to my deserts as individual or member of a heedlessly exploiting group. He is the compassionate one who ministers to my needs: the

---

26. See Outka, Agape, 255.

27. Barth, Church Dogmatics IV/2, 808.

stranger who takes me in; the father and mother, sister and brother. In him the image of the universal redeemer is seen as in a glass darkly. Christ is my neighbor, but the Christ in my neighbor is not Jesus; it is rather the eternal son of God incarnate in Jesus, revealed in Jesus Christ. The neighbor is in past and present and future, yet he is not simply mankind in its totality but rather in its articulation, the community of individuals and individuals in community. He is Augustine in the Roman Catholic Church and Socrates in Athens, and the Russian people, and the unborn generations who will bear the consequences of our failures, future persons for whom we are administering the entrusted wealth of nature and other greater common gifts. He is man and he is angel and he is animal and inorganic being, all that participates in being.[28]

In defining "neighbor," it is important to note that Jesus commanded his followers to love their *enemies*.[29] According to Ethelbert Stauffer, "In one demand Jesus consciously opposed Jewish tradition, namely, the demand to love one's enemies."[30] This is a new demand of a new age, the coming Kingdom of God, and it points to grace. Victor Furnish bids us remember that "this whole section of Matthew's 'Sermon' stands under the heading of 5:20 which urges that one's righteousness 'exceed' that of the scribes and the Pharisees. Love of enemies is thus a further distinguishing mark of the higher righteousness and of Christian discipleship."[31]

---

28. Niebuhr, Purpose of the Church, (New York: Harper & Brothers), 38.

29. Matthew 5:43-44.

30. Gerhard Kittel and Gerhard Friedrich, eds., and Geoffrey W. Bromiley, trans., Theological Dictionary of the New Testament, Vol.1 (Grand Rapids, Mich.: Eerdmans, 1964), 46.

31. Ibid., 48.

How is one to define the content of neighbor-love? For Nygren, this is not a special problem, because for him loving our neighbor amounts to God's *agape* being channeled to the neighbor through us. Since the subject of *agape* is God, the same four features of *agape* mentioned earlier apply. But for those theologians who believe neighbor-love has to do with a human *agape* that is elicited by but not identical with divine love or grace, neighbor-love is often defined by what Outka calls "equal regard," by which he means "a regard for the neighbor which in crucial respects is independent and unalterable" and "is for every person qua human existent."[32] Barth basically agrees that in *agape*-love the essential humanity of the other is respected; there occurs an I-Thou encounter, a perception of the other and a self-disclosure, genuine conversation, the offering and receiving of assistance, and all this with joy. There is therefore self-giving with no expectation of return, "identification with his interests in utter independence of his attractiveness."[33] To be sure, "equal regard" for these theologians does not always mean identical treatment nor does it mean submission to the exploitation of the other.

Kierkegaard, too, emphasizes that neighbor-love is "the eternal equality in loving," which is the opposite of showing partiality, as is the case with earthly love or friendship.[34] But, above all, it is H. Richard Niebuhr who gives a moving description of the meaning of love of neighbor in terms of rejoicing, gratitude, reverence and loyalty:

> Love is rejoicing over the existence of the beloved one; it is the desire that he be rather than not be; it is longing for his presence when he is absent; it is happiness in the thought of him; it is profound satisfaction over everything that makes him great and glorious. Love is

---

32. Outka, 9.

33. Barth, Church Dogmatics IV/2, 745.

34. Kierkegaard, Works of Love, 48.

gratitude; it is thankfulness for the existence of the beloved; it is the happy acceptance of everything that he gives without the jealous feeling that the self ought to be able to do as much; it is a gratitude that does not seek equality; it is wonder over the other's gift in companionship. Love is reverence: it keeps its distance even as it draws near; it does not seek to absorb the other in the self or want to be absorbed by it; it rejoices in the otherness of the other; it desires the beloved to be what he is and does not seek to refashion him into a replica of the self or to make him a means to the self's advancement. As reverence love is and seeks knowledge of the other, not by way of curiosity nor for the sake of gaining power but in rejoicing and in wonder. In all such love there is an element of that "holy fear" which is not a form of flight but rather deep respect for the otherness of the beloved and the profound unwillingness to violate his integrity. Love is loyalty; it is the willingness to let the self be destroyed rather than the other cease to be; it is the commitment of the self by self-binding will to make the other great. It is loyalty, too, to the other's cause--to his loyalty.[35]

In addition to "equal regard" as the normative meaning of neighbor-love, some theologians emphasize "self-sacrifice" and others "mutuality." Reinhold Niebuhr, for instance, contends that "disinterested love" is bound to end in self-sacrifice in this life.[36] However, Outka rightly points out that the meaning of a concept such as self-sacrifice is much more difficult to isolate than that of equal

---

35. Ibid., 35.

36. Niebuhr, The Nature and Destiny of Man, Vol 2, 72. This is cited in Outka, Agape, 24.

regard.37 On the other hand, theologians as different as Williams, D'Arcy and Tillich insist that *agape*-love need not be "disinterested" but may be expressed in mutual personal and social relationships. They argue that relationships between friends and even in communities need not be poisoned by nefarious self-love but may embody genuine equal regard.38

Another major issue centers around the question of "self-love." Jesus said that the second great commandment, like unto the first (which is to love God), is this: "You shall love your neighbor as yourself."39 Are we commanded to love ourselves, or does Jesus merely *presume* self-love to be our "natural" condition and thus command us to love the neighbor as we already love ourselves without being commanded to do so? Is not self-love the essence of eros-love rather than of *agape*-love? Is it not sinful self-centered love? Finally, does not *agape* require an object, an "other" who is opposite the lover, a beloved to whom one gives oneself? If so, is it possible for a self to love its own self?

In his ethical analysis of *agape*, Outka sets forth four different value judgments of "self-love": (1) as wholly nefarious (self-love is basically "acquisitiveness," the self seeking its own desired ends); (2) as normal, reasonable, prudent (self-love is not especially praiseworthy but not necessarily blameworthy); (3) as justified derivatively (if Christians are to love their neighbor, then they are responsible for developing and using all their natural capacities in order to benefit others); (4) as a definite obligation (self-love as self-respect may refer to laudable attitudes limited not to prudence but to courage, e.g. sticking to a job though one's heart is not in it; or self-love as coincident with neighbor-love).40

---

37. Ibid., 25.

38. See the discussion of "mutuality" in Outka, Agape 34-37.

39. Matthew 22:39; Mark 12:31; Luke 10:27.

40. Outka, Agape, 55-74.

Doctrine of Love

Nygren, who believes he is also rightly interpreting Paul and Luther, condemns self-love as being inevitably that erotic, egocentric love which is the very opposite of neighbor-love. "*Agape*," he states, "excludes all self-love. Christianity does not recognize self-love as a legitimate form of love."[41] Many New Testament scholars, however, dispute Nygren's claim that the "as ourself" in the second great commandment means that love of neighbor must replace love of self, i.e., that we must love our neighbor as we have been in the habit of loving ourselves. Rist believes the obvious interpretation is "that we should love our neighbors in the same way as we love ourselves. Thus we shall love both ourselves and our neighbors equally, because both we and they are children of God."[42] Warnach states that while true *agape* is never egoistic or egocentric, *agape* does not exclude orderly self-assertion and self-love.[43] Furnish thinks "as yourself" means simply to love the neighbor as you already naturally love yourself, but he cautions that it also means that the neighbor can be no more avoided than one's own self.[44] Bultmann warns that although self-love is presupposed in the command, it is not something we need to learn and cultivate but a natural tendency we need to overcome.[45]

Barth is reluctant to speak of self-love, because he believes love must have an object; but when he discusses self-love in the context of the second great commandment, he finds it at most not blameworthy but also not a definite obligation. He, like most others, makes a distinction between healthy self-esteem and sinful selfishness, but he believes we must always be on guard against the tendency toward the latter. Unlike Nygren, he distinguishes sharply between an acquisitive

---

41. Nygren, Agape and Eros, 217.

42. Kegley, Philosophy and Theology, 170.

43. Ibid., 148.

44. Furnish, The Love Command, 50.

45. Rudolf Bultmann, Jesus and the Word, trans. L. P. Smith and E. H. Lantero (New York: Charles Scribner's Sons, 1958), 116.

notion of eros and human nature.⁴⁶ D'Arcy, on the other hand, is an example of a theologian who defends self-love as a definite obligation, taking self-love and neighbor-love to be always coincident.⁴⁷

One further issue of importance must be mentioned, namely, the relation between love and justice. Here again Outka presents a convenient and lucid discussion of what is a notoriously difficult subject that engages Christian ethicists with special urgency.⁴⁸ "Justice" as a concept is itself very difficult to define. Most agree that it has something to do with the notion of suum cuique: giving each person his or her due. Most also agree that love must assume the form of justice when one is dealing not with a particular neighbor but with a neighborhood. In Paul Ramsey's words, "Justice may be defined as what Christian love does when confronted by two or more neighbors."⁴⁹

Outka distinguishes between such different concepts of justice as (1) similar treatment for similar cases (what is right for one person cannot be wrong for another similarly circumstanced); (2) to each according to his merit or works (advantages or disadvantages are to be apportioned on the basis of a person's efforts or achievement); (3) to each the same thing (equal consideration of and identification with the interests of each person); (4) to each according to his needs (differential treatment based on the need of persons for what is essential for their life and welfare). Concluding that none of these concepts of justice coincides with equal regard, Outka nevertheless believes that "the overlap is greatest between *agape* and a notion of

---

46. On Barth's view of these matters, see Outka's chapter on "Karl Barth on Agape" in his book Agape, especially 227.

47. See Outka, 73.

48. Ibid., 75-92.

49. Paul Ramsey, Basic Christian Ethics (New York: Charles Scribner's Sons, 1950), 243.

Doctrine of Love 205

justice which is egalitarian."⁵⁰

With respect to the relationship between *agape* and justice, three positions become evident in the relevant literature: they can be viewed as opposed, distinguished, or identified. In Outka's judgment, the first position is represented by Nygren; the second in varying ways by Reinhold Niebuhr, Emil Brunner, and Gérard Gilleman; and the third by Joseph Fletcher. Nygren, he claims, sees *agape* and justice opposed in Jesus' parable of the laborers in the vineyard (Matthew 20:1-16). Justice in this case would be "to each according to his works," but God's love is "unmotivated" and cannot be regulated by such a principle. Niebuhr, according to Outka, sometimes finds the requirements of love and justice to be compatible, sometimes not. In the first instance, *agape* may involve doing more than justice requires but never less; in the second, *agape* and justice may imply conflicting kinds of actions between which one must choose, and without the advantage of an absolute priority either way. Fletcher is selected to represent the position that identifies love and justice, for he writes: "Love and justice are the same, for love is justice distributed, nothing else."⁵¹ Fletcher refuses to confine love to one-to-one relationships and would change the commandment to read, "You shall love your neighbors as yourself." Justice, then, is love coping with situations where distribution is called for.

What becomes clear is that the three positions identified and illustrated above assume different notions of justice. In these complex matters, the most Outka can say in general is that *agape* will most likely affect priorities when dealing with questions of justice: needs will precede merit, other sorts of differences will be played down, and privilege will always have to be justified.

This brief, limited, and all too simplistic review of issues and positions regarding love in recent theological and ethical writings

---

50. Outka, Agape, 92.

51. Joseph Fletcher, Situation Ethics: The New Morality (Philadelphia: The Westminster Press, 1966), 87. Cited in Outka, Agape, 85.

affords some background against which Bonhoeffer's doctrine of love can be projected. Even though many of these writings have been published since Bonhoeffer's death in 1945, it is hoped that they will prove helpful in distinguishing and evaluating Bonhoeffer's own contribution to what tend to be perennial themes and issues.

III. THE CONCEPT OF LOVE IN BONHOEFFER'S WRITINGS

Love is a central concept in Bonhoeffer's theology from beginning to end. Therefore an examination of his understanding of love in his various writings should shed light on the development of Bonhoeffer's theology and ethics, as well as indicate his stand on many of the issues regarding love that have been delineated above. This presentation of what Bonhoeffer actually wrote about love from time to time will generally follow a chronological order.

A. THE EARLY YEARS: 1927-1933

The Communion of Saints (Sanctorum Communio), Bonhoeffer's first work, was a dissertation presented to the Theological Faculty of the University of Berlin in 1927, when he was only twenty-one. Its sub-title was "A Dogmatic Inquiry into the Sociology of the Church," and the investigation discloses even at this young age a rich and profound grasp of the meaning of Christian love.

Projecting backward according to what he called "the logic of dogmatics," Bonhoeffer posits love in humanity's primal state, whether between God and humankind or between humans, to entail a communion between I and I. This community of immediate and mutual love is a community of ruling and serving: God rules over humankind by limitless serving; among humans this changes to mutual service under the rule of God. When sin enters in through the Fall, these relationships undergo drastic alteration. Community is broken, love of self replaces love of others, and from this follows humankind's autonomy, estrangement, the will to dominate, and bondage to self. In the midst of this tragic situation, God acts to bring about reconciliation--the Word becomes flesh! The love of God revealed in Jesus Christ's life, crucifixion, and resurrection is brought to the hearts of humans by the Holy Spirit. Hearts are thereby made new with a will for good, and a new community called "church" arises. This community has love as its life-principle: this means that in it the thou of the other person meets my I no longer as law but as gospel, which is to say it becomes an object of love. Mutual love and service are again made possible by Christ, who fulfills my claim on the other I by loving me and thereby freeing my I from its self-bondage and letting me love the other. New social relationships are established; old social attitudes are overcome. Faith recognizes and receives God's lordship; love makes the Kingdom of God actual.[52]

Bonhoeffer states that a humanitarian viewpoint fatefully confuses eros and *agape*. The New Testament, he asserts, defines love in two distinct ways: positively, as the love of God revealed in Jesus Christ; and negatively, as our love of ourselves. Thus our point of departure, he insisted, must not be from our love for God or for other humans, but only from the love of God which reveals itself in the cross of Christ, in our justification, and in the founding of the Church, and from our egoistic attitude toward ourselves. The former shows us love's foundation, its depth and meaning, the latter the hardness with which that love turns against ourselves. Although the moral command to love is not specifically Christian, the reality of love, in Bonhoeffer's view, is present only in Christ and his church. Christian love, then, has a special meaning, which Bonhoeffer details in the following statements:

1. Christian love is not a human possibility. It has nothing to do with the humanitarian ideas of affection, sympathy, eroticism, and so on.

2. Christian love is possible only through faith in Christ and through the work of the Holy Spirit. It has its basis in obedience to the work of Christ and means that we surrender our will to Christ and make no claim on God or our neighbor.

---

52. CS, 40-44, 118-136.

3. Christian love, as an act of the will, is purposive. God's will for the other human is determinative, and the will of God is that the other be subject to God's lordship. How to carry out this aim varies according to circumstances and must be perceived by each individual by himself or herself.

4. Christian love loves the real neighbor. This is not because of the other human's attractiveness, but because he or she acts as a thou and makes me experience God's claim in this thou. Moreover, insisted Bonhoeffer, love is not directed to God *in* the neighbor but to the concrete thou. It is at this point that Bonhoeffer criticizes Karl Barth for suggesting in his The Epistle to the Romans that we are to love "the One" in the neighbor. No, protests Bonhoeffer, we are not to love God in the neighbor, but the neighbor himself or herself. Other humans are of supreme significance in themselves. The other is to be loved by placing our entire self at his or her service.

5. Christian love knows no limits. It seeks the realization of God's lordship absolutely everywhere. Therefore, God's command to love our neighbor must be obeyed without any reservations.

Bonhoeffer sums up his view of neighbor-love by stating that it is our will for God's will for the other human being. We are not called to love the neighbor in God's place or to love God in the neighbor; rather, we are to put the neighbor in our own place and to love the neighbor instead of ourselves.[53]

The church, as Bonhoeffer defines it in The Communion of Saints, is a community in which persons are not only *with* one another but also *for* one another. Being for one another is actualized through an act of love which Bonhoeffer believed could take place in three

---

53. CS, 120-122. For Bonhoeffer's extensive controversy with Barth's interpretation in The Epistle to the Romans, see note 47 on 226-227. Besides Bonhoeffer's disagreement with Barth over whether the object of Christian love is God *in* the neighbor or the neighbor himself/herself, Bonhoeffer has another difference with Barth over the conception of communio. For Bonhoeffer, "to be one" with God and with one's neighbor is altogether different from having communion with either; Barth, he claims, makes the two things synonymous. Where there is only love of the One in the other, warned Bonhoeffer, there is ultimately a creeping danger of Romanticism.

ways: (1) renunciatory, active work for our neighbor; (2) prayers of intercession; and (3) the mutual granting of the forgiveness of sins in God's name. With all of them, emphasized Bonhoeffer, it is a question of abandoning oneself for the neighbor, being ready to do and bear everything in the neighbor's stead, and, if need be, to sacrifice oneself, i.e. to act vicariously, for the neighbor. Even if vicarious action is seldom actualized, said Bonhoeffer, the intention is there in every genuine act of love.[54]

Love is not only the life-principle of the church but also the aim of the Kingdom of God. God's will, asserted Bonhoeffer, is to build a kingdom of persons in which God's love conquers and rules. Thus the divine love is both a means to an end and an end in itself; it serves to realize the community and reigns in it. The goal of God's will, then, is nothing other than the loving communion of the saints.[55]

The Communion of Saints, which won for Bonhoeffer his degree of Licentiate of Theology in 1927, was not published until 1930, and then in an abridged form. In the meantime, Bonhoeffer spent 1928-29 as a vicar in Barcelona, Spain, after which he returned to Berlin, where he wrote his habilitation dissertation on Act and Being, which was published in 1931 and gained for him the privilege of lecturing in theology at the University.

In Barcelona Bonhoeffer preached regularly and occasionally presented lectures to the German-speaking congregation. In both sermons and lectures, references to love are found from time to time. For instance, in a lecture entitled "What is a Christian Ethic?" he stated: "There are countless ways from man to God, and therefore there are also countless ethics, but there is only one way from God to man, and that is the way of love in Christ, the way of the cross."[56] At another point he admitted that the commandment of love is not

---

54. CS, 130.

55. CS, 183-184.

56. NRS, 37.

exclusively Christian, that it was already widespread at the time of Jesus. So what is new about Jesus' commandment of love? What is "new," he explained, is *who* said it: the one who is able to place humans before God, to reveal the divine will, and to set us free for ethical action.[57] In a sermon on the church, preached on 29 July 1928, Bonhoeffer cites three wonderful powers of the Christian community: offering, intercession and forgiveness of sins--all of which are summarized in the word "love," as God has shown it to us.[58]

Act and Being is a rather technical discussion of the concept of revelation and thus yields little material on the question of love. However, Bonhoeffer makes the following important statement about God's freedom, which has a definite bearing on God's love:

> In revelation it is a question less of God's freedom on the far side of us, i.e. his eternal isolation and aseity, than of his forth-proceeding, his *given* Word, his bond in which he has bound himself, of his freedom as it is most strongly attested in his having freely bound himself to historical man, having placed himself at man's disposal. God is not free *of* man but *for* man. Christ is the Word of his freedom.[59]

During the academic year 1930-31 Bonhoeffer was a Sloane Fellow at Union Theological Seminary in New York. From time to time he was asked to preach to American audiences, and the first time he preached in English he spoke on the "Love of God," taking as his text I John 4:16--"So we know and believe the love God has for us. God is love, and he who abides in love abides in God, and God abides in him." In the sermon Bonhoeffer spoke of how both Americans and Germans, indeed all peoples, are one in Christ. "God," he said, "has erected a strange, marvellous and wonderful sign in the world, where

---

57. NRS, 38-39.

58. GS V, 444.

59. AB, 90.

Doctrine of Love

we all could find him--I mean the cross of Jesus Christ, the cross of the suffering love of God."[60] Toward the end he exhorts the young people of his audience: "let us love one another, let us build in faith and love one holy Christianity, one brotherhood, with God the Father, and Christ the Lord, and the Holy Spirit as the sanctifying power."[61]

Returning to Berlin in the summer of 1931, Bonhoeffer took up his duties as a lecturer in theology at the University, a responsibility he carried out for the next two years. During the Winter semester of 1932-33, he presented an important set of lectures which were later published under the title <u>Creation and Fall: A Theological Interpretation of Genesis 1-3</u>. The work is shot through with insights on the nature and purpose of love. Bonhoeffer emphasizes God's love for what has been created prior to the creation of human beings, yet "God does not recognize himself in his work." So in the human creature God lovingly "creates his image on the earth." Humans are like the Creator in that they are free, but Bonhoeffer stresses that freedom is in truth a relationship of love between two persons. That is, being free means "being free for the other," because the other has bound me to him or her. The God who is free creates humans who are free for God. Thus "the creature loves the Creator because the Creator loves the creature."[62]

That humans are "created in the image of God," stated Bonhoeffer, means that they are created male and female in a relationship of love, a relationship that in an analogous way reflects God's love for humankind, a love revealed definitively in Christ. When Bonhoeffer interprets the story of Adam and Eve in Genesis 2, the further meaning of this relationship becomes evident. The other person, Eve, is the limit placed upon Adam by God that addresses him in both his freedom and his creatureliness. In mercy, explains

---

60. NRS, 73.

61. NRS, 80.

62. CF/T, 25, 35, 37, 38.

Bonhoeffer, the Creator knew that humankind's creaturely, free life can only be borne in limitation if it is loved, and so God created a companion for Adam who is simultaneously the embodiment of his limit and the object of his love. He is to love this limit and not to transgress it because of his love, which means that the two, who remain *two* as the creatures of God, become *one* body, i.e., belong to each other in love. "In the creation of the other person," wrote Bonhoeffer, "freedom and creatureliness are bound together in love." Sexuality, according to Bonhoeffer, is in its original sense the expression of this two-sidedness of being both an individual and being one with the other person, the ultimate realization of our belonging to one another. With the "Fall," however, the situation changes drastically: the limit is transgressed and one person no longer sees the other person in love, as grace. Here the story of creation and fall ends and becomes a part of the larger story of God's loving, redemptive activity on behalf of humankind.[63]

The center of the "larger story" was partially set forth in lectures on christology during the Summer semester of 1933, lectures that were later reconstructed from students' notes and published in the book Christ the Center. The word "love" is rarely used in this work, but in reality the whole theme has to do with the incarnation of God's love in the "humiliated One" who assumes our sinful flesh and atones for our sin on the cross: the God-Man Jesus Christ, who is the hidden center of human existence, history and nature; and who is present with us as Word, Sacrament and Church.

There is one final aspect of Bonhoeffer's doctrine of love that appears already in these early days of his career, and that is his love of the earth. He appreciated this theme in Nietzsche's writings, and it becomes apparent here and there in his own writing. For instance, in a lecture in November 1932 on "Thy Kingdom Come! The Prayer of the Church for God's Kingdom on Earth," he warns against otherworldly abandonment of the earth. Said he: "Whoever loves God... loves him

---

63. CF/T, 38, 61-62., 78.

Doctrine of Love 213

as Lord of the earth as it is; and whoever loves the earth loves it as God's earth. Whoever loves God's kingdom, loves it wholly as God's kingdom, but he also loves it as God's kingdom on earth."[64]

B. THE MIDDLE YEARS: 1933-1939

Adolf Hitler, head of the National Socialist party, was appointed chancellor of the Third German Reich on 30 January 1933. After that, nothing was the same for Dietrich Bonhoeffer or, for that matter, for any German. Soon what is called the German Church Struggle began between those Protestant churches that fought against any accommodation to the Nazis' racial and dictatorial policies (the "Confessing Church") and those that accepted and advocated those policies (the "German Christians"). From the outset Bonhoeffer was on the side of the Confessing Church, taking an active role in its founding and giving staunch support during the years of its existence. In the fall of 1933 he left Germany to become pastor of two German-speaking congregations in London. The move was a sign of his protest against the introduction of the government's anti-Semitic "Aryan Clause" into his own Church of the Old Prussian Union, as well as a chance to further ecumenical relations outside Germany on behalf of the Confessing Church.

The situation in Nazi Germany raised many questions for Bonhoeffer, not least of which concerned the doctrine of love. How does one love "the enemy," especially when the enemy claims to be within the church? How does one love neighbors who are innocent victims of unjust racial policies? These questions will increase in intensity as matters worsen in his homeland during the second half of the decade, and more and more Bonhoeffer will turn to thoughts of the *suffering* love of God and the divine call for humans to suffer for the oppressed. Already in London, however, in a sermon in early 1934 on the text, "My strength is made perfect in weakness" (II Corinthians

---

64. "Thy Kingdom Come!" trans. in John D. Godsey, ed., Preface to Bonhoeffer (Philadelphia: Fortress Press, 1965), 32.

12:9), Bonhoeffer said: "Our God is a suffering God. Suffering forms man into the image of God. The suffering man is in the likeness of God."65

On four successive Sundays in the fall of 1934 Bonhoeffer preached sermons on I Corinthians 13, Paul's great chapter on *agape*-love. This rich resource for Bonhoeffer's view of love, as it is filtered through his interpretation of Paul, provides more evidence of his sharp contrast between *agape* and eros and between love for God and neighbor, on the one hand, and self-love, on the other. In his final sermon, which fell on Reformation Day, Bonhoeffer warned that the church which is great in faith must be still greater in love. A church of faith--and be it the most confessionally true and most orthodox faith--which is not still more a church of pure and encompassing love, he said, is good for nothing.66

In the spring of 1935 Bonhoeffer was called back to Germany to lead one of the Confessing Church's Training Seminaries (Predigerseminare) for ministerial candidates who could no longer attend those of the Reich Church. Thus began his extraordinary teaching experiences, first at Zingst on the Baltic Sea and then at the "Brüderhaus" in the village of Finkenwalde, near Stettin. But during this period Bonhoeffer continued his work in the ongoing church struggle and as a pastor. An example of the former is his lecture on "The Question of the Boundaries of the Church and Church Union" in April 1936, in which he declared that it is no work of mercy for the church to deny its boundaries, such as those drawn by the pseudo-church of the "German Christians." "The true church," he said, "comes up against boundaries. In recognizing them it does the work of love towards men by honouring the truth. *Extra ecclesiam nulla salus*."67

---

65. GS IV, 182.

66. GS V, 534-560.

67. WF, 95.

Doctrine of Love

As a pastor Bonhoeffer often preached and occasionally conducted weddings for his students and others. His view of love in marriage emerges clearly in a wedding sermon in the summer of 1936. He chose as his text John 13:34: "A new commandment I give to you, that you love one another; even as I have loved you, that you also love one another." His emphasis in the sermon is that love as a commandment of Jesus Christ is different from love that comes out of the human heart. He stressed that of course we should also be thankful for the human love that is present in the wedding and which is supported and blessed by God's own affirmation of marriage as an institution. Nevertheless, warned Bonhoeffer, the love that comes from the human heart is unfortunately cursed by instability and a tinge of self-seeking. This is true in the best of circumstances, and so we need God's help if our love is to be everlasting, selfless and pure. And so Jesus gives us a new commandment: that we should love one another as he has loved us. That is something new! Bonhoeffer then proceeds to describe the love of Jesus Christ for us--that it is a love which is eternal, which avoids no pain or suffering to help us, which loves us as we are, which forgives us our sins, and which prays and intercedes for us daily. Bonhoeffer ends the sermon with this exhortation: "Love one another not only as husband and wife but as Christians."[68]

In 1937 Bonhoeffer published The Cost of Discipleship, a major work that culminated many years of wrestling with Jesus' Sermon on the Mount (Matthew 5-7). That its message of what it means to be a follower of Christ in the modern world was sharpened by the deteriorating situation in Germany can hardly be gainsaid, but these words of Jesus had been a challenge to Bonhoeffer in a personal way since the early 1930s.[69] What was entailed, I think, was not a matter simply of curbing his own ego-strength but also of facing

---

68. GS IV, 463-465.

69. For an illuminating discussion of Bonhoeffer's problems with his own ego-strength during the 1930s, see SCH, Chapter IV.

squarely for himself the age-old theological problem of the relation between justification and sanctification, and in his own particular Lutheran heritage, the problem of law and gospel. How, indeed, are faith and love to be related? If we have "faith," does that mean that we no longer have to be concerned with "good works," with loving acts?

Bonhoeffer obviously wanted to overcome an attitude that was widespread in his own church that since salvation according to Luther is "by faith alone," obedience is not of great concern. But, argued Bonhoeffer, this is to turn the "costly grace" of Jesus Christ into the "cheap grace" of doing as little as possible. This is to completely misunderstand Luther, who never dreamed of faith without obedience, without discipleship. And so Bonhoeffer stated his basic thesis in two propositions that are equally true: "only he who believes is obedient, and only he who is obedient believes."[70]

To support and illuminate this thesis, Bonhoeffer devotes the major part of The Cost of Discipleship to a detailed exposition of the Sermon on the Mount. All of Jesus' teachings have a bearing on the meaning of Christian love, but none sharpens the definition of love so much as his command that we love our enemies: "You have heard that it was said, 'You shall love your neighbor and hate your enemy.' But I say to you, Love your enemies and pray for those who persecute you...."[71] Here in this one word "love", wrote Bonhoeffer, the whole of the message of the Sermon is summed up. Jesus bids us to overcome our enemies by loving them. But who are our enemies? They are those "who are quite intractable and utterly unresponsive to our love, who forgive us nothing when we forgive them all, who requite our love with hatred and our service with derision." Love asks nothing in return, but seeks those who need it, and who need it more than those who are consumed with hatred and devoid of love? As to how love should behave, Jesus gives the answer: bless, do good and

---

70. CD, 69.

71. Matthew 5:43-44.

Doctrine of Love

pray for your enemies without reserve and without respect of persons.[72]

Bonhoeffer stressed that in loving our enemies, not only in thought and word but in deed, we are taken along the way of the cross and into fellowship with the Crucified. And the more we travel this way, the surer is the victory of our love over the enemy's hatred; for then it is no longer simply our own love but the love of Jesus Christ, who for the sake of his enemies went to the cross. It is this kind of self-sacrificing love that is to distinguish the Christian. After all, we all find it easy to love those who are lovable or who love us, but the Christian is called by Christ to do more than what comes naturally, to do the extraordinary, the unusual, the peculiar, the "perisson." This "more," this "beyond-all-that," is, according to Bonhoeffer, the way of self-renunciation, of unreserved love for our enemies, for the unloving and unloved, for our religious, political, and personal adversaries. In short, it is the love of Jesus Christ, who went to the cross.[73]

In his Sermon on the Mount Jesus spoke not only of the extraordinary character of the love to which his disciples are called, but also its hidden nature. Bonhoeffer emphasized that the genuine work of love is always a hidden work, something self-forgetful, spontaneous, and unpremeditated, which to all appearances is quite ordinary and natural. Because love is hidden, it can never be a visible virtue or a habit that can be acquired. Our calculating and self-interested ways are brought to an end, for we look not to ourselves but to the Christ we are following. Thus genuine love spells the end of the "old Adam" in us, and we recover our true nature in the righteousness of Christ and in our fellow human beings. The love of Christ crucified, wrote Bonhoeffer, is the love which lives in those who follow him.[74]

---

72. CD, 164-165.

73. CD, 165-166., 169.

74. CD, 176-179.

The Cost of Discipleship is a tour de force on behalf of Christian obedience. Without jeopardizing the Reformation doctrine of justification by grace through faith alone, Bonhoeffer nevertheless pulls out all the stops to arouse Christians in Germany to the dangers of "cheap grace" and to instill discipline in their lives. His concern was not merely for the intra-church struggle. More and more he sensed that a time of widespread persecution by the Nazi government was approaching. "Our adversaries," he wrote, "seek to root out the Christian Church and the Christian faith because they cannot live side by side with us, because they see in every word we utter and every deed we do, even when they are not specifically directed against them, a condemnation of their own words and deeds."[75] The commandment to love their enemies and forego revenge will grow even more urgent!

The members of the Confessing Church during the 1930s surely were justified in seeing themselves as victims of the state, although much of their energy was spent in fighting against the "German Christians" and later against the so-called "intact" Lutheran Churches that broke the united front that had been forged at the Confessional Synods of Barmen and Dahlem. What seems strange to us today, with our 20-20 hindsight, is the lack of reference, even in writers like Bonhoeffer, to the plight of the Jews, who were to be the ultimate victims of the Nazis. Bonhoeffer took cognizance of "the Jewish question" in an article in 1933,[76] but the focus of concern at that time was more on Jewish Christians who were being affected by the Aryan Clause than on the Jews themselves. How Christians should love Jews was a much neglected question.

Bonhoeffer's seminary at Finkenwalde was closed by the Gestapo in September 1937. The next year he wrote Life Together, a book which discusses various aspects of Christian community and

---

75. CD, 168.

76. "The Church and the Jewish Question," in NRS, 216-225. For a discussion of this matter, see Eberhard Bethge's essay on "Dietrich Bonhoeffer and the Jews" in ER, 43-96.

Doctrine of Love

was based on the actual experience of living life together at Finkenwalde. Christian community, he asserts, is like the Christian's sanctification, that is, a gift of God which we cannot claim. It is not an ideal to be realized, but a reality created by God in Christ in which we may participate. It is a spiritual (geistliche) rather than a human-psychic (seelische) reality. Spiritual reality is based on the clear Word of God in Jesus Christ, human reality on the dark urges and desires of the human mind. The community of the Spirit is based on truth and its essence is light; the human community of spirit is based on desire and its essence is darkness. In the former, *agape*-love abounds, in the latter, eros.[77]

It is evident that Bonhoeffer now returns to the distinction between *agape* and eros he had earlier delineated in The Communion of Saints, but here in Life Together the contrast is drawn even more sharply. He puts it this way: human love (eros) is directed to the other person for his own sake; spiritual love loves the other for Christ's sake. Human love is based on its desire to enjoy and control; spiritual love wants only to serve others and has its source in Jesus Christ and his Word. Spiritual love is from above and thus quite new, strange and incomprehensible to earthly love. Human love constructs its own image of the other person; spiritual love recognizes the true image of the other person to be the image received from Jesus Christ, the image Christ embodied and would bestow on all human beings. Human love produces human subjection, dependence, constraint; spiritual love creates freedom of others under the Word of God. Human love breeds hothouse flowers; spiritual love creates the fruits that grow healthily in the rain and sunshine of God's outdoors.[78]

Bonhoeffer warns that any true community life of Christians depends upon the ability on crucial occasions to distinguish the difference between human community and spiritual community, between a human ideal and God's reality, between a collegium pietatis

---

77. LT, 30-31.

78. LT, 34-37.

and the one, holy, catholic Church. Some of the questions to ask on such occasions are these: Are you willing to dissolve a fellowship that has become false for the sake of genuine fellowship? Can you love an enemy, one who resists fellowship? Do you have a principle of selectivity that excludes the weak, the insignificant, the different, the seemingly useless? And are you willing to suffer for Christ and his Church?[79]

C. THE FINAL YEARS: 1939-1945

By 1939 Bonhoeffer's life began to change dramatically. His options were running out. He had long since been forbidden to teach at the University, his make-shift work with ministerial candidates of the Confessing Church was fast drawing to a close, the church struggle had run out of steam, Germany was headed for war, and he himself was threatened with conscription. It would not be long before the Nazis would forbid him from publishing, from speaking in public, and even from residing in Berlin. Yet he still had powerful family and ecumenical church connections. Through the latter, he arranged an invitation to come to Union Theological Seminary in New York as a visiting lecturer, but no sooner had he arrived in June 1939 than his conscience told him to return to Germany. After all, he loved his people and must share their destiny. So in less than a month he sailed back to a rapidly deteriorating situation. War broke out in September. Through family connections, specifically his brother-in-law Hans von Dohnanyi, he entered the underground resistance movement dedicated to the overthrow of Hitler. In 1940 he became a civilian employee of Army Military Intelligence (the Abwehr) as a "cover" for his resistance activities and to keep him from being drafted into the army.

From 1940 until his arrest on 5 April 1943, Bonhoeffer's "churchly" work lessened and his "worldly" work increased. He had entered "the great masquerade of evil," and during three Abwehr-sponsored trips to Switzerland and one to Sweden he used his

---

79. LT, 34, 37-38.

ecumenical church contacts to further the cause of the resistance. It was precisely during these years of conspiratorial activity, when he was cut off from many of his friends and activities in the Confessing Church and in vital touch with his family, that he began working on a book on ethics, which he considered to be his magnum opus. His view of reality was no less centered on Jesus Christ, but now he felt a special urgency to delineate how worldly reality is related to God-in-Christ. He certainly did not believe that he was any less related to Christ, any less Christian, in his worldly activity than in his churchly activity. Indeed, the whole idea of dividing reality into two spheres, the "secular" and the "sacred," he considered to be mistaken. And so he wanted to write an ethical treatise that would do justice to reality as a whole, reality in which God and world must be distinguished but never separated, where they are held together in a "polemical" unity.

Bonhoeffer's Ethics was never completed. Fragments were written and hidden at various places in Germany, to be collected and collated and published posthumously by his close friend and biographer, Eberhard Bethge. The result is, in spite of its fragmentary character, a substantial work which provides snapshots, as it were, of Bonhoeffer's thought in motion. As always, his thought is Christ-centered, but now the horizons of Christ's dominion are being constantly pushed back. Despite the presence of Bonhoeffer's characteristically disciplined thought, the work has a kind of fresh, exhilarating quality to it, as if the author was moving in a number of exciting directions almost simultaneously.

In dealing with such a rich and complex book as Ethics, it is impossible here to do more than hit the high points of his thinking about even this one topic of "love." Fortunately, one of his chapters is entitled "The Love of God and the Decay of the World." In this he contrasts the disunity of the fallen world, full of conflicts and ethical problems because everything is based on the knowledge of good and evil, with the world of recovered unity that one finds in the New Testament, a unity brought about by God's reconciling act in Jesus Christ. One of the sub-headings in this chapter is called "Love," and in dealing with this concept we find Bonhoeffer sounding some familiar notes, but some new ones, too.

Bonhoeffer emphasizes once more the difference between God's love and what passes for love from a human point of view. Love is not a human attitude or conviction or deed. Love is God Himself. Or better: *God* is love. Thus to know what love truly is, we must learn its meaning from God's self-revelation, that is, from Jesus Christ. Bonhoeffer asserts that the New Testament defines what love is by unambiguously pointing to the concrete action and suffering of Jesus Christ. But love is not what he *does* and what he *suffers*, but what *he* does and what *he* suffers. Love is always he himself, always the revelation of God in Christ.

At this point in his Ethics, Bonhoeffer opens up what appears to be a new area in his discussion of *agape*-love. Heretofore he has emphasized the discontinuity between human love and divine love, between love from the human viewpoint and love as defined by God. But now he concedes a connection between the two. He states that even though *agape* acquires an entirely new connotation in the New Testament message, it is still not entirely disconnected from what we understand by "love" in ordinary parlance. This does not mean, he insists, that the biblical concept of love is a particular form of what we already know generally by this word. Rather, the contrary is the case: the biblical concept of love alone is the foundation and truth and reality of love, so that any natural notion of love contains truth and reality only in so far as it participates in God's love in Jesus Christ.

For sinful humans who live in disunion from their origin in God, it is love that unites them again to their origin. Thus, states Bonhoeffer, love is the reconciliation of humankind with God in Christ. Love is something that happens to us, something passive, that overcomes our disunity with God, with one another, with ourselves, and with our world. It is the transformation of our entire existence by God, so that we are "being drawn into the world as it lives and must live before God and in God." Since it is not our choice, love is nothing less than our election by God.

Doctrine of Love

If this is so, asks Bonhoeffer, then in what sense can we speak with the New Testament of love as a human activity, of the love of humans for God and their neighbors? Bonhoeffer's answer is that to love God means to accept willingly our being elected and engendered in Christ. At this point Bonhoeffer makes an important distinction. We must not think of the relationship as one in which divine love merely precedes human love in order to set human love in motion as a love that is now an independent, autonomous human activity. On the contrary, stresses Bonhoeffer, the love with which humans love God and their neighbors is strictly God's love. There is no other love. Thus even here the love of humans remains purely passive: loving God is the other aspect of being loved by God, and being loved by God implies loving God. The two do not stand side by side but go together.

Here the reader is faced with some frustration in trying to determine more exactly what Bonhoeffer means. He explains that "passivity" in this context is not to be understood psychologically but in terms of our existence before God, that is, theologically. Passivity here does not mean that our thoughts, words, and actions as whole human beings are to be excluded in our loving. But at this point, just when we would like to have more explanation, the chapter ends abruptly and remains unfinished.[80]

In his chapter on "History and Good" Bonhoeffer deals extensively with the crucial concept of responsibility and outlines a "structure of responsible life" that includes deputyship (Stellvertretung), correspondence with reality (Wirklichkeitsgemässheit), pertinence (Sachgemässheit), and the acceptance of guilt. He also deals with two presuppositions of responsible life: conscience and freedom. It could be argued that all of this discussion about responsibility has to do with love, particularly as it is related to the question of justice in society. Where Bonhoeffer specifically mentions the concept of love, however, is in the section on "the acceptance of guilt." Here he points

---

80. E, 49-54.

out that Jesus was not concerned with the proclamation and realization of new ethical ideals or with himself being good, but rather with love for real human beings who were burdened with guilt. A love which left them alone in their guilt would not be love for the real man or woman. As one who acted responsibly in the historical existence of humans, Jesus became guilty, and this solely out of his love for humankind. As one who loved selflessly and one who was free from sin, Jesus entered into the guilt of sinful humanity and took this guilt upon himself. Responsible persons, Bonhoeffer emphasized, will follow Jesus' lead and not shirk from entering into the guilt of others for the others' sake.[81]

The chapter on "History and Good" that is incorporated in Ethics is Bonhoeffer's second draft of this material. The first sketch, which he abandoned in favor of this revision, is published in Volume 3 of his collected writings (GS III) and is focused much more on the theme of love. Bonhoeffer states there that *love* is the content of Jesus Christ's responsibility for humankind, *freedom* its form. Love in this case is both God's love actualized for humans and the return of human love to God. On the one hand, Jesus Christ is the incarnate love of God for humanity--not a proclaimer of abstract ethical ideals but one who concretely lives out the love of God. And so humans are called not to the realization of ideals but into a life in the love of God, which means a life which fulfills God's command to righteousness in deputyship for others.[82]

The love of which the gospel speaks, wrote Bonhoeffer, differs from philosophy in that it is not a method of intercourse with humans but rather a being drawn and drawing into an event, namely, into the fellowship of God with the world which was accomplished in Jesus Christ. "Love," then, is not to be looked upon as an abstract attribute of God, but as this actual event of God's loving humankind and the world. Likewise, Bonhoeffer continues, "love" is also not to be seen

---

81. E, 240-242.

82. GS III, 466-467.

Doctrine of Love

as a human attribute, but as human beings' actually belonging to one another and with one another and the world on the basis of God's free love for each of them. Furthermore, just as God's love became subject to misunderstanding and ambiguity when it entered the world, so Christian love will also be subject to misinterpretation and even condemnation when it becomes "worldly." Any attempt on Christians' part to keep from "getting their hands dirty" in the world represents a false perfectionism that shows disdain for the incarnation of God. The purity of Christian love will be proved precisely in its worldly form, not in its aloofness from the world. From this perspective, advises Bonhoeffer, it is not only possible but imperative to understand historical action as Christian action, that is, as action whose origin is the incarnate love of God.[83]

The Sermon on the Mount, Bonhoeffer declares, is nothing other than the proclamation of the incarnate love of God. As such, it calls us to love other human beings and to renounce whatever might hinder this task. In a word, it demands *self-denial*. Renunciation of our own happiness, rights, righteousness, worth, power and success becomes our preparation for loving our neighbor. Our "natural" perspective is distorted and misled by self-love, but the love of God frees our view so that we attain a clear perception of reality, of our neighbor and world, and only so do we come to know our real responsibility. Thus the Sermon on the Mount places us before the necessity of responsible actions in history.[84]

God's love, according to Bonhoeffer, encompasses the whole of reality in itself. Just as there is no limit of the love of God for the world, so likewise there can be no limit to the human love that derives from it. It is applicable to all the various spheres and relationships of life. Thus, writes Bonhoeffer, either the Sermon on the Mount concerns us at all times and in all places, or it concerns us not at all. A limited love, after all, would not have had to go to the cross. But

---

83. GS III, 474-475.

84. GS III, 475-476.

Jesus died on the cross because God loved the entire world, and this same love calls us to the whole world, too.[85]

If the Sermon on the Mount is validly applicable to the historical activity of humans, argues Bonhoeffer, then this means it is valid in the political sphere, especially Jesus' words about self-denial and loving the enemy. In Bonhoeffer's opinion, only abstract pseudo-realistic thinking designates self-assertion as the sole law of political action and self-denial as the sole law of Christian action. To see them in this manner, as exclusively opposed, sets up an intolerable double morality. Bonhoeffer points out that such an understanding bypasses the reality of the incarnation and, as a result, neither the "worldly" nor the "Christian" is comprehended. That God's love for the world also encompasses political action, and therefore that the worldly form of Christian love also can assume the form of those fighting for self-assertion, power, success and certainty--this, states Bonhoeffer, can only be grasped where the incarnation of God's love is taken seriously. Here the limits, or better, the background of the law of self-assertion in political action is revealed. Political action means to perceive responsibility. It cannot take place without power. Power enters into the service of responsibility....[86]

Bonhoeffer's first draft of "History and Good" breaks off at this point. Bethge thinks it was probably begun in the summer of 1941. It was rejected by Bonhoeffer, who then began again in more detail. Bonhoeffer seems to be thinking through, from a theological point of view, his own involvement in the resistance movement. For this reason, it is a very important (and largely overlooked) document for assessing Bonhoeffer's political activities as a Christian in the "worldly" sphere. Bonhoeffer may have rejected it precisely because he thought it might be read as too self-serving.

Much that Bonhoeffer writes in other sections of Ethics are variations on the theme of love. A few examples must suffice: Living

---

[85]. GS III, 476-477.

[86]. GS III, 477.

Doctrine of Love

and increasing in love is the precondition of "proving" the will of God. Reconciliation comes by the perfect love of God--not by a general idea of love but the really *lived* love of God in Jesus Christ. God's love for humankind has proved stronger than death. The church is the place where testimony and serious thought are given to God's reconciliation of the world with himself in Christ, to his having so loved the world that he gave his Son for its sake. The central message of the New Testament is that God loved the world and reconciled it with himself in Christ.[87] "Christian formation" is nothing other than conformation with Christ in the form of love, and "preparing the way" in the realm of the penultimate is human love that is related to and dependent upon God's loving act of justifying humankind by grace alone (the ultimate). One could go on and on, but now we must turn to Bonhoeffer's thoughts after he was incarcerated in Tegel Military Prison in Berlin.

Bonhoeffer, along with Dohnanyi and others, was arrested by the Gestapo on 5 April 1943, on suspicions relating to an attempt of some members of the Abwehr to help a few Jewish employees escape into Switzerland. In January he had become engaged to Maria von Wedemeyer, but the engagement was not announced until after he entered Tegel Prison. During his imprisonment Bonhoeffer passed much of his time in reading and writing. He carried on extensive correspondence with his parents and family, his fiancée, and his friend Eberhard Bethge, who by this time had been conscripted into the army and was serving in Italy. Some of Bonhoeffer's letters passed through the hands of the prison censors, but the majority were smuggled out uncensored through the good graces of friendly prison orderlies. This correspondence was ended when he was moved on 8 October 1944 to the Gestapo prison in the Prinz-Albrecht-Strasse, a move caused by the discovery of papers implicating him in the resistance movement.

Bonhoeffer's letters, poems and other papers from prison reveal at once the human and the Christian that were so inseparable in this

---

87. E, 39, 70, 78, 202, 204.

man. Even under these arduous prison conditions, including interminable interrogations and frequent wartime air-raids, he lived a disciplined life of prayer and study, and he thought deeply about those things that mattered most to him. How much he loved his family, his fiancée and his friends shines through his letters. And how much he felt their love for him does too. All of this human love, he knew, was grounded in God's unfathomable love for this world, and as he pondered that fact he came to his brilliant insights about the need for a "non-religious interpretation" of the great biblical concepts relating to God's action in Christ, the action which he believed was eventuating in the world's "coming of age."

Included in Letters and Papers from Prison, but actually written by Bonhoeffer to a few close friends at New Year 1943, is a tract called "After Ten Years." In it he reflects briefly on a number of common experiences they had had during the past decade. The writing abounds in aphorisms, which is also true of his prison letters, and sometimes the subject is love. For instance, under the heading "Contempt for Humanity?" he writes: "We must learn to regard people less in the light of what they do, and more in the light of what they suffer. The only profitable relationship to others--and especially to our weaker brethren--is one of love, and that means the will to hold fellowship with them. God himself did not despise humanity, but became man for men's sake."[88] Under "Sympathy" he writes: "We are not Christ, but if we want to be Christians, we must have some share in Christ's large-heartedness by acting with responsibility and in freedom when the hour of danger comes, and by showing a real sympathy that springs, not from fear, but from the liberating and redeeming love of Christ for all who suffer."[89]

In one of his letters from prison, Bonhoeffer criticizes those people who want to be done with the earth and go to their heavenly home. He admits that heaven is our ultimate destination but thinks we

---

88. LPP, 10.

89. LPP, 14.

Doctrine of Love

ought not long for it prematurely. What we should do, he admonishes, is to to love and trust God in our *lives* here and now, and in all the good things God sends us, that when the time finally comes (but not before!) we may go to God with love, trust and joy. To drive his point home, Bonhoeffer continues, "But, to put it plainly, for a man in his wife's arms to be hankering after the other world is, in mild terms, a piece of bad taste, and not God's will."[90] Later, in the same vein, Bonhoeffer associates pious otherworldliness with "religiousness" and warns that we ought not write off this world too soon but should drink our cup of life here to the lees![91] In another letter he says that it is only by living completely in this world--in its duties and problems, successes and failures, experiences and perplexities--that one learns to have faith.[92]

While in prison Bonhoeffer seems to become all the more appreciative of human, earthly love, though never apart from God's love. In a sermon written for the wedding of Bethge and his niece Renate Schleicher, he extols their love for each other, but then says that marriage is more than that: "It is not your love that sustains the marriage, but from now on, the marriage that sustains your love."[93] He discusses friendship many times and composes a moving poem to "The Friend," but he confesses it is hard to classify friendship among the mandates of God.[94] He says that the Old Testament book Song of Songs is best read as an ordinary love song and that this is probably the best "christological" exposition.[95]

Perhaps the best understanding of the relation between human

---

90. LPP, 168.

91. LPP, 191-192.

92. LPP, 369-370.

93. LPP, 43.

94. LPP, 181, 192, 388.

95. LPP, 315.

love and divine love at this point in his life is found in Bonhoeffer's exposition of what he calls the "polyphony of life." He writes as follows:

> There's always a danger in all strong, erotic love that one may lose[96] what I might call the polyphony of life. What I mean is that God wants us to love him eternally with our whole hearts--not in such a way as to injure or weaken our earthly love, but to provide a kind of *cantus firmus* to which the other melodies of life provide the counterpoint. One of the contrapuntal themes (which have their own complete independence but are yet related to the *cantus firmus*) is earthly affection. Even in the Bible we have the Song of Songs; and really one can imagine no more ardent, passionate, sensual love than is portrayed there.... Where the *cantus firmus* is clear and plain, the counterpoint can be developed to its limits. The two are 'undivided and yet distinct', in the words of the Chalcedonian Definition, like Christ in his divine and human natures. May not the attraction and importance of polyphony in music consist in its being a musical reflection of this Christological fact and therefore of our *vita christiana*?[97]

Bonhoeffer's own life, fragmented as it was, displayed to a remarkable degree the polyphonous character of which he spoke so eloquently in this passage. He never had the opportunity to develop the many exciting and tantalizing ideas that were expressed in his letters and papers from prison, and yet even in their incompleteness one senses something whole and harmonious: a truth just breaking forth.

---

96. An egregious error has been made in the English translation here; "love" is found there instead of the correct "lose."

97. LPP, 303.

At great loss to us all, Bonhoeffer was eventually removed from the Gestapo prison in Berlin, was shuttled from one concentration camp to another, and on 9 April 1945 was hanged to death at Flossenbürg. His body was burned and his ashes, like his spirit, was scattered abroad by the winds of the world. A simple plaque in the Protestant Church in Flossenbürg commemorates his death in these words: "Dietrich Bonhoeffer: A Witness of Jesus Christ among his Brothers."

IV. CONCLUSION

After this survey I think there can be no doubt about the major role that the doctrine of love played in Dietrich Bonhoeffer's theology and ethics. He was convinced that his own church and probably most of the mainline Protestant churches of the West had become purveyors of "cheap grace" and in doing so had betrayed the proper biblical and Reformation understanding of the interrelationship between faith and love, justification and sanctification. Like Paul and Luther, he never wavered in his conviction that we are saved by God's grace alone, through faith alone; what God had done for us in the life, death and resurrection of Jesus is pure gift, to be received with empty hands and glad hearts. But also like Paul and Luther, he knew that this gift of the Holy Spirit calls forth in the believer a grateful response of obedience that encompasses the whole of one's life. True faith will always be active in love.

So Bonhoeffer's theology and ethics can be looked upon as a corrective for cheap grace wherever it is found in the church. If Karl Barth's early efforts can be seen as an attempt to correct a liberal theology which had turned into a religious ethic without transcendent foundations, then Bonhoeffer's contribution was to reclaim concrete ethics for Barth's dialectical theology. When Barth was insisting on the revelation of the Word, Bonhoeffer was insisting on the response of the Cross. This is what the "cost of discipleship" is all about.

Bonhoeffer's is a theology of love par excellence, and his

concept of love is centered firmly on the cross of Christ. That cross represents the epitome of a joyful self-sacrificing life for others, and this is exactly the life of love that Bonhoeffer advocated for Christians. Bonhoeffer never doubted that Christian love was a free response to God's love for humankind, but he believed that the freedom of the Christian was not jeopardized by, but indeed required informed discipline. This is why he, like Luther, wrote clarifying expositions of the Sermon on the Mount and the Ten Commandments. Bonhoeffer was convinced that Christian love calls the followers of Christ to do more than others, to take the surprising and extraordinary action. This is why the hallmark of his doctrine of love is Jesus' teaching that we should love our enemies, which of course is not unrelated to Jesus' death on the cross.

To recapitulate some of the features of Bonhoeffer's doctrine of love, we can state the following:

(1) God's love for the world, incarnated in Jesus Christ, provides the foundation, norm and possibility for all Christian love.

(2) The New Testament word for God's love is *agape*, the love which is lived out in a life of utter and sacrificial self-giving on behalf of others.

(3) *Agape*-love is best exemplified by Jesus' suffering and atoning death on the cross, but it can be seen throughout his life and teachings, especially in his Sermon on the Mount and his command to love one's enemies.

(4) From a Christian perspective, there are essentially two kinds of love that should not be confused: love for others (*agape*) and self-love (eros). Both can generate the same power and passion, but one has its origin in God's love and is outgoing, the other originates in the dark desires and urges of the human heart that has "fallen" away from God and is selfish.

(5) Love for God is not only possible but is an imperative which entails worship and service. Love for God cannot be reduced to faith or neighbor-love, but love of neighbor is certainly a sign of a true love of God, because to love God is to want to do God's will and God's

will is that we love one another.

(6) Love for the neighbor cannot be limited. It applies to the neighbor far and near; it applies to Christians and non-Christians; it applies to individuals and to groups; it applies to personal life and to political life; it applies to the rich and the poor. Who the neighbor is and how best to love that neighbor cannot be decided casuistically but only in the concrete situation and with prayer for God's guidance.

(7) We do not love God *in* the neighbor but the *real neighbor* himself or herself. Likewise, it is *we* who do the loving, not God. Nevertheless, while we are not mere "pipelines" for the passage of God's love to the neighbor, there is a mystery involved in the relationship between our human action and God's action. We do not act apart from the work of the Holy Spirit upon and within us.

(8) Love is an act, not an attitude or warm feeling or sentiment.

(9) Philia, the New Testament word for friendly, warm affection, can be subsumed under *agape* as an aspect of "mutuality," that is, the mutual love between persons. However, the danger is ever present for such love to become eros instead.

(10) Christian love demands responsible action in society; while pursuing the ideal of equalitarian justice, it will focus its attention on the less fortunate and the most vulnerable, taking on the role of deputyship and representation on their behalf.

Bonhoeffer's basic doctrine of love seems not to have changed much during his lifetime. Its christological center remains the same among all the changes of his circumstances. Nevertheless, he seems to grow in his understanding of the wide dominion of Christ, especially under the impact of the experiences of the resistance movement and his imprisonment. God's presence in and suffering for the *world* comes to the fore, the sharp edges between God's love and our earthly, "natural" love become worn down, and faith is now to be realized only in a life of love lived out in the very midst of a non-religious world-come-of-age. Even the church can be the church only by existing for others, that is, by concrete examples of love.

Perhaps the most felicitous expression of Bonhoeffer's mature understanding of the relation between our love for God and our earthly loves is found in that prison letter where he writes about the polyphony of life. As in the music of a fugue, where there is a basic theme or cantus firmus to which all other melodies are counterpoint, so the Christian life should have a polyphonous character: the love for God is the cantus firmus and all our earthly loves the contrapuntal melodies. As long as the cantus firmus is clear and plain, the earthly loves can be developed to their limits.

I hope this essay has convinced the reader that Bonhoeffer's doctrine of love is not only central to his theology and ethics, but that its richness and pertinence make it worthy of study. Its fruitfulness ultimately will be borne out only in practice, as we ourselves act lovingly in our time and place. Fortunately, here too Bonhoeffer is helpful. For he not only taught about love; he attempted to live a life of love in his own time and place. Thus he is one of those rare teachers whose life is as important--if not more important!--for the subject-matter of his teaching as are his words. We should be thankful for his witness--and give the glory to God!

VII

GROUND UNDER OUR FEET

A Reflection on the Worldliness of Dietrich Bonhoeffer's Life and Thought

Charles C. West

Dietrich Bonhoeffer was a secular Christian. To explore the meaning of this paradox is the purpose of this essay. The paradox is not new. It was more than thirty years ago when Bonhoeffer's <u>Ethics</u> and <u>Letters and Papers from Prison</u> first appeared, projecting a vision for secular people still disturbed by God, of the style and direction of a worldly life in Christ. Since then people of a vast variety of faiths and experiences have given this vision their own forms, claiming Bonhoeffer as inspiration. Meanwhile each new revelation about his own thought and life has illuminated and deepened the mystery of what it meant to him to be Christian and worldly, at once. The paradox still guides and eludes us.

This essay has three theses. First, Dietrich Bonhoeffer's own particular world--of bourgeois aristocracy rooted in German culture and Prussian integrity--was the substance of his life, the soil in which he grew, the ground under his feet, as he himself put it more than once. He was an aristocrat of that world. Personal or social alienation was foreign to his being. Theologically this expressed itself in a sense of the penultimate that was close to theonomous: grasped by the ultimate and open to its mystery, in its secularity.

Second, Bonhoeffer's profound awareness of the fragility of this world, of the vanity of its, and of his, self-justification, was rooted in no social analysis or experience, but rather, from his earliest years, in a sense of ultimate reality that not only transcends the world, but questions and transforms the world at the center of its existence. God, in and for the world, negates for him every effort of the world to provide itself with ultimacy, whether by ideals and religions which sanctify existing order or by ideologies and utopias which sanctify its overthrow. It is Christ who gives the world its true secularity. In him the world can be affirmed in its maturity at the very time when it is falling apart.

Third, this experience and this theology of Christ and the world is fundamentally different from two others onto which it has too often been grafted: the Marxist dialectic of alienation, struggle and liberation on the one side, and the anxious search of liberal culture for ultimate self-confidence on the other. The proletarian experience was strange to Bonhoeffer. So was knowing the world as a human project with a religious superstructure. He could not easily understand what drives some people to seek salvation by revolution and others by the endless expansion of knowledge, power and wealth. But in his particular limitation and concentration of theological experience he has gone beyond the conflict between Marx and the bourgeois religious society which Marx criticized, to create a new context for Christian life, or perhaps to rediscover a very old one: the penultimate, secular task of preparing the way for Christ in a world whose ultimate reality he already is.

I. THE GOODNESS OF THE WORLD

Bonhoeffer was a child of his world. Eberhard Bethge puts it succinctly:

> Dietrich Bonhoeffer could not stand to leave faithfulness to the earth to Friedrich Nietzsche. Antaeus

the son of Gaea--unconquerable as long as his feet were on the ground--crowned Bonhoeffer's 1928 reflections on ethics in Barcelona, and Antaeus illustrated his talk of the ethics of earthly responsibility in Tegel in 1943.[1]

There are two dimensions to the symbol of Antaeus. This son of the goddess Earth lived a life of struggle. For Bonhoeffer in 1928 this meant ethical behavior in the midst of the needs, the conflicts, the decisions of the immediate world around him, from which there is no escape into general ideals and principles. Ethics is a matter of history, a child of the earth. Only in this context comes God's call to responsible action.

But the mythical giant also drew strength from the ground under his feet. It was not only an arena for conflict but a source of nourishment. It was the root, the power and the order of his being. This ground, for the young theologian working for the first time outside his own country, was not a general symbol but a specific experience.

> There is a German ethic and a French ethic, just as there is an American ethic, and none is more ethical than the others, but all are firmly fixed in the nexus of history, and all have in our time been decisively influenced by the tremendous experience of the world war, as it has been seen through different eyes.

Today he would certainly have added, an Indian, a Chinese, a Latin American ethic and several more. In any case a particular nourishing tradition, with a particular perspective and way of life, was in his mind when in the summary of his Barcelona lecture on ethics he wrote:

> Whoever would leave the earth, who would like to escape from the need of the present, loses the strength which continually upholds him by mysterious eternal

---

1. GS III, 7 (my translation).

powers. The earth remains our mother as God remains our father, and only the one who remains true to the mother, will she lay in the father's arms. This is the Christian hymn of the earth and its need.2

What, then, is the character of this earth which is raised (to be sure, only in this one youthful burst of rhetoric) to become the consort of God? It has its physical dimension, certainly. The rolling hills of central Germany harmonized with Bonhoeffer's spirit. He rejoiced in well-performed activities in which the body interacts with nature. He radiated health, strength and confidence in the capacity of that which is natural in life to re-establish itself ever anew, in its order against formless vitalism, and in its underlying givenness against human organization.3 An estate well managed, a game well played, a bodily life enjoyed to the full in labor and recreation, food, drink, clothing and sex in the context of family and property--these are all for him expressions of natural right, of the created goodness of the world, and as such arenas of human fulfillment and responsibility.

This earth has also its cultural dimension, with both a religious and a secular expression.4 Perhaps in fact one should not separate them. The music of Bach or the magnificent Christian art and achitecture of Rome were for him as worldly in their religious expression as the gods of Greek and Roman antiquity are religious in their secularity. Bonhoeffer had learned early from Barth that religion is a human enterprise, as self-centered and as much in need of divine justification as any other human activity. But religion as a form of that secular enterprise known as culture--directed in Christ away from the effort to embody the ultimate, and toward the expression of

---

2. GS III, 58; English Translation, NRS, 47, somewhat altered.

3. E, Ch. IV, "The Natural," 147-149.

4. The word "culture" as used here corresponds to the German word Kultur, and refers to works of art, literature, music, etc. which symbolize the meaning of life. For the other meaning of the word, corresponding to the German Bildung, see below.

Ground Under Our Feet 239

meaning in human life illuminated by ultimate mystery--this Bonhoeffer enjoyed in forms as varied as Paul Gerhardt's hymns, Black American spirituals, descriptions of Greek gods[5] and, from afar, the vision of Gandhian spirituality.[6]

Neither physical life nor cultural works as such, however, bring us to the heart of Bonhoeffer's world. For this we must turn to the historical reality of human society, in both its intepersonal and its collective dimensions. The real ground under his feet was an historically developed texture of sociality with its personal values and relations, its sense of order and wholeness as a community, and its disciplined, responsible aristocracy called to give it leadership. Let us say a word about each of these aspects in turn.

II. GROUND: THE COMMUNITY OF PERSONS

Bonhoeffer throughout his life worked to deepen and clarify the interpersonal world which was his heritage, to understand it as a creative tension--sometimes even a conflict--between the free integrity of the individual and the claim of the other person. His earliest work, The Communion of Saints, places this tension in the primal state of humanity before the fall and sin take their toll.[7] On the one hand personal being is structurally open to sociality:

> The I and the Thou are fitted to one another in infinite nearness, in mutual penetration, forever inseparable, resting on one another in inmost mutual participation, feeling, and experiencing together, and sustaining the general stream of spiritual interaction.[8]

---

5. LPP, 333. Letter to Bethge, 21 June 1944.

6. DB, 329-330.

7. CS, Ch. III. See also Clifford Green's exposition of this chapter against its intellectual background: SCH, Ch. II.

8. CS, 48.

On the other hand the very condition of this is that personal being be also structurally closed:

> I is real only in the relation with the Thou. Clearly then [the person] is not just the reservoir for a certain amount of objective spirit--but an active bearer and member in this whole context of relations.[8]

There is an objective social spirit but it becomes real only in individual embodiment. The bonds in which it is expressed--language, will, service, love--presuppose not a solidarity which submerges persons but the action of persons relating to one another.

> God does not desire a history of individual persons, but a history of the community of persons. Nor does he desire a community which absorbs the individual into itself, but a community of persons.[9]

He goes so far as to say that human community, in its expressions of marriage and family, religious community and state, to which he later gave the name "mandates," is not a pre-personal given structure, but rests upon the wills of the persons who are their members.[10] God alone, the ultimate Thou, gives the I being and command absolutely, for only God is infinite sovereign love. But it is God who presents every I with a human Thou who is also created in the divine image. Thus is the stage set for the penultimate history of human persons with one another in their differences, their conflicts, their cooperation and reconciliation in realizing human community (Gemeinschaft) or society (Gesellschaft).

The interplay between the person and the other remains Bonhoeffer's theme to the end of his life, but it changes in form.

In Life Together we find him working out the theme within the Christian community, developing the interplay of the day alone and

---

9. CS, 52. Translation altered to render Mensch as "person."

10. CS, 53.

Ground Under Our Feet 241

the day together, and sharply contrasting seelische Gemeinschaft as a self-centered romantic ideal with the community of the Spirit wherein persons are related through Christ. In Ethics Chapter IV the theme comes up again as part of a discussion of human rights in the penultimate sphere. "The individual comes into the world with a natural right of his own,"[11] he says flatly. It is based on his or her participation in the form of the natural which is that movement of the created world, which is directed after the Fall toward the coming of Christ. It has therefore a social structure and direction which negates sheer self-expression. But this structure may not take the form of organization, which coerces the person into ways contrary to freedom. Rather it expresses the direction in which human relations may grow and deepen. Bonhoeffer was able to take only the first step along this road, defining the sphere of freedom for life and bodily existence against the powers that threaten it. The notes at the end of this unfinished chapter show the task that lay ahead of him:

> The natural rights of the life of the mind. The natural right to work and property.--The natural right to fellowship. The natural right to piety. The natural right to happiness. The right of mental and bodily defense.[12]

How Bonhoeffer would have finished this is an open question. It probably was also for him. Everything would have depended on the interplay developed between the individual rights already described and those which in their very nature depend on mutuality. Some sense of the direction the natural might take for him is found in a few notes on Bildung which are immediately appended to the above. They suggest the picture of a cultivated person as a generalist in knowledge and awareness, "assimilating the world as a whole and carrying it within oneself," sensitive to other cultures and people, modest, open

---

11. E, Ch. IV, 153.

12. E, 186.

to the new, but rooted in "family, friendship and small groups."[13]

All of this, as Renate Bethge has pointed out, drawing on personal memories, reflects the personal values and relations which the Bonhoeffer family admired and tried to practice. We find it still to be the theme in the literature from prison, asserted against the background of catastrophe which might have called it all in question. In "Thoughts on the Day of Baptism of D. W. R. Bethge" Bonhoeffer eloquently describes the past virtues of the two homes out of which the child's parents had come and then adds:

> By the time you have grown up, the old country parsonage and the old town villa will belong to a vanished world. But the old spirit, after a time of misunderstanding and weakness, withdrawal and recovery, preservation and rehabilitation, will produce new forms. To be deeply rooted in the soil of the past makes life harder, but it also makes it richer and more vigorous.[14]

In "After Ten Years" this confidence is based on an explicit faith in God. But remarkably, the picture of the "man come of age which emerges from the letters that deal with this theme, embodies some of the same poise of free responsibility in interpersonal relations and in dealing with history and nature, without a conscious grounding in Christian faith. Not only is the religious a priori outgrown; no ultimate is assumed.

> The world that has become conscious of itself and the laws that govern its existence has grown self-confident in what seems to be an uncanny way. False developments and failures do not make the world doubt the necessity of the course that it is taking; they are

---

13. E, 187. Cf. Renate Bethge, "'Elite' and 'Silence' in Bonhoeffer's Person and Thought," in ER, 293-306.

14. LPP, Enlarged Edition, 295.

accepted with fortitude and detachment as part of the bargain, and even an event like the present war is no exception.[15]

Such people Bonhoeffer would like to claim for Christ, not in their need and weakness, not in the boundaries of their capacities, but in the center of their power and goodness and life.[16] Some of them were his collaborators in the conspiracy against Hitler's life, dedicated to the same risks as he. Some were his relatives and friends. Their culture was the ground under his feet as well; their mother earth was also his. It is their sense of the natural which at its best is open to the coming of Christ.

In <u>Ethics</u> Chapter III, which, as Clifford Green's research confirms, was written before, and possibly as foundation for, what is said about the natural in Chapter IV, Bonhoeffer sets forth forcefully the false absolutes that can beset and destroy this responsible worldliness: reason that withdraws from an unreasonable world or imposes on it a rationality that favors the stronger party; fanatic devotion to principle that distorts real human need; conscience that deceives us under pressure; duty that cannot break with evil authority; freedom that loses itself in compromise; and private virtue that withdraws from public responsibility. Against these he calls on the reality of the world as it is known at one with God in Jesus Christ.[17] Conformity to Christ renews the secularity of the world. But it is *secularity* which is renewed: the give-and-take of interpersonal relations among free people who know their mutual dependence, who do not submerge their identities in any human group or principle, but who discern and build together, in conflict and in reconciliation, the law and structure of responsible community. If one

---

15. LPP, 326.

16. LPP, 282.

17. E, Ch. III, 65-70. See also the recapitulation of these in "After Ten Years," LPP, 4-5.

may use the image of a scale, Bonhoeffer's concepts of the penultimate and the natural in Ethics Chapter IV would be the fulcrum. The evangelistic plea for faith in Chapter III is in one pan; the affirmation of a world come of age in the best of the culture that he knew, is in the other. Where the weight must come down will depend on the world's balance in any given time and place.

III. GROUND: ORDER AND WHOLENESS

This brings us to the second level of Bonhoeffer's sociality: the role of order and wholeness in an interpersonal world. In The Communion of Saints he draws on the sociologist Ferdinand Tönnies to distinguish two forms of this order: Gesellschaft (society) and Gemeinschaft (community). The choice was not felicitous. It oversimplified the variety of social structures and relations, and fitted too easily the dichotomy between liberal individualist and conservative romantic concepts of politics. In places Bonhoeffer seemed to fall into this dichotomy. With one part of his being he yearned for Gemeinschaft and described it in terms that border on transcending secularity altogether.

> A community is a concrete unity. Its members must not be thought of as individual: the center of action does not lie in each member, but in all together.[18]

It is a collective person "in the eyes of God, the all-embracing person."[19] Its existence furthermore does not depend on human purpose.

> A community is permeated with value as history is, and as value itself, lies beyond intramundane limitations. Communities of blood, such as family and race--historical communities, such as the people and the nation--communities of destiny, such as marriage and

---

18. CS, 51.

19. CS, 52.

friendship--in their nature as communities they are all from God to God.[20]

On the other hand Bonhoeffer knew even in those early years that community in this sense is an ideal. His next step, for which the ground was already laid in The Communion of Saints, was to move beyond idealism, precisely in its seductive Hegelian form that had so permeated German culture, to a more penultimate sense of the socially real. There was no way open for him toward pragmatism and empiricism. Here his cultural ground differed fundamentally from that of an American for whom this would be the basic social experience and temptation. He could never have developed Tönnies' concept of Gesellschaft into a theory of social harmony in the style of Adam Smith and his followers, or into a concept of political order through constitutionally regulated balance of power such as that of American democracy. Instead he introduces the idea of authority (Herrschaft) in contrast to power (Gewalt), as a way of directing human wills toward social order. In power there is a mechanical domination of one will by another. In authority

> there is presupposed an understanding of the command by the one who obeys. This is sociologically significant in so far as in an association of power there can be no community, whereas in one of genuine authority community is not only present, but for the most part realized.[21]

With this the seed was planted. The plant, however, had to be drastically pruned. The events of the next few years revealed vividly the demons hidden in community ideals based on race, people and nation. At the same time a grotesque distortion arose in Nazism of Bonhoeffer's picture of authority-based community. It made him clarify both the aristocratic base and the penultimate character of

---

20. CS, 61.

21. CS, 58-59.

authority. In his radio talk of 1933 he drew a sharp contrast between the "messianic concept of the Leader" and the "originally matter-of-fact (sachlich) idea of political authority (Autorität)."[22] The Leader's authority grew out of the yearning of the people for an authority-based community and their failure to seek it in the objective realities of function and office, orders and institutions by which society lives, and in the knowledge, ability, and experience appropriate to these offices. The Leader's authority is entirely from below, from the concentrated will of the people who transfer their rights to him, and therefore his authority rests on a wrong foundation. It has no structural limits and therefore seeks to transcend the penultimate in its messianic claims. True authority is not delegated but recognized. It adheres in the offices which express the orders of life, and the person is the steward of authority in serving the office--such as parent, teacher, judge or official.

Two important shifts have happened here. The orders of society are no longer seen as communal in their ground of being. No longer do they express a collective personality which acts as a subject in I-Thou relations. They have instead become part of the structure of a penultimate world, the objects of maintenance and cultivation by those called to office in them. Co-ordinately, then, the concept of authority--functional, responsible, sachlich and limited, exercised by those called and qualified for it--is greatly strengthened.

From here it is only a step to the wonderfully open and unfinished thoughts on the subject in the Ethics. Theologically the way had been prepared in 1932 before Hitler came to power when Bonhoeffer joined Karl Barth and others in an attack on the nineteenth century doctrine of "orders of creation." "Every human order," he wrote, "is an order of the fallen world and not of creation." Only in Christ who has fulfilled the law, who brings and promises a new world, can we learn what we are to do.

Therefore we are completely directed to Christ.

---

22. NRS, 199.

Ground Under Our Feet

> Therefore we also understand the whole world order of fallen creation as directed toward Christ and the new creation. What was for us dark and hidden comes into a new light. Not that we suddenly know from Jesus Christ which conditions we are to regard as orders of creation and which not, but that we know that *all* orders of the world only subsist in that they are directed toward Christ. They all are preserved by God as long as they are still open for Christ, they are *orders of preservation* not orders of creation.... (They) are functional forms against sin and in the direction of the Gospel. *Every order*, be it the oldest and most holy, *can and must be broken up* when it grows hardened and self-enclosed and no longer allows the proclamation of revelation to come in.23

In a later lecture the same year he described one order of preservation, the state, as, with the church, a vehicle for the kingdom of God on earth.

> The kingdom of God assumed form in the state insofar as here the orders of existing communities are maintained with authority and responsibility. Lest mankind fall apart through the desires of individuals who want simply to go their own way, the state takes the responsibility in a world under the curse for the preservation of the orders of communities, such as marriage, family and nation.24

But it does this only in continual openness to the divine miracle

---

23. "Zur theologischen Begründung der Weltbundarbeit," a lecture given to a youth peace conference in Czechoslovakia, July 1932 (GS I, 150-151). Cf. also Clifford Green's discussion, SCH, 247-249.

24. "Dein Reich komme," public lecture in Potsdam-Hermannswerder, November 1932. Tr. in John Godsey, Preface to Bonhoeffer: The Man and Two of His Shorter Writings (Philadelphia: Fortress Press, 1965), 42.

proclaimed in the church that breaks through all human order and sin with new life in Christ. In this tension, for Bonhoeffer in 1932, the world lives and hopes: "The kingdom is always divided in this way: miracle as breaking through all order, and order as preservation in preparation for the miracle; but also miracle completely veiled in the world of orders, and order enduring completely by virtue of its being limited by miracle."[25]

The Ethics moves decisively beyond this. Powerfully assisted, if the historical critics are right, by Barth's exposition of "The Command of God",[26] the ontological foundation of supra-personal social orders is swept away and a Christ-centered understanding of mandate is put in its place. Mandates are "divinely imposed tasks," not "determinations of being."[27] They are commissions to human beings based on "the claiming, the seizure and the formation of a definite earthly domain by the divine commandment." They "are dependent solely on the *one* commandment of God as it is revealed in Jesus Christ."[28] The whole realm of ordered wholeness in the various areas of human life on earth (even, it should be noted, the order of the church which is one of the mandates) becomes not an ordained structure, but a divine calling and a human secular responsibility. Only the "domains" are presupposed, not how they shall be ordered. The ground under our feet is not orders of economic life, marriage and family, state, church or culture, but human relations justified and

---

25. Ibid., 40.

26. Church Dogmatics, II/2, Ch. VIII, "The Command of God." Cf. Larry Rasmussen's article in this volume for details. Bonhoeffer's indebtedness to Barth at this point is somewhat modified by the fact that his first treatment of the mandates in E, Ch. V, was probably written before his trip to Switzerland in May 1942 when he had a chance to read Barth's volume. Barth also, in later work, had some criticism of Bonhoeffer's concept of mandate (Church Dogmatics III/4, 14). The openness of the mandates to interpersonal formation under the command of God is, however, the profound common theme.

27. E, 207.

28. E, 287-292.

illumined by Christ, in all of these spheres, and beyond them.

Thus, a new approach to the forming of the common life radically relativized all tradition. Once again we do not know how Bonhoeffer would have proceeded to flesh out these mandates "with, for and against one another,"[29] and perhaps he did not either. There is some evidence--in his section on the mandate of the church and in his wedding sermon from prison--that the results would have been more traditional than his theology suggests.[30] If so, one reason could be found in the third element which defined his world: his sense of aristocracy.

IV. GROUND: THE RESPONSIBLE ELITE

The style and values of the family and culture in which Bonhoeffer grew up were aristocratic. It was an aristocracy of education, intellect and social status, strongly represented in the leadership of German society in the first decades of the century. But all of this was not an object of much reflection in those years, until it was brought into sharp relief by the barbarity of the Nazi movement. This is reflected in Bonhoeffer's thought. In The Communion of Saints his reference to authority is impersonal and almost casual. By contrast with the Nazi concept of leadership, he defined it more clearly. But it is the Ethics that states it most urgently and sharply.[31] With the disappearance of idealistic illusions about the spirit of community and with the battering of traditional social structures by what Bonhoeffer and his colleagues described as a revolt from the baser forces of human nature and society, everything came to depend on a faithful elite who would accept and carry out the mandates of God. In the world there are not orders of being, but there is an order

---

29. E, 291-292.

30. E, Ch. VII, 292-302; LPP, 41-47.

31. E, Ch. VII, 289-292, 293.

of relationships whereby certain people are called to be above and some to be below in the context of certain mandates. This is a personal relationship. It binds and limits both those who are in charge and those who follow in a common submission to God and a common responsibility. It is not determined by earthly power; in fact it may correct and challenge this power, for its essence is mutual service and sacrifice. The ultimate authority over these relationships is Christ himself, and all authority in the mandates derives from him and shares the form of his ministry and passion. He is the ultimate aristocrat. But in his name and under his commission, leaders are called to penultimate authority and others are called to follow.

Who then are these leaders and how is their calling validated in the world? Here is where Bonhoeffer found himself in continual reconsideration, at the very end of his life. It took two related forms.

First, there was a continual tension between the principle that the elite should be determined by certain qualities of "sacrifice, courage and a clear sense of duty to oneself and society" which may come from all social classes, and the fact that these qualities had been taught and learned in the context of a particular class. Renate Bethge describes this interaction beautifully in her article on "Elite and Silence in Bonhoeffer's Person and Thought."[32] An old elite--that of Bonhoeffer's family and their associates--was being purged and deepened. A new elite--from all circles of society--was being called together in the struggle against Hitler. This was a worldly change in community, a shift in earthly ground, a new discovery of penultimate goodness in the world.

Second, there was the more profound tension between the elite and those who, for whatever reason, are at a disadvantage in the personal relations, the interplay of wills, and the give and take of life. The figure of Christoph in the Fiction from Prison, especially in his encounter with Heinrich, the alienated man without "ground under his feet" in the drama, reflects a haunting question to the calling and the

---

32. ER, Ch. X.

actions of the aristocrat. The world of history, culture and responsible personal relations in the context of respect for the integrity of others bears a promise. We are nourished by mother earth. It is good to have social ground under our feet. But how are we related in Christ to those who are not so endowed? It is time to move to the second thesis.

V. THE FRAGILITY OF THE WORLD

Eberhard Bethge writes in his biography about Bonhoeffer's spiritual development:

> He set out on the path to theology from an essentially worldly base. First of all there was the "call" that came to him in his youthful vanity to do something special in life. The intellectual curiosity plunged him into theology as a branch of knowledge. Only later did the church come into his field of vision. Unlike theologians who have come from church and theological families and have discovered the existence of the "world" only later, Bonhoeffer set out on his journey and eventually discovered the church.[33]

True, but what cut the path that led this scion of a worldly family to become so completely a church theologian? On the evidence of Bethge's own account, it was not the search for religious answers to worldly questions. It was not the drive for personal wholeness or ultimate security. Dietrich Bonhoeffer was never religious in the metaphysical and individualistic sense he described in his letter from prison.[34] The path in fact is more an exploration of the relational field than a journey from place to place: the relation between divine action and human response in this good but fragile and

---

33. DB, 28.

34. LPP, 285-286.

mismanaged world. One can speak of occasions, as Bethge does, which spurred this exploration: Dietrich's search for independence in a science-oriented family; the profound effect in the family of his brother Walter's death in the war; the fact that although the family was not churchgoing, prayers, Scripture and hymns were a part of its daily routine.[35] But the evidence seems clear, as far back as we have signs of his spiritual life, that it was not his own or the world's problems that led him to search for God; rather it was awareness of God that made self and the world problematic.

We see this in those childhood efforts to think eternity which his sister Sabine reports.[36] We see it in the remarkable reminiscence on glorifying and fearing death as a boy which he penned in 1932, and in the reappearance of this theme in the drama fragment from prison.[37] Death in the world seems ultimate. Only in Christ do we know it as a gateway to life. To make of it a self-glorifying scene even in faith is in the next breath to be terrified by its reality. To seek life without limit, responsibility and order in the world is to court death, as the curious stranger in the drama fragment suggests. Yet to face death as an aristocrat who makes an ultimate of the order, culture and authority for which he is responsible, is to be ridden by the despair of it, as the figure of Christoph in the drama movingly portrays. We see it most sharply of all in a poignant memory, also in the 1932 document, of an incident in school years before. His teacher had asked what he intended to study and he had answered, "Theology," and flushed with embarrassment. A moment of surprise followed, then a quiet answer.

---

35. DB, 20-28.

36. Sabine Leibholz-Bonhoeffer, The Bonhoeffers: Portrait of a Family, 38. Quoted in DB, 23-24.

37. DB, 24; FP, 13-47. The entire drama fragment is concerned with the theme of death as the nemesis of the values and order of the world, and the ways of defining or cooperating with it. It is, curiously, an almost Stoic-Epicurean debate with hardly a suggestion of the message of the New Testament, but with a profound sense of judgment on a penultimate society that had tried to incorporate the ultimate.

Ground Under Our Feet

That was all. But for the boy,

> the moment swelled into pleasure, the classroom expanded into the infinite. There he stood in the midst of the world as the herald and teacher of his knowledge and his ideals. They all had now to listen to him in silence and the blessing of the Eternal rested on his words and on his head. And again he felt ashamed. For he knew about his pitiful vanity.... How often he had tried to master it. But always it crept back again and it spoiled the pleasure of this moment. Oh, how well he knew himself at the age of seventeen. He knew all about himself and his weaknesses. And he also knew that he knew himself well. And through the corner of that piece of self-knowledge his deep vanity again forced an entry into the house of his soul and made him afraid.[38]

One feels moved to apologize to Bonhoeffer for this intrusion into his personal life. The only excuse for it is to demonstrate something which is true not only of him but of us all, whatever our condition: where the Word of God is present, it defines for itself the human situation. When this happens, the world--private or public--is grasped at the center of its ideals, its plans, and its powers whatever they may be, and is placed in the context of a reality it does not control. Human efforts to direct and define the ultimate goals of life have the smell of death about them, even though they be efforts by a people seeking liberation, efforts by aristocrats seeking creative order, or efforts by a dreaming boy to project a theological vocation.

Bonhoeffer's most powerful theological statement of this is in the first pages of <u>Creation and Fall</u>.

> "In the beginning, God created the heavens and the earth." Thus the Bible begins with God's free

---

38. DB, 25-26.

affirmation, free acknowledgement, free revelation of himself.[39]

God acts "in the beginning." All human existence and action is in response to, in relation with, this God. God makes himself known as the beginning in the middle of human life, through the biblical story. All human knowledge gains perspective, as knowledge of reality and not as deduction from hypothesized premises, through interaction with this revelation. *Then* it is that human action and human knowledge become in truth problematic. Then we see that the concept of beginning is not only an intellectual conundrum: the impossibility of conceiving an event before which there was no other, or a cause which is really first. It is a moral and spiritual temptation. The more we know about origins, the more we think we can control developments. The closer we are to the beginning, the more we ourselves try to be the source of what flows from it. So the world has a love/hate relationship with the beginning. It hates the beginning because the beginning reminds it of finitude, of limit, of end. On the other hand,

> the fact that we ask about the beginning is the innermost impulse of our thinking; for in the last resort it is this that gives validity to every true question we ask.... Man no longer lives in the beginning--he has lost the beginning. Now he finds he is in the middle, knowing neither the end nor the beginning, and yet knowing that he is in the middle, coming from the beginning and going toward the end. He sees that his life is determined by these two facets, of which he knows only that he does not know them.[40]

God directs human life toward the other person in the middle, and away from efforts to grasp the beginning. God comes as the

---

39. CF, 11.

40. CF, 10.

ultimate who is the Other, the Thou over against our I, in Christ in the midst of life. This defines us as persons. It defines the world in which we live. Free responsible human love, knowing the limit of the other whom God has given as grace and promise for us amid the non-human creation which we are to tend, is witness to the ultimate at work in a penultimate world. In the light of this, then, human efforts to provide themselves with their own ultimates (of tradition, of nation or of religion) or their own methodologies (reason in its technological or idealistic form, or organization, political or social) become problems not because they are imperfect or limited in reason and power, but because they destroy life in its reality.

> Man sicut deus is dead, for he has cut himself off from the tree of life. He lives out of his own self and yet he cannot live. That means that he is dead.

In this condition we live by divine mercy which preserves us in division from one another and from the earth. Our death is not the last word. "The death of death--that is the promise in this curse."[41]

The essential has here been said. It remains to illustrate. Bonhoeffer had throughout his life a sharp eye for structures of thought and of society which submerge the problem of human conflict and the mutual limitation of personal relationships in superhuman concepts and movements. Ideals and ideologies are deceivers in the world. They "vent their fury on a man and then leave him as a bad dream leaves the waking dreamer. The memory of them is bitter."[42] The first part of his first book was a careful analysis of a range of idealisms from Aristotle to Kant, Hegel and Fichte. Each of them with somewhat different emphases, he says, relate the subject, the

---

41. CF, 88-89.

42. E, Ch. VI, 216. The reference is specifically to ideologies. It is not certain exactly what ideologies Bonhoeffer had in mind. The context suggests political reformers with formulae for solving the problems of society. Would he have included Lenin, or even Kautsky? In any case the concept means an unreal imagined answer to human problems as a misguided form of engagement with them.

person, to some form of spiritual universal in which it finds its fulfillment and to which it is guided by some form of reason.[43] For Aristotle it is the polis or state. For the Stoics it is the universalized moral reason of the individual. For Kant, despite the genuine transcendentalism of his theory of knowledge, including moral knowledge, spirit "is the highest principle of form--so that spirit and the universal are identical and the individual loses its value."[44] Fichte finally depends on a universal consciousness which at times he calls God to overcome the separation between the I and the Not-I.[45] Hegel's synthesis is both metaphysical and social, but persons in relation are finally over-ridden by the spirit of the whole.

There are strengths he grants, in various of these, of course. The Stoics restored the integrity of the individual in a morally insensitive world. Kant established at least in principle the final philosophical criticism of the idealistic illusion of the union of the knowing mind with universal truth.[46] Fichte was most deeply aware of the challenge of other persons to understanding the world in idealistic categories.[47] Hegel brought back the question of ontology to philosophy.[48] All of them dealt with the problem of human conflict. But all of them ultimately--just insofar as they became closed and complete systems of thought--rested on the union between human reason and eternal goodness and truth. They are, he maintained, ways of escape from living in the middle and facing interpersonal reality there.

The young theologian's judgment on one or another of these

---

43. CS, Ch. II, 23-30.

44. CS, 23-30. See also AB, 19-30.

45. CS, 27, 211.

46. AB, 24.

47. CS, 212.

48. AB, 49.

philosophers could be questioned, but his insight into the German idealism they nourished was prophetic. It deepened in the next decade into personal experience of the judgment of God on the society he loved and which had nourished him. He saw his self-confident secularist world--whatever place it gave to God--lose its integrity and crumble. The section on "Inheritance and Decay" in the Ethics is his account of this. There was a corpus christianum. "Jesus Christ has made of the west a historical unit."[49] Its foundation is in him. In the Incarnation of Christ "history becomes a serious matter without being canonized." We are set in this history and must ask ourselves "about the present and about the way in which the present is taken up by God in Christ."[50] Western history is distinct in being determined by that question, inspired by it and judged by it. Now that it has lost the unity which that question provided--now that the church is divided and world-conforming Christendom is secularized by technology, the masses and nationalism--the Western world is on the brink of a void in which "everything established is threatened with annihilation.[51]

In this situation the self-confidence of a culture that once thought it could realize the purposes of God with or without his help, is gone.

> Reason, culture, humanity, tolerance and self-determination, all these concepts which until very recently had served as battle-slogans against the Church and against Christianity, against Jesus Christ himself, have now, suddenly and surprisingly come very near indeed to the Christian standpoint.... It is clear that it was not the Church that was seeking the protection and alliance of these concepts; but, on the contrary, it was the concepts that had somehow become homeless and

---

49. E, 92.

50. E, 89.

51. E, 105.

now sought refuge in the Christian sphere.[52]

They were children of the church and now returned to their origin. This is the context of Bonhoeffer's understanding of the world come of age. The maturity of the world is based on this brokenness. It is the maturity of people who know that they cannot and must not escape from the world into a religious realm, or count on some transcendent reason to explain and excuse what is. They may not be believers, but they are "good people" who will not surrender the values which give their world meaning, and who seek some basis in reality for putting their lives at stake for these values when destruction threatens.[53] It is to people like this, indeed to the person like this in himself, that Bonhoeffer could speak freely of God.

VI. GROUND: ULTIMATE AND PENULTIMATE

How can one speak in this world--of God? So far we have spoken of the world, not untheologically to be sure for Bonhoeffer's experience was itself rooted in revelation, but of the experience rather than of the revelation. How could we have done this so long, and still speak of Bonhoeffer? Only in order finally to pose the problem of worldliness in the terms in which he understood his own: as a problem within the human response to God's word and act. In any case the answer to the question is awesomely simple: to speak of God in this world one must speak of Christ. The corollary is also true: to speak of Christ is to speak of the reality of the world.

We are directed, then, to the incarnation. There--in the midst of the world, serving it and suffering at its hands--the ultimate reality of the world, its origin, its goal and meaning, in each day and year, is

---

52. E, 55.

53. This combination of the discussion in the Ethics and that in the well-known letters concerning "good people" and "man come of age" is, it seems to me, justified by the social context in which Bonhoeffer was living when both of these were written.

revealed.

> The point of departure for Christian ethics is not the reality of one's own self or the reality of the world, nor is it the reality of standards and values. It is the reality of God as he reveals himself in Jesus Christ.[54]

To participate in the reality of God in the world in Jesus Christ, to discern, serve and make known the way this reality is working and taking form, in short "the realization among God's creatures of the revelational reality of God in Christ," is the ethical task.

> The place which in all other ethics is occupied by the antithesis of "should be" and "is," idea and accomplishment, motive and performance, is occupied in Christian ethics by the relation of reality and realization, past and present, history and event (faith), or, to replace the equivocal concept with the unambiguous name, the relation of Jesus Christ and the Holy Spirit.[55]

Nevertheless, within this reality, there is a difference between being and action, between what really is and what is to be realized. Bonhoeffer uses the now familiar terms "ultimate" and "penultimate" to describe it. It is easy to misunderstand these terms. They do not refer to what will be in the last judgment but unfortunately is not now. They do not mean a perpetual tension between the true law of life and the relative choices in a sinful world (Reinhold Niebuhr) or any form of a static two-realms theory in the traditional Lutheran sense. Nor do they mean the difference between what is and what will be as soon as we build it. The ultimate (Bonhoeffer sometimes calls it Christ, sometimes the work of Christ, sometimes the "justification of the sinner by grace alone") is actively present in the world both as origin

---

54. E, Ch. V, 189-190.

55. E, 190.

and root of our existence, and as goal of our work. It qualifies the penultimate, gives it both legitimacy and limit. "A thing becomes penultimate only through the ultimate, that is to say, at the moment when it has lost its own validity."[56] Human works and human relationships are not good in themselves by some endowment from the Creator. We cannot come to each other by ourselves in some "natural" fellowship, because the way is blocked by our own ego.[57] Human works and relationships are given their value, in each time and place, by the calling and forgiveness of God in Christ. In this context, they prepare the way for the coming of Christ in his world.

This interaction has, it is not generally recognized, two levels. On the one level it is built into creation itself and something of its original form expresses itself even in a fallen world. "God," he wrote in Act and Being, "is not free of man but for man. Christ is the word of his freedom."[58] The being of God is being-for. Human beings are created in his image, in relationship with one another. A blessed penultimacy is present in human life from the beginning. Once again, Creation and Fall:

> Man's limit is in the middle of his existence, not on the edge. The limit which we look for on the edge is the limit of his condition, of his technology, of his possibilities. The limit in the middle is the limit of his true existence.... The limit is grace because it is the basis of creatureliness and freedom.... Grace is that which supports man over the abyss of non-being, non-living, that which is not created--and all this nothingness is only conceivable to Adam in the form of

---

56. E, Ch. IV, 133.

57. LT, 16-17.

58. AB, 90.

the given grace of God.[59]

The limit, furthermore, is the other person. He is to be for her and she for him, in their mutually limiting differences and their mutually binding love. Here, in the relationship, is the image of God, precursor of the relation between Christ and his people. Or, to put it in terms which Bonhoeffer borrowed from the New Testament,

> Christ stands in the center, between me and myself, between the old existence and the new. So Christ is at the same time my own boundary and my rediscovered center.[60]

This, Bonhoeffer points out, is an ontological not a psychological statement. Human personality, thought, and feelings still have their penultimate locus in me. But Christ as the center is a statement of our ultimate reality: our judgment and our justification.

In Christ we know therefore that the ground under our feet is good, even while it is under judgment. We know that in these fragile human relationships, in these mandated yet broken spheres of the common life, in the depths of culture--in Bonhoeffer's case a definite bourgeois culture--there is something blessed, something that will guide the future out of the past, something that will reappear after judgment and bring fruit from the soil of tradition. There is a cantus firmus to life in loving God with all our heart and mind and soul and strength, a direct response to the ultimate of God's own love. But within this, and because of it, the polyphony of human loves can be developed to the full.[61] Bonhoeffer developed this image with regard to personal erotic love, but it could apply as well to the range of human relations, to art, to social improvement and to the transformation of nature to enhance human life. So it was in the

---

59. CF, 51-52.

60. CC, 62-63.

61. LPP, 303.

beginning before the fall. So it is now. Who knows that it will be otherwise when the kingdom comes? The penultimate life is already in this sense everlasting.

On the other level the relation between the ultimate and the penultimate takes on a sharper and more dialectical form to cope with the world of human self-centeredness, brokenness and fear. All human work displays an attempt to possess and contain the ultimate, as well as divine guidance toward participation in the life, death and resurrection of Christ. Shame is a testimony to the division between human beings and God, and a means of making that division tolerable in human relations by covering that which would destroy them.[62] Conscience is the human effort at self-justification before God, aimed at human goodness, and it is a guide to human insight in responsible action in the context of faith.[63] The law is used by the Pharisee, yet it is also a limit and guide to understanding the being and direction of other persons, institutions and things, in faith.[64] The mandates of marriage, labor and the state can become centers of self-assertion, yet they are also spheres of responsible relation and action. The natural is properly defined as that which, after the fall, looks forward to the coming of Christ.

All of these are experienced in human life, not in their original created form and purpose, but in the combination of judgment and grace with which Christ confronts the world. They are spheres of struggle between human self-assertion and divine guidance. They have therefore an authoritarian, coercive element in them. They rest not on some order of being the knowledge of which is accessible to each person's reason, but on "a concrete relation between the giver and the receiver of commands."[65] This in turn is rooted in the all-

---

62. E, Ch. I, 20-23.

63. E, 24-26; 242-248.

64. E, 26-37; 236-238.

65. E, Ch. VII, 273.

embracing concrete commandment of God which is neither a general structure of law nor "positivistic" assertion of divine inspiration in each situation, but takes "a definite historical form" with relation to the historical powers at work. "God's commandment, which is manifested in Jesus Christ, comes to us in the church, in the family, in labor, and in government." Human authority is commissioned and proved by the work of Christ giving form and direction to these mandated forms of human relationships.[66]

There is something of Luther's dialectical relation of law and grace in this perception, but there is, in substance at least, more of Calvin. Bonhoeffer moves beyond Luther's acceptance of the institutions of this world as agents of the law in restraining sin, to the forming and transforming power of Christ himself in a sinful world, in and through its institutions, and its moral sensitivity. The "third and principal use, which pertains more closely to the proper purpose of the law,"[67] namely to guide and discipline the Christian in the way of sanctification, is dominant in his understanding. Self-denial by participation in Christ, which Calvin describes as the sum of the Christian life, is for him the promising discipline of secular obedience. Above all, Calvin's affirmation of the humanizing task of secular institutions as a witness to the ultimate kingdom is Bonhoeffer's as well.[68] Indeed, one can say that Bonhoeffer's conception of penultimate responsibility in a sinful world is authentically post-Calvinist. Calvin was still "religious." Concern for the holy life apart from worldliness still preoccupied him overmuch. The law, for all its thrust toward freedom in his thought, still remained, like the majesty and omnipotence of God, too a-historical. For Bonhoeffer the penultimate task is to prepare the way for the coming of Christ. The law is discerned in the being and direction of things, ideas and

---

66. E, 286.

67. Calvin, Institutes of the Christian Religion, II.vii.12.

68. Ibid., IV.xx.2.

institutions toward this end.[69]

Yet there is something of Luther the man and the theologian in the spirit of this penultimacy. It comes out in a remarkable passage from one of the prison letters:

> My thoughts and feelings seem to be getting more and more like those of the Old Testament, and in recent months I have been reading much more of the Old Testament than the New. It is only when one knows the unutterability of the name of God that one can utter the name of Jesus Christ; it is only when one loves life and the earth so much that without them everything seems to be over that one may believe in the resurrection and a new world; it is only when one submits to God's law that one may speak of grace; and it is only when God's wrath and vengeance are hanging as grim realities over the heads of one's enemies that something of what it means to love and forgive them can touch our hearts. In my opinion it is not Christian to want to take our thoughts and feelings too quickly and too directly from the New Testament.... One cannot and must not speak the last word before the last but one. We live in the penultimate and believe the ultimate don't we? Lutherans(so-called!) and pietists would shudder at the thought, but it is true all the same.

And, lest the point be missed, he continues:

> Why is it that in the Old Testament people tell lies vigorously and often to the glory of God (I've collected the passages), kill, deceive, rob, divorce, and even fornicate (see the genealogy of Jesus), doubt, blaspheme and curse, whereas in the New Testament there is nothing of all this? "An earlier stage" of religion? That

---

69. E, Ch. VI, 236-238.

is a very naive way out; it is one and the same God.[70]

All of this must be understood christocentrically! The whole Bible is, as for Luther, the cradle of Christ. The faith that makes it possible to struggle for a blessing with all the lust for life and power at one's command, is the justification of the sinner by grace alone. This was Luther's spirit. But this justification plunges one into the world's responsibilities with a hope and a direction that themselves give ethical guidance in wrestling with the powers and ambiguities of life. Here Luther is left behind. The freedom of a Christian, given in the commandment of God which is "the permission to live as a human being before God,"[71] is a freedom to explore relationships and build institutions, not only to do what is appropriate (sachgemäss) beyond the law (Luther's pecca fortiter), but to discover the law of human relations, even in the family and the state, as Christ takes form in them. There are no two realms.

> It is now essential to the real concept of the secular (Weltliche) that it shall always be seen in the movement of being accepted and becoming accepted by God.[72]

But there is a profound participation in the way of the cross:

> By this-worldliness I mean living unreservedly in life's duties, problems, successes and failures, experiences and perplexities. In so doing we throw ourselves into the arms of God completely, taking seriously not our own sufferings, but those of God in the world--watching with Christ in Gethsemane.[73]

In this world, qualified by the suffering and risen Christ, death

---

70. LPP, 157. Letter to Bethge, 5 December 1943.

71. E, Ch. VII, 281.

72. E, Ch. V, 198.

73. LPP, 370. Letter to Bethge, 21 July 1944.

is a moment in the free, responsible and hopeful life. Suffering is, as for Christ, the companion of action, and the whole is, in the reality of the Redeemer's work, moved to blessed penultimacy despite itself. This is the life of faith in a world that lives from its own ultimates cut off from the tree of life, and so cannot live.

One more word must be said to make this picture clear. The church is one of the mandates in a penultimate world. It is not a realm set apart from the sin, struggle and historical task of that world, but that part of the world itself where the word of God is spoken and heard.

> The church is a piece of the world, a lost, godless world, under the curse, a complacent, evil world. And the church is the evil world to the highest degree because, in it, the name of God is misused, because in it God is made a plaything, man's idol. Indeed it is simply the eternally lost, anti-Christian world if it emerges from its ultimate solidarity with the evil world and sets itself up, boasting against the world. But the church is a piece of qualified world, qualified by God's revealing, gracious word, which, completely surrounded and handed over to the world, secures the world for God and does not give up. The church is the presence of God in the world. Really in the world, really the presence of God. The church is not a consecrated sanctuary, but the world, called by God to God.[74]

This paradox of the church is stretched to the limit in Bonhoeffer's writings. Sectarians of the right and of the left have drawn upon these writings for their purposes. In The Cost of Discipleship some passages read as if indeed a consecrated community were separated from an alien world, claiming space there only for its proclamation and the common life of its members, until

---

74. NRS, 153. GS III, 286. The essay is from 1932.

the world is judged.⁷⁵ Among the Letters and Papers from Prison are statements that sound as if the church itself were no longer the bearer of the Word, and must be renewed as a community of hidden discipline with a radically reformed lifestyle of holy worldliness in order that the Word may be heard.⁷⁶ Because Bonhoeffer was so much a part of the church (it seemed closer to him than even the social ground of his being which he was able in faith to analyze), ecclesiology was never for him a solved problem. But to take either his passionate identity with the church over against the compromised Christian expressions of a Nazified world, or his radical disillusion with even the Confessing Church's witness in time of crisis, as the center of his churchmanship, is to see him in distorted light. Bonhoeffer was no sectarian. The reality of Christ being realized in the world, the way for his coming being prepared there, requires an interpersonal community of response and witness to that reality as one sphere of human relations.

> A life in genuine worldliness is possible only through the proclamation of Christ crucified; true worldly living is not possible or real in contradiction to the proclamation or side by side with it, that is to say, in any kind of autonomy of the secular sphere; it is possible and real only "in, with and under" the proclamation of Christ.⁷⁷

This liberates other spheres of human relations--family, culture, labor, government--to realize their penultimate character, whether by way of confrontation and judgment (which is also judgment on the church itself as one of the mandates) or the polyphonic elaboration of the fullness of human life which is nourished by the cantus firmus of the love of God. The church hears the divine judgment on the world

---

75. Cf. Ch. IV, "The Church of Jesus Christ and the Life of Discipleship."

76. LPP, 281, 286, 299-300, 381-383.

77. E, Ch. VII, 297.

first of all as a judgment on itself for its complacency and pretensions, and shares this word with the rest of the world. The church is the very heart of a blessed secularity, where God's limiting and liberating presence in Jesus Christ points an anxious and broken world toward the wonderful freedom of mutual dependence and responsibility.

VII. GROUND: BONHOEFFER'S AND OUR OWN

The world that formed Dietrich Bonhoeffer is different from our own. There is no use pretending that he was at heart an equalitarian and a democrat, or in his outreach a proto-proletarian. A society which affirms that "all men are created equal," in which individual rights to life, liberty and the pursuit of happiness come first and governments are instituted to secure these rights, "deriving their just powers from the consent of the governed," was strange to him. Rebellion against authority, first ecclesiastical (Pilgrims, Puritans, Baptists, Quakers) then political, which undergirded both the religio-cultural pluralism and the constitutional covenant of American society, was far from his experience. His brief encounter with it produced some sharp critical insights, about the nominalism of Anglo-Saxon thought, the limitation of all earthly power, the technical and administrative attitude toward the state, and above all about the peculiar kind of world-conformity which a vital religious pluralism produces: "Protestantism without Reformation."[78] But he did not give us there the bridge we seek. We must ask the question for ourselves. What does this man's faith, standing on the ground of a quite different world from the American, or indeed from the European of the present generation, have to say to our discernment of Christ taking form amid the welter of powers--industrial, financial, technological and scientific--and the fragmented communities--national, cultural, familial--of the late twentieth century, in a world where all authority is questioned?

---

78. NRS, 92-118. GS I, 323-356.

Before taking up this question, let us make the opposite point. Bonhoeffer's experience was as strange to the proletarian as it was to the equalitarian democrat. It is not that he failed to recognize the problem. Already in <u>Communio Sanctorum</u> he proclaimed that "the hope for our 'bourgeois' church lies in a renewal of its life blood, which is only possible if the church succeeds in winning the proletariat."[79] He saw them at that time, to be sure, more as a spiritual need than as a social movement, a mass seeking to become a true community; but he was deeply aware that the church must take form among them in a way that would express their world in Christ. In <u>Christ the Center</u> he was more specific:

> For the working class world, Christ seems to be settled with the church and bourgeois society. There is no longer any reason why the worker should encounter Jesus Christ. The church is all one with the fossilized sanctions of the capitalist system.

Yet in spite of this Christ is present even here:

> The worker does not say, "Jesus is God." But when he says "Jesus was a good man" he is at any rate saying more than when the bourgeois says "Jesus is God." God for him is something that belongs to the church. But Jesus can be present on the factory floor as the socialist, in politics as the idealist, in the workers' own world as the good man. He fights in their ranks against the enemy, capitalism. Who are you? Are you our brother and Lord? Is the question merely evaded here? Or do they, in their own way, put it seriously?[80]

But his final and most painful recognition is in the last scene of the drama fragment from prison. Christoph, the self-assured

---

79. CS, 191.

80. CC, 35.

aristocrat, seeks out Heinrich, a proletarian. They both are soldiers. They both face death. But friendship is not natural. Heinrich is suspicious, even resentful of this personal approach:

> Man to man--you always say that when you want to silence the voice of the masses, of the common people, that lives in us. You dislike this voice; you want to rip us out of the community in which alone we are something, and you know perfectly well that you needn't fear us any longer once you confront us as individuals. As individuals we are completely in your hands--for we aren't individuals, we are the masses or nothing.

Christoph pleads for mutual trust, for self-confidence on both sides, for a constructive approach to rebuilding the world, until Heinrich stops him:

> We want something much simpler: ground under our feet so we can live. That is what I called foundation. Don't you feel the difference? You have a foundation, you have ground under your feet, you have a place in the world; for you there are self-evident values which you can uphold and give your lives for, because you know your roots are so deep that they'll make new growth.--If one wants to live, there must be ground under one's feet--and we don't have this ground. Therefore we are blown about, hither and yon, by the storm.[81]

Bonhoeffer was wrestling here with a human relation that went beyond his understanding but which he knew held the key to a worldly blessing. It may have been about this time that he penned the paragraph, "the view from below," where he speaks of looking at history "from the perspective of the outcasts, the suspects, the

---

81. FP, 44-46.

maltreated, the powerless, the oppressed, the reviled," as a rewarding experience.[82] But for all this, the central world view of the proletarian remained a mystery to him, especially in its concepts of mass solidarity, of revolutionary liberation and even of socialism as a structure of society. He was not the precursor of liberation theology, but a believer to the end that the secular openness of a humanity come of age, whether in wealth or poverty, in authority or in submission to it, expressed more faithfully a penultimate Christian ethic.[83] What then does this man have to say to the masses of alienated humanity today?

Let me suggest, as answer to both the above questions, three thoughts.

First, Bonhoeffer leaves us all with the question: What is the ground under our feet? Unless we face this honestly and without slogans, we deceive ourselves and others also about our faith. Ground is not just an ideology. It is not a system of ideas about ourselves and our society. It is rather the whole combination of human relations, including the traditions, the values, and the ways of living, which have been bred in us and which we find good. It is what we have learned and taken into ourselves, whether from books or mass media or personal relations. It is what we find meaningful in this penultimate world. Ground is more than personal development and individual interests. It involves a sense of society, whether or not we organize it in the spheres of family, labor, culture, church and state as Bonhoeffer did. But ground is also more than politics, more than a sense of

---

82. LPP, 17.

83. I am here taking issue with Clarke Chapman: "Bonhoeffer stood at the threshold of a social ethic as liberation theology would define the term." ER, 156. Bonhoeffer had a social ethic, defined more by his life and occasional writings than by systematic treatise, except for portions of the Ethics. But it specifically rejected the substitution of collective categories such as "class" and "solidarity" for interpersonal spheres of life, and the continuity between human struggle and divine salvation, for which liberation theology is known. Chapman shows well how Bonhoeffer has been used in Latin America. Now the controversy needs to be sharpened between them.

solidarity in oppression, and struggle. Life is interpersonal in many more complex ways than political concepts can grasp.

Christ confronts the ground of our lives with continual transforming judgment. He is the person who holds the key to its reality and its creativity. In Bonhoeffer's case we see that judgment at work in a constant questioning and reforming of his sense of aristocratic and authoritative structures, beginning in his earliest writing, which confronted the idealism of German Christian culture with the reality of the church. How does this happen in American pluralist democracy? Among poor and exploited peoples in the third world? How do we all understand the ground under our feet within the reality of Christ?

Second, what is really the brokenness of our world? What are the forms of self-justification, the religious or pseudo-religious ultimates we throw up to protect ourselves against breakdown? There are a thousand analyses in the Western world which try to answer these questions, on the basis of as many different world views. We, however, are asked by Bonhoeffer to face them theologically, and to ask the first question first. How are we--personally, communally, collectively--caught in patterns of life that direct us away from responsibility to the other person and toward some effort at ultimate control of our destiny? What names do we give to the structures of thought and power that give us assurance of success? How then do we see the world in conflict and destruction when these are confronted by the crucified Lord? Here are our tools of analysis, as relevant to defense and economic policy within a developed nation as they are to personal vocational planning, or to the strategy of social revolution in an oppressed land.

Third, what is for us the style and discipline of penultimate action where we are? For Bonhoeffer it is personal action, in a context of responsible and qualified companions, with concrete human welfare in view. It is relative action, aware of the possibility of divine judgment, ready for repentance and change in the light of new human events. It is action that does not claim to be good in itself, but only to be appropriate and realistic. It is action for human community in its various mandated spheres. As such it is free and witnessing action which points even opponents and enemies to the judgment and grace of God. Persons, not ideals to be realized or institutions to be preserved, are its concern. To create human community, not social structures in themselves, is its object. Immediate faithfulness in the human situation, not long-range plans that sacrifice the present, and therefore reform where possible, not revolution, is its method. Shall this style be ours? Or can we, as penultimate witnesses to God's justifying grace, defend another?

WORKS CITED

See also "Abbreviatons"

Althaus, Paul. Communio Sanctorum. München: Chr. Kaiser Verlag, 1929.

Barth, Karl. "No!" in John Baillie, ed., Natural Theology. London: Geoffrey Bles, 1946.

Barth, Karl. Anselm: Fides Quarens Intellectum. London: SCM Press, 1960.

Barth, Karl. Church Dogmatics II/2. Edinburgh: T. & T. Clark, 1957.

Barth, Karl. Ethics, trans. G. W. Bromiley. Grand Rapids, Mich.: Eerdmanns, 1981.

Barth, Karl. The Epistle to the Romans, trans. Edwin Hoskyns. London: Oxford University Press, 1933.

Bell, George K. A. Christianity and World Order. London: Hodder and Stoughton, 1940.

Bethge, Eberhard. "The Editing and Publishing of the Bonhoeffer Papers." Andover Newton Bulletin LII.2 December, 1959.

Bethge, Eberhard. Am gegebenen Ort: Aufsätze und Reden. München: Chr. Kaiser Verlag, 1979.

Bethge, Eberhard. The Challenge of Dietrich Bonhoeffer's Life and Theology. Chicago Theological Seminary Register LI.2 February, 1961.

Bonhoeffer, Dietrich. Schweizer Korrespondenz 1941/42. Im Gespräch mit Karl Barth, ed. Eberhard Bethge München: Chr. Kaiser, 1982; Theologische Existenz Heute, N. 214

Bramsted, Ernest K. Aristocracy and the Middle-Classes in Germany. Chicago: University of Chicago Press, 1964.

Brunner, Emil. The Divine Imperative, trans. Olive Wyon. Philadelphia: Westminster Press, 1947.

Bultmann, Rudolf. Jesus and the Word, trans. L. P. Smith and E. H. Lantero. New York: Charles Scribner's Sons, 1958.

Burnaby, John. Amor Dei: A Study of St. Augustine's Teaching on the Love of God as the Motive of Christian Life. London: Hodder and Stoughton, 1938.

Calvin, John. Institutes of the Christian Religion. Volume I, II, Philadelphia: Presbyterian Board of Christian Education, 1936.

D'Arcy, M. C.,S.J. The Mind and Heart of Love: A Study in Eros and Agape. New York: Henry Holt, 1947.

Day, Thomas. Dietrich Bonhoeffer on Christian Community and Common Sense. New York: Edwin Mellen Press, 1983.

Fletcher, Joseph. Situation Ethics: The New Morality. Philadelphia: The Westminster Press, 1966.

Forastiori-Braschi, Eduardo, et al. eds. On Text and Context: Methodological Approaches to the Contexts of Literature. Editorial Universitaria: Universidad de Puerto Rico, 1980.

Furnish, Victor Paul. The Love Command in the New Testament. Nashville and New York: Abingdon Press, 1972.

Gerth, Hans and C. Wright Mills, eds., From Max Weber. New York: Oxford University Press, 1946.

Godsey, John D. Preface to Bonhoeffer. Philadelphia: Fortress Press, 1965.

Helmreich, Earnest Christian. The German Churches under Hitler. Detroit: Wayne State U. Press, 1979.

Horan, Dennis J. and David Mall, eds. Death, Dying, and Euthanasia. Frederick, Maryland: Aletheia Books, University Publications of America, Inc., 1980.

Kegley, Charles W., ed. The Philosophy and Theology of Anders Nygren. Carbondale and Edwardsville: Southern Illinois University Press, 1970.

Kierkegaard, Søren. Works of Love. Princeton: Princeton University Press, 1946.

Kittel, Gerhard and Gerhard Friedrich, eds., and Geoffrey W. Bromiley, trans. Theological Dictionary of the New Testament, Vol.1. Grand Rapids, Mich.: Eerdmans, 1964.

Klassen, A.J. ed. A Bonhoeffer Legacy: Essays in Understanding. Grand Rapids, Michigan: William B. Eerdmans, 1981.

Lehmann, Paul. "The Foundation and Pattern of Christian Behavior," Christian Faith and Social Action. New York: Charles Scribner's Sons, 1953.

Long, Edward L., Jr. A Survey of Christian Ethics. New York: Oxford University Press, 1967.

Lovin, Robin W. Christian Faith and Public Choices: The Social Ethics of Barth, Brunner, and Bonhoeffer. Philadelphia: Fortress Press, 1984.

Meinecke, Friedrich. Machiavellism, trans. Douglas Scott. New Haven: Yale University Press, 1951.

Merrell, Floyd. A Semiotic Theory of Texts. Berlin, New York, Amsterdam: Mouton de Gruyter, 1985.

Moffatt, James. Love in The New Testament. London: Hodder and Stoughton, 1929.

Morris, Kenneth Earl. Bonhoeffer's Ethic of Discipleship: a Study in Social Psychology, Political Thought, and Religion. University Park and London: Pennsylvania State University Press, 1986.

Müller, Hanfried. Von der Kirche zur Welt. Leipzig: Koehler & Amelang, 1961; 2nd edn. Leipzig & Hamburg, 1966.

Niebuhr, H. Richard. The Purpose of the Church and Its Ministry. New York: Harper and Brothers, 1956.

Niebuhr, Reinhold. The Nature and Destiny of Man, 2 volumes. New York: Charles Scribner's Sons, 1941, 1943.

Nowak, Kurt. 'Euthanasie' und Sterilisierung im 'Dritten Reich'. Göttingen: Vandenhoeck & Ruprecht, 1977.

Nygren, Anders. "Eros and Agape," in A Handbook of Christian Theology. New York: Meridian Books, 1958.

Nygren, Anders. Agape and Eros: A Study of the Christian Idea of Love. Part I, trans. by A. G. Hebert. London: SPCK, 1932; Part II, Vol. I, trans. by Philip S. Watson. London: SPCK, 1938; Part II, Vol. II, trans. by P. S. Watson London: SPCK, 1939

Ott, Heinrich. Wirklichkeit und Glaube. Zurich: Vandenhoeck und Ruprecht, 1966.

Ott, Heinrich. Reality and Faith: The Theological Legacy of Dietrich Bonhoeffer, trans. Alex A. Morrison. Philadelphia: Fortress Press, 1972.

Outka, Gene. Agape: An Ethical Analysis. New Haven and London: Yale University Press, 1972.

Paton, William. The Church and the New Order. New York: Macmillan, 1941.

Peck, William Jay "From Cain to the Death Camps: an Essay on Bonhoeffer and Judaism." Union Seminary Quarterly Review, 28 Winter, 1973.

Petöfi, János S., ed. Text vs Sentence: Basic Questions of Text Linguistics, First Part. Hamburg: Helmut Buske Verlag, 1979.

Ramsey, Paul. Basic Christian Ethics. New York: Charles Scribner's Sons, 1950.

Rasmussen, Larry L. Dietrich Bonhoeffer: Reality and Resistance. Nashville: Abingdon Press, 1972.

Schäfer, Gerhard, ed. Landesbischof D. Wurm und der Nationalsozialistische Staat: 1940-1945, Eine Dokumentation. Stuttgart: Calwer Verlag, 1968.

Schlatter, Adolf. Die Christliche Ethik, Zweite Auflage. Stuttgart: Calwer Vereinsbuchhandlung, 1924.

Scholz, Heinrich. Eros und Caritas. Halle [Saale]: Max Niemeyer Verlag, 1929.

Soloviev, Vladimir. War, Progress, and the End of History. London: University of London Press, 1915.

Strauss, Leo. Persecution and the Art of Writing. Glencoe, Ill.: The Free Press, 1952.

Tillich, Paul. Love, Power and Justice. New York and London: Oxford University Press, 1954.

Tillich, Paul. Systematic Theology. Chicago: University of Chicago Press, 1963.

Van den Berk, M. E. M. "Bonhoeffer en de dood," in Tijdschrift voor Theologie Nijmegen, 1975.

Van den Berk, M.E.M. Bonhoeffer, boeiend en geboeid: de theologie van Dietrich Bonhoeffer in het licht van zijn persoonlijkheid,. Boom Meppel, 1974.

Warnach, Victor. Agape: Die Liebe als Grundmotiv der neutestamentlichen Theologie. Düsseldorf: Patmos-Verlag, 1951.

Weiland, J. Sperna "Ein Paar Gedanken über Freiheit" in Wie eine Flaschenpost: Oekumenische Briefe und Beiträge für Eberhard Bethge, eds. Heinz Eduard Tödt, et al. München: Chr. Kaiser Verlag, 1979.

Williams, Daniel Day. The Spirit and the Forms of Love. New York and Evanston: Harper and Row, 1968.

Zimmermann, Wolf-Dieter and Ronald Gregor-Smith, eds. I Knew Dietrich Bonhoeffer. London: E.T. Collins, and New York: Harper & Row, 1966.

INDEX

Abortion, 168
Abstract, 142, 144, 224,
    Abstraction, 48, 53, 104, 106
Abwehr, 77-78, 84, 86-87, 92, 94-95,
    100, 144, 151, 220, 227
Act and Being, 71, 112, 209-210,
    258
Actus directus, 154
"After Ten Years," 27, 228, 240
Agape, 190-196, 200, 202-205, 207,
    214, 219, 222, 232-233
Althaus, Paul, 191
America; American 19, 210, 235,
    237, 243, 266, 270
Ansatz, 8-12, 18, 25, 42, 44, 48, 50,
    53-54, 58, 60
Arbitrary killing, 147
Aristocracy, 78, 233, 237, 247
    Aristocratic, 88, 91, 158, 244,
    270
Aristotle, 168, 172, 183, 253, 254
Arrest, 11, 13, 15, 55, 68, 87, 92,
    126, 220, 227
Aryan Clause, 213, 218
Atomistic, 110-111, 115, 138
Augustine, (Bishop of Hippo), 191,
    193, 199
Authority, 85, 88-89, 91, 94, 98-99,
    156, 160, 195, 241, 244-245,
    247, 250, 261, 266, 269
Baillie, John, 19
Barcelona, 110, 116, 209, 235
Barth, Karl, 4, 47, 56-60, 69-76, 79,
    91-99, 116, 120, 122-123, 125,
    127, 131-132, 136, 154, 170,
    172-175, 191, 194-195, 197-
    198, 200, 203, 208, 231, 236,
    244, 246
Bell, George, 81, 92, 95
Benedictine, 10, 33, 84, 144, 152
Best Physician, 145, 154, 156, 157
Bethge, Eberhard, 3-4, 6-13, 15-26,
    29, 32, 34-35, 39-40, 42, 44, 48,
    50, 53, 55, 57, 103, 112, 114,
    120, 126, 133, 144, 221, 226-
227, 229, 234, 249
Bethge, Renate, 240, 248
Between the lines, 143, 146-147,
    150, 152, 165
Biologization, 148, 154
Bismarck, Otto von, 68, 89-90
Bodelschwingh, Friedrich, 160, 162
Bourgeois, 233-234, 259, 267
Brunner, Emil, 71-74, 91, 205
Bultmann, Rudolf, 191, 203
Calvin, John, 261
Canaris, W. W., 77, 100
Capital punishment, 147, 149, 158
Caritas, 191-194
Casuist, 233;
    Casuistic, 53, 79
Catholic ethics, 71, 140, 144, 153,
    (see Ethics)
Censor, 142, 227
Cheap grace, 218
Child, 177
Christ, 9, 15, 21-25, 30-31, 35-39,
    41, 43-44, 46, 49-50, 52-54, 59,
    77, 79, 81, 83, 90, 97, 98;
    Christ existing as community,
    112;
    Christ and good people, 34, 36,
    83
Christendom, 38, 80, 255
Christian, 19, 21, 35, 39, 43-44, 53,
    55, 57, 59, 60-61, 71-72, 81, 83,
    86, 91, 95, 97-99, 107, 112-113,
    118, 121;
    Christian life, 67, 75-76, 101,
    132-133, 137-138, 234, 261;
    Christianity, 83, 101, 136, 196,
    203, 211, 255;
    Christians, 23, 91
Christocentric, 86, 89, 91, 111, 126,
    149, 263
Christocratic, 106, 140
Christology, 22, 111-115, 118, 125,
    133-134, 137, 212;

Christological, 10, 24, 33, 43, 59, 149, 154, 229, 233; Christologically, 54, 59
Church, 11, 23, 25, 30-31, 35-36, 40, 56, 67, 73, 76, 79, 83, 86-87, 93, 97-98, 101, 112, 117, 120-121, 125, 128, 132-133, 134, 154, 160, 168, 170, 174, 178, 191-192, 196, 199, 206-210, 212-214, 216, 218, 220, 227, 231, 233, 245-247, 249, 255-256, 261, 264, 267, 269
Command, 22, 56, 94, 96, 103, 116-122, 124-128, 130, 132-133, 135, 137-138, 195, 203, 207-208, 216, 224, 232, 238, 243, 246, 260, 263
Commandment, 55, 57-60, 73, 87, 92, 96, 98, 100, 119, 121, 123-124, 126, 128, 131, 133, 202-203, 205, 209, 215, 218; Commandments, 48, 117, 198, 232
Communion of Saints, 112, 190, 206, 208, 209, 219, 237, 242, 243, 247
Community, 31, 36, 75, 98, 105, 118, 163, 198-199, 206, 208-210, 218, 237, 239, 242-243, 247-248, 264, 267, 268, 271
Compromise, 90, 93, 241, 265
Concrete, 53, 88, 208, 222, 224, 231, 233, 242, 260, 270; Concrete situation, 110, 116, 119; Concreteness, 112, 126, 138, 142, 153, 164
Confessing Church, 23, 30, 67, 68, 74, 75, 76, 78, 82, 83, 84, 93, 156, 213-214, 221, 265
Confession, 23, 31, 36
Conformation, 9-10, 21-22, 35, 50, 54, 103, 107, 110-111, 114, 138, 227
Conscience, 21, 26, 113, 120, 151, 220, 223, 241, 260
Conservative, 148, 158, 242
Conspiracy, 11, 77, 86, 87, 88, 92, 94, 100, 142, 151, 153-154, 159, 164, 221, 241
Contextual ethics, 109, 111, 115, 130, 138

Contraception, 168
Cost of Discipleship, 21, 75-76, 113, 115, 120, 154, 215, 218, 231, 264
Costly grace, 216
Coup d'etat, 87, 151
Creation, 59, 72, 98, 113, 119, 131, 156, 212, 244, 253, 258
Creation and Fall, 21, 154, 211, 251, 258
Culture, 23, 25, 30, 40, 72, 73, 82, 84, 86, 93, 97, 146, 233, 236, 240, 242-243, 247, 249, 250, 255, 259, 265, 269
D'Arcy, M.C., 202, 204
Das Gebetbuch der Bibel, 19
Death, 19, 54, 91, 142, 157, 159-160, 162, 196, 206, 227, 231-232, 250-251, 253, 260, 263, 268
Deed of free responsibility, 139, 158
Delbrück, Hans, 80
Dilschneider, Otto, 20, 22
Dilthey, Wilhelm, 6
Discipline, 36, 75, 96, 98, 218, 228, 232, 261, 265, 270
Dohnanyi, Hans von, 27, 68, 157, 220, 227
Duty, 26, 195, 241, 248
Earth, 109, 116, 211-212, 228, 235-236, 241, 245, 248, 252-253, 262, 266; Earthly, 219, 230, 233, 235, 246
Economics, 148, 246, 270
Elite, 247, 248
England, English, 81, 210
Epidemics, 148
Eros, 190-194, 202, 204, 207, 214, 219, 232-233
Espionage, 163
Ethics, 3-4, 9, 13, 18, 19, 21, 27, 31, 43-44, 52-53, 55-57, 59-61; Ethics, Catholic, 71, 140, 144, 153; Ethic of principles, 174
Etsi deus non daretur, 135
Ettal, 10-11, 17, 33, 42, 77, 84, 144-145, 152-153, 155
Europe, European, 88, 266
Euthanasia, 168, (see Chapter IV)
Evil, 20, 22, 37, 39, 48, 53, 70, 75, 77, 90-91, 117, 154, 220-221, 241, 264

Index

Extermination, 148, 159
Faith, 22, 23, 30, 36, 39, 44
Family, 72, 73, 97-98, 128, 153, 161, 220-221, 227-228, 236, 238, 240, 242, 245, 247-250, 261,263, 265, 269
Fanaticism, 26
Feil, Ernst, 12, 19, 24, 26, 29, 32-33
Fiction from Prison, 6, 248
Fides directa, 115
Fides reflexa, 115
Finkenwalde, 11, 74-76, 78-79, 153, 157, 214, 218
Fletcher, 205
Forgiveness, 35, 84, 93, 99, 113, 119, 168, 173, 209-210, 258
Formation, 31, 35, 77, 79, 81, 105, 107, 110, 113, 116, 130-133, 135, 137, 140, 227, 246
Fragment, 24, 58, 104, 145, 154, 156, 158-159, 164, 221, 250, 267
Fragmentary, 4, 7, 13, 104-105, 137
Freedom, 23, 30, 36, 48, 171, 177, 180-181
Friendship, 192, 200, 229, 240, 243, 268
Führer, 73, 161, 163, (see Hitler)
Gemeinschaft, 242
Germany, 80, 162, 176, 178, 214-215, 218, 220, 236;
    German, 11, 26, 67, 80, 89, 93, 150, 158, 190, 209, 213, 233, 235, 243, 247, 255, 270;
German Christians, 213-214, 218
Gesellschaft, 242
Gestalt, 108-109, 111-112, 115, 130, 133, 138, 140
Gilleman, Gérard, 205
Gleichgestaltung, 107
Good, 15, 16, 20, 22, 36, 37, 38, 41, 42, 43, 45, 46, 47, 50, 51, 55, 60, 70, 71, 75, 77, 86, 87, 89, 100, 109, 113, 117, 153-154, 155, 192, 207, 214, 216, 221, 223-224, 227, 229, 248-250, 254, 258-259, 267, 269-270;
    Good people, 23, 37-38, 256;
    Goodness, 236, 241
Government, 87, 89, 97, 98, 161-162, 163, 213, 218, 261, 265
Grace, 22, 36, 74, 139, 168-169, 184-185, 189, 193, 195, 199-200, 212, 218, 227, 231, 253, 258, 260, 262-263, 271, (see Costly grace)
Greece, Greek, 71, 142, 191-192, 236-237
Green, Clifford, 103, 241
Ground, 194, 233, 235, 237, 241, 243-244, 246, 248, 259, 265-266, 268-270, (see Chapter VII)
Guilt, 31, 35-36, 48, 69, 81, 147, 151, 158, 223
Harnack, Adolf von, 80
Hartmann, Nikolai, 71
Health, 148, 169, 236
Hegel, 253
Heroic efforts, 148
History, 11, 15-16, 36, 42-44, 46-49, 51, 74, 78-80, 82-87, 89, 93, 97-99, 105, 108, 115, 140;
    Historical, 31, 36, 46-47, 58, 79-80, 86, 109, 128, 130
Hitler, Adolf, 67-68, 73-74, 78-80, 82, 85, 88, 94-95, 99-100, 143, 150, 152, 159, 161, 163, 213, 220, 241, 244, 248, (see Führer)
Holy Spirit, 207, 211, 231, 233, 257
Humanists, 23
Humanity, 21, 23, 25, 30, 31, 37, 39, 41, 49-50, 79, 83, 105-106, 114, 123, 130, 132, 138, 140, 189, 192, 196-198, 200, 206, 224, 228, 237, 255, 269
Hustinx, A., 176
Ideology, 269
Imprisonment, 198, 227, 233
Incarnation, 9-11, 44, 49-50, 52, 111, 114, 140;
    Incarnate, 49-50, 54, 59, 109, 112, 114, 199, 224, 232
Incognito, 145, 156
Incurably sick, 146
Individual, 198, 208, 212, 237-239, 242, 254, 266, 269
Injustice, 163
Innocent life, 145, 147, 149, 154
Interrogations, 228
Jew, Jews, 88, 100, 143, 159, 163, 199, 218, 227

Joy, 92, 153, 200, 229, 232
Judgment, 79, 192, 195, 202, 205, 255, 259-260, 265, 270
Justice, 23, 25, 30-32, 36-37, 83, 204-205, 221, 223, 233
Justification, 10-11, 22, 31-32, 35, 37-38, 50, 81, 84-85, 139, 151, 189, 192, 195, 207, 216, 218
Kant, 70, 153, 253-254
Kierkegaard, 70, 191, 195, 200
Killing, 145-146, 149, 152, 162
Kingdom of God, 199, 207, 209, 245
Kirchenkampf, 23
Klein-Krössin, 9, 11, 17-18, 25, 31-34, 42, 48, 77, 78, 84, 86
Kleist-Retzow, Ruth von, 17, 78, 95, 100
Labor, 40-41, 87, 236, 260-261, 265, 269
Law, 23, 59, 85, 88-89, 111, 117, 119, 131, 152, 158, 195, 207, 216, 226, 240, 242, 244, 257, 261-263
Lehmann, Paul, 127
Letters and Papers from Prison, 4, 13, 61, 108, 114, 132, 140, 228, 233, 265
Liberal, 71, 98, 231, 234, 242; Liberalism, 70, 134
Liberation theology, 269
Life, 47, 59, 72, 75-76, 87, 91-92, 96-98, 111, 119, 126-130, 132-133, 138-139
Logos, 106
Loneliness, 171, 183
Longing, 192, 200
Love, 97, (see Chapter VII)
Luther, Lutheran, 70, 75, 115, 140, 151, 158, 191-194, 196, 203, 216, 218, 231, 232, 257, 261-263
Man come of age, 240
Mandates, 6, 33, 40, 43, 58, 87, 92, 97-98, 111, 115, 127-130, 132, 138, 229, 238, 246-248, 260, 264
Manuscript, 4, 6, 11-18, 24, 40-42, 45-46
Marriage, 72, 87, 97, 128, 177, 215, 229, 238, 243, 245-246, 260
Masaryk, Thomas, 168

Meinecke, Friedrich, 80
Mercy killing, 152, (see Euthanasia: Chapter IV))
Method, 56, 103-105, 107, 115, 120, 131, 133-134, 137, 139-140, 145, 153, 158-159, 224, 271
Monastery, 10-11, 33, 77, 84
Monks, 84
Moral, 162, 207, 226, 252, 261; Moral blackmail, 169
Morality, 67, 94, 128
Müller, Hanfried, 8, 103
Möser, Peter, 12, 16, 24-26, 32, 42, 48, 51-53
Nachfolge, 9, 11, 21, 22
Nachlass, 14-15
National Socialism, (Nazi) 23, 67, 72-73, 75-77, 82-83, 87, 90, 92, 98, 154, 157, 161, 163-164, 213, 218, 220, 243, 247, 265
Nationalism, 80, 255
Natural, 145, 153, 156, 168-169, 202, 222, 225, 233, 236, 239, 241-242, 258, 260;
Natural law, 72, 85, 111, 131, 152;
Natural life, 10, 27, 33. 40, 111, 147;
Natural right, 239;
Natural, the, 11, 41, 55, 60, 72, 85-86, 97, 99, 111, 132, 138,140
Nature, 78, 85-86, 97, 105-106, 140, 153, 155-156, 168-169, 184, 193-194, 199, 204, 212, 217, 236, 240, 259
Neighbor, 155, 195-199, 201-204, 207-208, 214, 216, 225, 232
Neo-orthodoxy, 134
Niebuhr, H. Richard, 196, 198, 200
Niebuhr, Reinhold, 201, 205, 257
Nietzsche, Friedrich, 212, 235
Non-religious, 6, 133, 136-137, 228, 233
Nygren, 190-192, 194-195, 197, 200, 203, 205
Ontological, 106-107, 139, 246, 259
Orders(of creation and preservation), 72, 119, 244-246, 248
Origin, 7, 20-21, 23, 25, 30-32, 37, 44, 50, 119, 131, 156, 157, 194, 222, 225, 232, 257, 258

Index

Oster, Hans, 27, 77
Ott, Heinrich, 107, 140
Outka, Gene, 197, 200-202, 204, 205
Outline, 7, 14, 16, 19, 26-37, 40-42, 45-47, 55, 60, 77, 85, 87, 104, 133
Paper types, 4, 11, 14-20, 23-24, 26, 31-34, 37, 42, 48, 58, 78, 104
Particularity, 142
Paton, William, 81, 88, 95
Paul(the Apostle), 70, 123, 197, 203, 214, 231
Peace, 36, 57, 98, 114, 118, 125, 134
Penultimate, 149, 227, 234, 238, 242-244, 248, 253, 257-265, 269-271, (see Orders of creation and preservation)
Permission, 98, 121, 126-127, 160, 263
Person, 48, 71, 85, 87, 90, 105, 200, 204, 207-209, 211, 219, 233, 237-242, 244, 246-249, 251-254, 259-260, 265, 270;
Personal, 33
Philia, 192, 233
Plato, 192
Play, 127
Polyphony, polyphonic, 109, 230, 234, 259, 265
Positivism of revelation, 136
Power, 82, 91, 117, 135, 153, 201, 211, 225-226, 232, 234-236, 239, 241, 243, 248, 251, 253, 261, 263, 266, 270
Powerless, 269
Pre-ethical, 128-129, 130, 138
Proletariat, 234, 266-269
Psychiatrist, 176
Quarantine, 148
Radicalism, 70
Ramsey, Paul, 204
Rasmussen, Larry, 12, 56-57
Reasons, 150;
Reasons of state, 150, 152
Reference communities, 152
Reformation, 11, 30, 80, 192, 214, 218, 231, 266
Relativism, 110
Religion, 72, 136, 194, 234, 236, 253, 262;
Religionless Christianity, 136

Religious, 162-163, 169, 172-173, 217, 229, 231, 234, 236, 238, 240, 249, 256, 261, 266, 270
Repentance, 159, 168, 172, 270
Resistance movement, 150-151, 153, 220-221, 226-227, 233
Responsibility, 26, 47-48, 73, 88-91, 93, 97-99, 151, 155, 169, 177, 189, 223-226, 228, 235-236, 240-241, 245-246, 248, 250, 261, 266, 270
Revelation, 21, 51-52, 79, 108, 112, 210, 222, 231, 245, 252, 256, 257
Revolution, 69, 234, 270-271
Rights, 23, 36, 41, 111, 115, 162, 225, 239, 244, 266;
Rights of natural life, 169
Risk, 74, 91, 151
Rist, Benjamin, 197, 203
Ritschl, Albrecht, 191
Roman Catholicism, 79, 85, 98-99, 152, 199
Rome, 236
Sacrament, 105, 117, 212
Sacrifice, 174-175, 182-183, 192, 201, 209, 217, 232, 248, 271
Scheler, Max, 71, 191
Schlatter, Adolf, 153, 170-172
Schleiermacher, Friedrich, 191
Scholz, Heinrich, 191
Science, 30-31, 106, 153, 250, 266
Secularity, 236, 241-242, 266;
Secular, 221, 233-234, 236, 246, 255, 261, 263, 265, 269;
Secularized, 255
Seeberg, Reinhold, 191
Self-justification, 171, 234, 260, 270;
Self-killing, 173-175;
Self-murder, 173-174;
Self-surrender, 192
"Sermon on the Mount," 75, 89, 113, 119, 215-217, 225, 232
Shame, 21, 260
Simplicity, 76
Sin, 72, 168-169, 172-173, 178, 185, 206, 212, 224, 237, 245-246, 261, 264
Situational ethics, 174
Socialism, 269

Society, 70, 87, 98, 148, 223, 233-234, 237-238, 242, 244, 247-248, 253, 255, 266-267, 269
Socrates, 142, 199
Sperna Weiland, 177
Spirit, 160, 219, 231, 236, 238-240, 247, 254, 262-263
State, 72-73, 128, 146, 150, 218, 238, 245, 247, 254, 260, 263, 266, 269
Stauffer, Ethelbert, 199
Sterilization, 168
Strauss, Leo, 142-143
Success, 54, 68, 80, 225-226, 270
Suffering, 30, 135, 156, 211, 213, 215, 222, 232-233, 256, 263
Suicide, 34, 167-176, 179, 181-185, (see Chapter V)
Sutz, Erwin, 71, 170
Technology, 80, 255, 258
Teilhard de Chardin, 140
Telling the Truth, 6, (see Truth)
Temptation, 83, 94, 243, 252
The Cost of Discipleship, 22
Theologia crucis, 135
Thomas Aquinas, 140
Thou, 113, 196, 200, 237-238, 244, 253
Tillich, Paul, 202
Treason, 158
Troeltsch, Ernst, 134
Truth, 23, 30-31, 37, 71, 75, 82-83, 98, 214, 219, 222, 230, 254, (see Telling)
Tyrannicide, 151-152, 158, 164-165
Tödt, Ilse, 4
Ultima ratio, 152, (see Reaons of State)
Ultimate, 148, 212, 218, 237-238, 240, 250-251;
  Ultimate and penultimate, 10, 32-38, 40-41, 84-86, 103, 111, 132, 140, 149, 227-228, 234, 238-239, 242-244, 248-249, 253, 256-262, 264-265, 269-271, (see Orders)
Unconscious Christianity, 115
Unethical, 167-168
Van den Berk, M.F.M., 175-181
Vitalism, 236
Vocation, 90, 251

Von Kirschbaum, Charlotte, 47
War, 81, 118, 147, 149, 151, 157-159, 162, 163, 220, 235, 241, 250
Warnach, Victor, 197, 203
Weakness, 134-135;
  Weak, 135, 143, 148, 162, 213, 220, 228, 240-241, 251
Weber, Max, 90-91
Wedermeyer, Maria von, 100, 227
Western world, 36, 81, 255, 270
Wisdom, 93
World-come-of-age, 133-134, 136-137, 233
Worldliness, 59, 132, 135, 233, 241, 256, 261, 263, 265
Wurm, (Bishop) Theophil, 146, 158, 160, 162-163, 164
Zettel, 4, 14-15, 19-20, 22-23, 26-27, 29, 31-32, 34, 37, 45, 55

TORONTO STUDIES IN THEOLOGY

1. Robert Ross, **The Non-Existence of God: Linguistic Paradox in Tillich's Thought**
2. Gustaf Wingren, **Creation and Gospel: The New Situation in European Theology**
3. John Meagher, **Clumsy Construction in Mark's Gospel: A Critique of** *Form-* **and** *Redaktionsgeschichte*
4. Patrick Primeaux, **Richard R. Niebuhr on Christ and Religion: The Four-Stage Development of His Theology**
5. Bernard Lonergan, **Understanding and Being: An Introduction and Companion to** *Insight*
   Edited by Elizabeth Morelli and Mark D. Morelli
6. Geffrey Kelly and John Godsey, editors, **Ethical Responsibility: Bonhoeffer's Legacy to the Churches**
7. Darrell J. Fasching, **The Thought of Jacques Ellul: A Systematic Exposition**
8. Joseph T. Culliton, editor, **Non-Violence—Central to Christian Spirituality: Perspectives from Scripture to the Present**
9. Aaron Milavec, **To Empower as Jesus Did: Acquiring Spiritual Power Through Apprenticeship**
10. John Kirby and William Thompson, editors, **Voegelin and the Theologian: Ten Studies in Interpretation**
11. Thomas Day, **Dietrich Bonhoeffer on Christian Community and Common Sense**
12. James Deotis Roberts, **Black Theology Today: Liberation and Contextualization**
13. Walter G. Muelder, **The Ethical Edge of Christian Theology: Forty Years of Communitarian Personalism**
14. David Novak, **The Image of the Non-Jew in Judaism: An Historical and Constructive Study of the Noahide Laws**
15. Dan Liderbach, **The Theology of Grace and the American Mind: A Representation of Catholic Doctrine**
16. Hubert G. Locke, **The Church Confronts the Nazis: Barmen Then and Now**
17. M. Darrol Bryant, editor, **The Future of Anglican Theology**
18. Kenneth Cauthen, **Process Ethics: A Constructive System**
19. Barry L. Whitney, **Evil and the Process God**
20. Donald Grayston, **Thomas Merton: The Development of a Spiritual Theologian**
21. John J. McDonnell, **The World Council of Churches and the Catholic Church**
22. Manfred Hoffmann, editor, **Martin Luther and the Modern Mind: Freedom, Conscience, Toleration , Rights**

23. Erich Voegelin, **Political Religions,** Translated by T. J. DiNapoli and E. S. Easterly III
24. Rolf Ahlers, **The Barmen Theological Declaration of 1934: The Archeology of a Confessional Text**
25. Kenneth Cauthen, **Systematic Theology: A Modern Protestant Approach**
26. Hubert G. Locke, editor, **The Barmen Confession: Papers from the Seattle Assembly**
27. Barry Cooper, **The Political Theory of Eric Voegelin**
28. M. Darrol Bryant and Hans Huessy, editors, **Eugen Rosenstock-Huessy: Studies in His Life and Thought**
29. D. Thomas Hughson, editor, **Matthias Scheeben on Faith: The Doctoral Dissertation of John Courtney Murray**
30. William J. Peck, editor, **New Studies in Bonhoeffer's Ethics**

DATE DUE

JAN 4 '89			
AP 5 '90			
NO 7 '90			
JE 25 '92			
AP			
DE 21 '94			
SE 13 '02			

```
BJ              30028
1253
.B6153   New studies in Bonhoef-
N49          fer's ethics.
1987
```

HIEBERT LIBRARY
Fresno Pacific College - M. B. Seminary
Fresno, Calif. 93702